Narendra Modi, Prime Minister of India

"An inspiring and extraordinary story of an 'improbable politician', who rose to lead Singapore after the legendary Lee Kuan Yew. The biography offers invaluable insights into how Goh Chok Tong walked tall 'in his own shoes' overcoming challenges and defeating difficulties in the path of Singapore's consolidation. And how his strengths and values reflect and also reinforce those of Singapore. This volume whets our appetite for the second volume of the biography."

Ban Ki-moon, former United Nations Secretary-General

"Engaging and thought-provoking insights drawn from the leadership of one of Asia's most eminent statesmen. Emeritus Senior Minister Goh Chok Tong sheds inspiring light on the values, vision and valour of the new Singapore dream — both inclusive and sustainable — in our changing world."

Sir John Major, former Prime Minister of the United Kingdom

"Goh Chok Tong is a friend whom I cherish. But, more important than that, he has been instrumental in building a Singapore that is confident of its future at home, and respected widely overseas. Chok Tong views the world not only through the prism of what events mean for Singapore, but also what they presage for the wider world. In short, he is a true statesman."

John Howard, former Prime Minister of Australia

"Goh Chok Tong, both as Defence Minister and later the second Prime Minister of Singapore, was integral to the great success of that country since its foundation as an independent country. I knew him well in both capacities. His insights were always sharp, his commitment to the continued success of his country unconditional, and the importance he placed on close links between Australia and Singapore was never in doubt. I continue to value his friendship and opinion on contemporary issues."

Tung Chee-hwa, former Chief Executive of Hong Kong SAR

"*Tall Order* is more than the personal story of Goh Chok Tong. In his own words, it is 'a book about Singapore's transition from Mr Lee Kuan Yew to the next generation'. As I see it from outside, Chok Tong played a strategic and indispensable role in ensuring that this passing of the baton was a smooth and inspiring progression. This book is a living testimonial of contemporary politics. It is also an account of modern day administration that followers of government and politics should not miss."

Tommy Koh, Ambassador-at-Large of Singapore

"The story of Goh Chok Tong, our second Prime Minister, is an inspiration for young Singaporeans, especially those from humble families. There is no glass ceiling for Singaporeans, if you are able, hardworking and lucky. I love the book."

Chan Heng Chee, Ambassador-at-Large of Singapore

"*Tall Order*, a biography of Goh Chok Tong, is a must-read for all who are interested in the modern political history of Singapore and political succession. A treasure trove of frank insights into the internal workings of cabinet and government decision-making, this book stands with the two volumes of Lee Kuan Yew's memoirs as major contributions to understanding governance and politics in Singapore. The full interviews with Goh make riveting reading."

Ho Kwon Ping, Executive Chairman of Banyan Tree Holdings

"Goh Chok Tong's life story firmly rebuts the adage that nice guys finish last. He is the Singaporean equivalent of Everyman — the honest, hardworking and congenial colleague or neighbour who does not intimidate you with his brilliance or oratory but is the decent bloke who's destined to succeed. With his authentic, unique and disarming style, and an incisive and decisive personality which belies his outward casualness, Goh Chok Tong has left his imprint on Singapore as its second Prime Minister. This book, full of personal insights and anecdotes, reflects the man and the leader."

> *"We owe a debt to make lives better for all,*
> *and not just for ourselves."*

Goh Chok Tong, in a speech on Compassionate Meritocracy given in 2013.

Dear Reader,

All royalties from the sale of this book will be donated to two charities I started: namely, *EduGrow for Brighter Tomorrows* for children from disadvantaged families, and the *Mediacorp Enable Fund (MEF)* to support the integration of special-needs Singaporeans into society and the workforce.

EduGrow aims to help underprivileged children break out of the low-income trap. Through intensive mentoring and education support, *EduGrow* tackles income inequality and social mobility at its roots.

MEF supports people with disabilities to maximise their potential through early intervention beyond the financial reach of their families. *MEF* also raises awareness and focuses on their achievements and abilities instead of their disabilities.

Thank you for joining me in building a kinder, gentler Singapore.

Goh Chok Tong

TALL ORDER

---THE---
GOH CHOK TONG
---STORY---

Volume 1

PEH SHING HUEI
Winner of the Singapore Literature Prize

W📖 World Scientific

NEW JERSEY · LONDON · SINGAPORE · BEIJING · SHANGHAI · HONG KONG · TAIPEI · CHENNAI · TOKYO

Foreword by Goh Chok Tong

I did not choose politics. It chose me. Then Minister for Finance Hon Sui Sen invited me to stand for elections. He was looking for a successor. At the party interview, Dr Toh Chin Chye, chairman of the People's Action Party (PAP), asked me why I wanted to be an MP. It was at the tip of my tongue to say, "But you asked me."

Succeeding Lee Kuan Yew was a tall order. I was chosen by the second-generation Ministers to lead in December 1984. Mr Lee Kuan Yew then appointed me Deputy Prime Minister. But four years later, he publicly declared that I was not his first choice as Prime Minister. Whatever his doubts and reasons, my colleagues stood by me. Lee Kuan Yew handed me the premiership in November 1990.

My heavy burden was lightened by a strong, able, tightly-knit team. They deserved much credit for Singapore's successful transition from the Old Guard to the next generation. The public was also empathetic. Their encouragement gave me strength. I thank them.

It was an unexpected journey. Certainly, my rise was unimagined. I did not prepare for it. I learnt on the job. Much to the early consternation of Lee Kuan Yew, I did it my way.

I had never intended to write my memoirs. My grassroots leaders — Patrick Ng, Chua Ee Chek, Kok Pak Chow, Ng Hock Lye, Tan Jack Thian — persuaded me. They wore me down with their argument that I have valuable experience to impart to Singaporeans. So I agreed to this authorised biography by Peh Shing Huei, a writer with journalistic flair. Peh has managed to tell a vivid story of my early years and the first half of my political career, capturing not only my contributions but also my stumbles.

I agreed to my story being told to achieve three objectives.

One, to encourage present and future generations of Singaporeans to consider political office, regardless of their background or upbringing. The book narrates my transformation from an introverted, studious, reserved person to Prime Minister. I was unprepared for a life in politics. I lacked the multilingual and public-speaking skills. I was uncomfortable in the limelight.

I was not politically ambitious. Had I failed as Prime Minister, I would still hold my head high. I had answered the call to duty, and devoted my life to it. I have given my best. I can proudly rest.

Two, this book and its sequel should also tell the story of my generation and the second-generation leaders. Ong Teng Cheong, an architect, Ahmad Mattar, a lecturer, S. Dhanabalan, a public servant and banker, Lim Chee Onn, a naval architect and administrative officer, Tony Tan, a banker, S. Jayakumar, a law professor, Lim Boon Heng, a naval architect, and others, like me were helicoptered into the political arena at different times.

None of us set out to be the Prime Minister. The person chosen to head the team would be *primus inter pares*. He would lead and the rest would support and complement him. There was no manoeuvring or jostling to get to the top. There was camaraderie. There was trust. There was friendship. We shared a common mission of preparing and taking over the heavy responsibility of looking after Singapore.

Finally, my story of working with Lee Kuan Yew, and to a lesser extent, his son Hsien Loong, holds intriguing lessons too. Most relationships between top men and their successors do not end well. But ours did. We made it work.

Lee Kuan Yew was perceived to be a demanding man, an authoritarian. Some even called him a dictator. Many believed that he wanted to build up a Lee dynasty. But I never doubted that he was looking for the best men and women to carry Singapore forward — probably nobody outside the family knew him as well as I did. How I survived working under him is more than a matter of curious interest.

We lunched regularly before and after I became Prime Minister. We discussed international and regional developments, bilateral relations with neighbours, domestic challenges and politics. From time to time, he asked about my children and grandchildren and talked about his. However, his big family was Singapore. Their interests were always on his mind. The need to bring good men and women into politics to look after Singapore was a constant refrain.

I did not take it personally when rebuked by Lee Kuan Yew either

privately, in Cabinet or publicly, humiliating though it was. He was my mentor, master and teacher. I understood where he was coming from. I swallowed my medicine without bitterness. I pushed on.

He put across his views robustly but never imposed them on me. He always made it clear that I had to take the decision. He was respectful of me as Prime Minister, and insisted on observing public protocol. He helped me to succeed as Prime Minister. For that I am grateful.

Likewise, I did what I could to help Hsien Loong succeed as Prime Minister. Loong is now preparing the next team and its leader to take over from him. Our political succession has been smooth so far. I hope this book will motivate Singaporeans to do their part and contribute to their better understanding of how to secure Singapore's future.

Goh Chok Tong
Prime Minister of Singapore
November 1990 – August 2004

Timeline

1941

May 20: Goh Chok Tong is born — the first of five children of Goh Kah Khoon and Quah Kwee Hwa

1942

Moves to Johor and Pahang in Malaya following Japanese invasion of Malaya and Singapore; returns to Singapore in 1945 after the war

1949-1954

Studies at Pasir Panjang English School

1955-1960

Studies at Raffles Institution

1979

Starts new Ministry of Trade and Industry as its first minister; and is elected to the People's Action Party's (PAP) central executive committee as second assistant secretary-general

1977

Leaves NOL and is appointed Senior Minister of State for Finance

1976

Enters politics, wins new Marine Parade constituency with 78.62 per cent of the votes and is elected a Member of Parliament

1981

Switches portfolios to become Minister for Health and Second Minister for Defence

1982

Takes over as Minister for Defence, but stays on at the Ministry of Health as its Second Minister for Health to implement MediSave

1984

Moves up as PAP's assistant secretary-general

1964

Graduates from University of Singapore with a first-class honours degree in economics; joins the Administrative Service and starts work in the Economic Planning Unit in the Prime Minister's Office

1965

Marries lawyer Tan Choo Leng

1967

Graduates from Williams College, Massachusetts, with a Master of Arts in Development Economics

1973

Takes on top job in NOL as its managing director

1969

Joins Neptune Orient Lines (NOL) as planning and projects manager

1968

Becomes father to a pair of twins: daughter Jin Theng and son Jin Hian

1985

Chosen as First Deputy Prime Minister, a clear sign he is heir apparent to Lee Kuan Yew; remains Minister for Defence

1989

Becomes PAP's first assistant secretary-general

1990, Nov 28

Sworn in as the second Prime Minister of Singapore; remains Minister for Defence

Contents

Part 1: The Young Goh

Introduction

Chan Heng Chee stepped into the office of Goh Chok Tong for lunch feeling an unease which the academic found hard to explain. It was not her first meeting with the then First Deputy Prime Minister of Singapore, a man whom she has known since their student days in the former University of Singapore. Goh noticed her discomfort. "She was looking around and seemed somewhat nervous. I asked why and she said 'There is a climate of fear. The ISD is everywhere'," he said, referring to the Internal Security Department (ISD), Singapore's domestic intelligence agency. "She then said that if someone says something about the government, the authorities would come down very hard on the person." The encounter in 1987 shocked Goh. "I knew that there was this fear element, I just did not know it was that bad, that pervasive, that even lunch with me would be scary," he observed wryly.

The meeting to discuss the setting up of the Institute of Policy Studies came soon after the much-publicised and controversial Marxist Conspiracy in 1987, when 22 English-educated Singaporeans were detained without trial under the Internal Security Act. "People were taken in," said Chan, then a liberal political scientist who later became Singapore's long-time ambassador to the United States. "If you are criticising the PAP, you could be locked up. They were after the English-educated professionals and intellectuals. It cast a pall on the atmosphere. There were whispers around of what the ISD did." Her fear left a deep impression on Goh. "I like people to be fearful but they must be the right people — your criminals and terrorists," he shared with his characteristic humour. "But when it got to the stage where everybody was fearful — they say something and they are fearful… that is not good. That is not the kind of society I would like to govern."

The encounter, coming three years before he would succeed Lee Kuan Yew as Prime Minister, would turn out to be "an instrumental moment," said Goh, in crafting a new vision for his country. When US President George H. W. Bush articulated his desire for a "kinder and gentler" nation in 1988, Goh found the signature phrase which captured the new Singapore he would lead. He had the support of his colleagues, said Lee Hsien Loong, who would succeed him as leader. "It was timely. We supported it. There are still hard truths which are at the bottom of it, which do not go away," he said. "But in terms of our approach and our balance, our capacity to give weight to some of these softer aspects of developing the society, we could do a lot more."

What Goh did not bargain for was resistance from the man he was replacing. Lee Kuan Yew did not like Goh using the phrase "kinder and gentler," revealed the latter. He felt it telegraphed softness, and more importantly, weakness in the new leader and by extension the ruling People's Action Party (PAP). Instead, he passed to Goh a seminal text of political philosophy — *The Prince* by Niccolo Machiavelli — urging the younger man to subscribe to the tenets of the 16th century book. In short, to govern, it is always better to be feared than loved.

Goh took a read and put the book aside. He did not like the Machiavellian approach. "No, I did not agree. I never told him I didn't agree with this way of governing," he said. "I just did the things I believed in. If I told him, he would say 'No, no, you better follow me'. And we would clash. So, I just did things my way. I never told him his style was wrong going forward, this is the way, that you must be kinder and gentler." His voice and speech coach Sue Greenwood, who also trained other ministers in the 1980s, remembered him sharing his approach to governance: "He said 'Lee Kuan Yew does not have the time to deal with people he has written off. But I want to do it my way. I don't want to hurt people'."

The contrasting styles of these two prime ministers underpin a leadership succession story that has since been simplified to one which was peaceful, smooth and even bland. The reality had more kinks than a cursory glance of history would provide. The handover from Lee to Goh was in no way rocky, but there were detours, drama and even hints of intrigue on Goh's unlikely rise to the top. Setbacks happened on more occasions than the popular narrative has since assumed. He was clearly different from Lee and his refusal to embrace his mentor's ways wholesale led to him not being the strongman's choice as successor. It was not the first rebuff he had to endure in life. In many ways, Goh was not preordained for a career which would reach the highest office of the land. His journey was a tall order.

His family was so poor that when his father passed away, they could hardly afford the burial. He showed little inclination for politics when young: all four childhood friends interviewed for this book said they were shocked when the quiet "Chok" joined politics. He was effectively monolingual in English, lacking not only other language skills but also the communication craft. In the words of Greenwood: "He had no understanding of how to persuade an audience."

Yet, in a remarkable story which reflects as much his personal abilities and values as the meritocratic system built by his predecessors, he succeeded. He was a man who once marvelled at a flush toilet when he first moved into a Housing and Development Board (HDB) public flat, and later championed a massive nationwide upgrading of said flats for Singaporeans. He was a man who simply wanted to earn $200 more a month so that he could give his family a better life, but progressed to present the government budgets by his late 30s. He was an ordinary man who went on to lead an extraordinary life.

Strangely, the story of Goh Chok Tong's incredible rise has not been as well known as most would expect of a former Prime Minister of an extremely successful young country. There have been a handful of coffee table books on the man, more visually heavy than prose-driven. In 2009, there was a compilation of essays by scholars on the policies during his years as Prime Minister. Beyond that, it has largely been a blank. In comparison, the views, insights and life of Lee Kuan Yew have been extensively covered in books, documentaries and even a musical.

Part of the reason could lie in the allure of the first — Armstrong over Aldrin; Nehru over Shastri. As the founding father of modern independent Singapore, Lee captures the romantic narrative of a new nation. Goh, as the second man, does not engender as strong a symbology as the exploratory mission of the first commander. But another big factor behind the muted traction of the Goh story could lie with the man himself.

Goh was, and still is, incredibly private about his life, especially when it touches on his family. He was happy, even loquacious, to share about his childhood, parents and family roots back in southern China. During a tour of the former Pasir Panjang English School, which is now a halfway house for drug addicts, he excitedly showed off the toilet he used and the assembly ground where he stood. Old friends from Raffles Institution remembered him walking around the school's Bras Basah campus, after all had left, to say farewell when he was graduating.

But he would not let such sentimentality come at the expense of his nuclear family's privacy. They fall strictly beyond the out-of-bound markers. His wife, lawyer Tan Choo Leng, declined to be interviewed for this book. So did their twin children, filmmaker Jin Theng and doctor-entrepreneur Jin Hian. Goh himself became visibly protective during our interviews about his wife, children and six grandchildren, stressing that they have always led quiet lives and that they would like it to remain so. He also recounted how he learnt later from his children of their discomfort when growing up in the public glare of their father.

More than that, Goh seems to have a chronic unwillingness to inflate his personal work and achievements, a trait which is almost counter-intuitive for a politician. Through the dozen interviews conducted for this book, he often downplayed the milestones in his life or was cursory with the accomplishments. For instance, upon taking over the management of loss-making national shipping line Neptune Orient Lines (NOL), he asked his chairman to give him three years to make it profitable. When asked why he was that bullish, Goh replied that his intention was quite the opposite: "I was giving him notice that I needed three years to turn the company around, in case they expected me to turn it around in two years or one year!"

More often than not, after sharing on the development of a major policy which he introduced and implemented, such as the Total Defence concept or national health savings plan MediSave, he would quickly dismiss his work as "just common sense." And when pressed on why he believed a participatory democracy would be welcomed in Singapore after the tough leadership of Lee, he replied it was not borne out of any philosophy. He simply felt that that was the way to go, an instinct which he found hard to break down and make sense of, let alone storify.

For numerous major episodes of his life which we discussed and sparred over, he often concluded his role in them as happenstance, a semi-serendipitous feat which others could have achieved too. At times, he seemed almost embarrassed to be devoting that much time to speaking about himself. So he switched, as he often did when talking about himself, between the first and second person. In the dialogue between himself and our team of writers and researchers, he used "I" and "you" interchangeably to describe himself, with the latter popping up far more frequently. Otherwise, he preferred to turn the attention to others, attributing the work to a group effort rather than individual brilliance.

Over and over again during the interviews, he stressed that he was far from unique among the second-generation leaders of Singapore and that his thoughts and achievements were both shared and executed by his colleagues as well. Several of them, for example, brought their private-sector experience into government and persuaded Lee and the Old Guard to change policies, he said. Goh called their market-based push the "transformational thinking" of his generation. "I played a big part, but there were others too," he said. "So I think you should speak to them as well."

This willingness to share the limelight accounts for a large part of his success. A key strength of his leadership was the ability to draw good people consistently to work with him. When he became PM, Lee Hsien Loong went so far as to call Goh's team "one of the strongest Cabinets we ever had, even (compared to) now." "He can get good and strong people to work for him," said Lee. "Mr Lee Kuan Yew's Cabinet depended on a few strong men... but Mr Goh had many strong ministers... more than half a dozen people, each very strong in his own area. And he was able to make it all work together." His colleagues felt they could confide in him, said old friend and fellow politician Othman Haron Eusofe. "You can get close to him, and that allows him to rally people," he said. "He is a man with a lot of friends." Even his political opponents admitted he is a nice man. Veteran opposition leaders Chiam

See Tong and Lee Siew Choh described him as a "true gentleman" and "extremely likeable chap" respectively in an *Asia Magazine* story in 1989.

Yet, instead of extolling the big achievements in his career, Goh enjoyed reminiscing about the micro changes which he mooted, an attention to the minutiae not unlike his predecessor Lee Kuan Yew. During his time as Health Minister in the early 1980s, some of his fondest memories were of changes to nurses' uniforms from the standard white to brighter hues, with each hospital deciding on the design and colour of the uniforms. "I get satisfaction in those. They are little things but they are tangible and they make a lot of sense," he said with a gentle smile.

Transport Minister Khaw Boon Wan, who was a young officer in the Ministry of Health (MOH) under Goh in the early 1980s, explained: "Those were small things, but they were symptomatic of something. When it is an MOH-run hospital, everything is standard or standardised. So, one uniform applied to all. Whereas, he wanted a different hospital to acquire different characteristics." It is also symptomatic of Goh's own philosophy towards governance — a general bent towards a smaller, less rigid, and kinder government. "His subsequent political thought on town councils — it followed the same thinking," said Khaw, referring to the devolution of public estate management which Goh introduced in 1988.

Despite his reticence, Goh's rise to the top of Singapore politics is a remarkable and relatable story — a very real tale of improbable success which this book looks to capture. His background is no different from many Singaporeans, said several of those interviewed. In particular, it is a sharp break from Lee, said S. Dhanabalan, a fellow second-generation leader. "Goh Chok Tong was seen more as a person whom people could identify with," he said. "Lee Kuan Yew was a bit too lofty, you know. But Goh Chok Tong was seen as one of the people — that is his strength." Chan agreed: "He is a typical Singapore boy who went to a neighbourhood school and who speaks with the Singapore tune and rhythm. And people identify with that," she observed. "They found him very authentic."

This first of two volumes spans Goh's birth in 1941 — seven months before the first bombs were dropped on Singapore by the Japanese during World War II — till 1990 when he became Prime Minister. The second volume, to be released later and separately, will focus on his years as the premier and to the present day. In the first volume, a key theme is political succession. How did a man who was chosen neither by life nor his predecessor manage to rise to the top? What did he achieve and what setbacks did he suffer on the long journey which was never his first career choice?

Answers to these questions fill the gaps in the story of the man, of course. But more importantly, given his pre-eminent and central position in Singapore's narrative, they also form a critical component of the country's history. To obtain the answers, my team and I had 12 interview sessions with Goh in his office at the Istana, an unprecedented access to the former Prime Minister. Over the course of a year, I was joined by *The Straits Times*' Editor-at-Large Han Fook Kwang and my team of writers from The Nutgraf — Sue-Ann Chia, Aaron Low and Pearl Lee. Each session focused on either a theme or a period in history, or both. The robust exchanges between the team of five and Goh ensured every meeting was both draining and exciting.

While there were instances when Goh stonewalled, particularly when speaking about his family, he was usually generous with his answers. For the first time, he revealed many private conversations with Lee Kuan Yew and some of his own deepest thoughts and feelings during times of despair, such as during the 1981 Anson by-election. In one particularly memorable interview, Goh came with a folder containing a confidential PAP report on Prime Minister Lee Hsien Loong's interviews to be a candidate in the 1984 general election. Goh wanted to illustrate the transparency of the party's recruitment process and dispel once and for all the belief that Lee Hsien Loong was handpicked by his father.

The topics dealt with in this book are serious: economic downturn, political battles and leadership succession. However, during the interviews, the atmosphere was relaxed, as Goh alternated effortlessly between the solemnity of an elder statesman and the jocularity of a family uncle. He was never afraid or hesitant to let fly a self-deprecating joke. Once, when there was a pause during a question to describe his role between Lee Kuan Yew and Lee Hsien Loong, he quickly offered his own answer: "Seat warmer?"

More than his time, he also offered me and my team access to classified exchanges between Cabinet ministers on policies and the PAP's post-mortem of its election results. To complete the research, I referred to open sources such as books, journals, magazines, newspapers, and records of Parliamentary Debates. There were also interviews with

Goh's childhood friends, teachers, NOL staff, former Cabinet colleagues, Members of Parliament, civil servants, grassroots leaders, academics, observers, diplomats and PM Lee Hsien Loong. A rare opportunity to speak to Goh's second aunt, Goh Shu Er, who is his father's younger sister, threw up many insights into his family, as she shared details which even he was unaware of.

This biography takes a chronological approach, with an additional layer of themes to provide structure. It is divided into four sections. In the first, it looks at Goh's younger days from birth till his early working years in both the government and NOL. The second section jumps into his political career and tells the story of how he was groomed by Lee Kuan Yew for bigger jobs, while tripping up as he came to terms with a changing electorate. The Goh brand of politics and leadership begins to emerge in the third section, as he learnt to flex his muscles even as he endeavoured to create a more consultative relationship between the government and the governed. In the last segment, the final lap of his journey to the top job had a few surprising bumps, as he revealed previously undisclosed negotiations between Lee and him on how and when the handover should take place.

This book is not a comprehensive recap of Goh's life and earlier career. Episodes, such as his time as Defence Minister, have been condensed in the interest of readability. I did not seek to write an A-Z account of the man and the many diverse fields, sectors and people he had influenced and changed.

Every chapter ends with an extract of the dialogue between him and the team of writers, a format which I believe captures not only

Goh's voice authentically, but also the unscripted spontaneity of the interviews. At the end of the book, Goh offered his thoughts on the chapters in an Afterword, a useful tool which allows the reader to hear his voice directly. But there is one anecdote which both of us did not include in the book. At the end of every interview, Goh would ask me: "You still think this book is worth doing?" My answer, every single time, was an unequivocal yes. A journey of such a tall order is certainly a story worth telling.

Peh Shing Huei

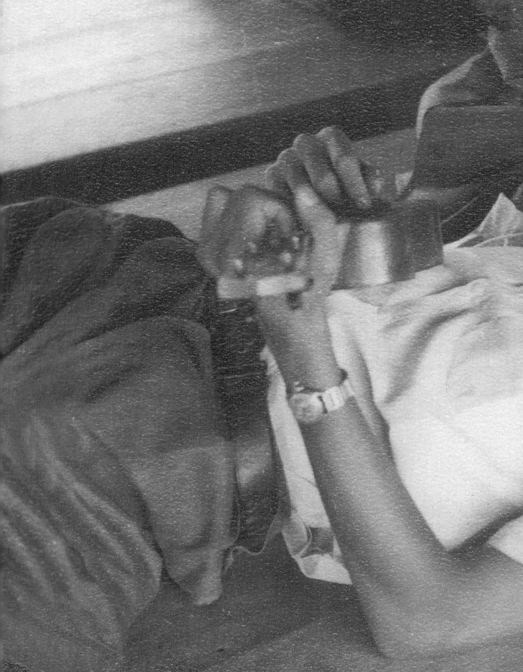

The
Young Goh

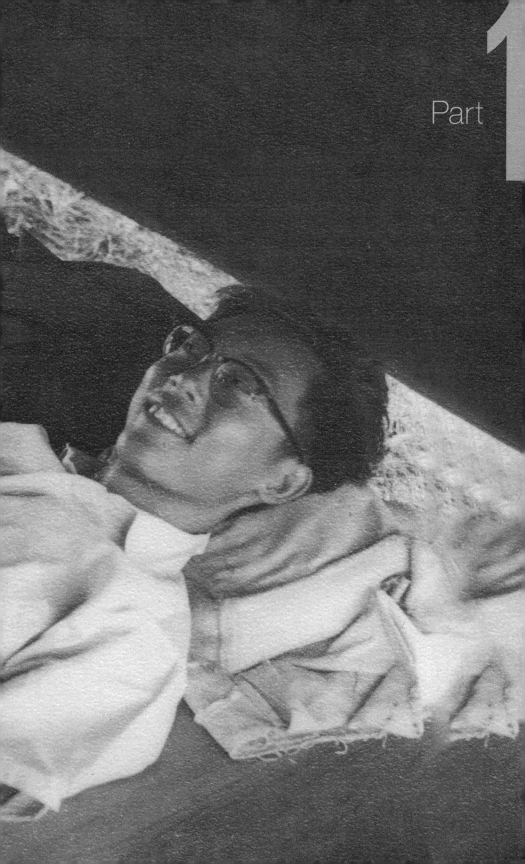

> How would I have known
> that life turned out this way?

Chapter 1

The Coup

"I never thought that he would be Prime Minister."

Tan Cheng Bock, childhood friend of Goh Chok Tong,
in an interview for this book.

I t started with a coup — on campus. It was the time of the year again to elect office bearers to the Historical Society of Raffles Institution (RI), the top school in Singapore. And as was usually the case, the senior students studying history were expected to fill the positions with little fanfare. But a bunch of younger boys in the science stream — none of whom studied history — had different ideas. They had five classes of students in their cohort while their seniors had only three. Through sheer numbers, they knew they could outvote the older boys. "One man, one vote, we knew we would win," said Lim Jit Poh, one of the plotters in 1958. They did so, not out of any noble beliefs, but only to do something mischievous. They won, much to the consternation of the teachers and senior boys, including one S. Jayakumar, who would rise to be Deputy Prime Minister of the country.

The young upstarts had a secret weapon — a quiet, amiable and incredibly tall boy named Goh Chok Tong, who was clueless about the takeover. He was watching from the sidelines, amused, when the time came to nominate the new chairman of the society. Someone shouted: "I propose Goh Chok Tong." The chosen one was shocked. "I said, 'What? What?'," he recalled, with a laugh. "Then someone said 'I second him'. I did not protest. And I was elected. That was the first coup. I was just the fall guy."

His classmates knew what they were doing. "Whenever we wanted to do anything naughty, we would push Chok to the front," said Lim. "Once the teachers saw him, they were okay. They knew he was a responsible boy." Goh's closest childhood friend, Lee Keow Siong, who was also at RI, said that teachers liked Goh. "He's a goody-goody." It was true. One of the teachers, Eugene Wijeysingha, described Goh as a student who "came through as a very reliable and upright person to both his teachers and fellow schoolmates." "His build and towering physical stature, notwithstanding, he was gentle in his approach, friendly and entirely sociable," he shared.

The episode left a strong impression on Goh, who called it half-jokingly in a speech at an RI reunion in 1988, as his "first taste of politics." But what followed took on greater significance. It would lead to his first meeting with a man who would not only be his mentor, but also define his life. The new Historical Society team decided to hold two talks and invited the two most prominent politicians of the day — former Chief Minister David Marshall, and leader of the opposition PAP Lee Kuan Yew. "So we went to David Marshall and he said yes," said Goh. "We went to Lee Kuan Yew at Malacca Street, that was his office, without making an appointment. Schoolboys did not know anything about appointments. We just walked there, climbed up the steps and told someone we were there to see Lee Kuan Yew and he was very good, he came out of the room and he saw us. We explained that we would like to invite him to speak to RI boys, and he asked about the topic. We said 'Landmarks of Democracy,' and he said yes."

The positive replies got Goh worried — about his oratory skills as he had to give a speech, and his sartorial tastes. He did not know how to dress for the occasion. "I never had long pants," he said. "So I looked around and found some old clothing left behind by my father. I found a pair of white pants, or rather, yellowish-white pants. I tried them on and I told an aunt to help me lengthen them a bit. So I had a collared white shirt, which was my school uniform, and my father's old pants." The talks were packed, but Goh could barely recall what Lee and Marshall said in their speeches.

"I was wondering what I should say because I had an opening speech and, at the end, I got to round up," he said. "I can tell you, I was quite nervous. First, it was before the school crowd. Second, it was Lee Kuan Yew and David Marshall." But what lingered in Goh's mind was Lee's impressive oratory skills. "Just spoke off the cuff. Many of us afterwards felt he would be our future Prime Minister just based on his performance," he recalled. "The students were spellbound." Goh would have no idea at that point that his career, and life, would become so intimately tied to Lee's in the coming decades. The pair, according to Goh, never spoke about their first meeting: "I never asked him. I do not think he remembered. He had given so many talks."

The campus coup and the talks gave an early insight into the layered personality of Goh, one which became increasingly evident as he made an unlikely climb to Singapore's highest office over the next 30 years. Despite his imposing height — 1.89m — he did not have ambitions of similar stature, let alone the appetite or desire to scheme and plot to succeed at all costs. He lacked, nor desired to have, the killer instincts of his schoolmates who engineered the putsch. His old RI friend, Tan Cheng Bock, who later joined him in politics, said Goh was never aggressive. "He's too kind, too soft, too much of a gentleman," he shared. Yet, when placed in positions of responsibility, Goh had the abilities to complete the tasks reliably and competently. These were strong characteristics.

But in 1958, when politics in Singapore was turbulent and ruthless, such traits of a young man seemed as far removed from politics as possible. By his own admission, he had no interest in politics at that age. In the speech he made at the RI reunion in 1988, he said: "Thirty years ago, I could not imagine myself being a politician. I was not clear as to my own ambition. I did aspire to be a journalist, but never a politician. The thought never crossed my mind. I am sure none of you had expected me to be one either." He was right. Lee Keow Siong said: "He was so shy. I was surprised that such a shy person would join politics and become such an effective politician." When asked if Goh had any interest in politics in school, Lee Keow Siong's reply was emphatic — "nil."

In an impoverished post-war society full of political actors fighting each other over colonialism, socialism and capitalism, among others, Goh had neither the personality nor the inclination for the rough and tumble of politics. At a time when his family was struggling to make a living, the larger national struggles for independence and freedom were luxuries he could ill afford. Money was important, he said repeatedly. Tan Hwee Hock, who was his teacher in both Pasir Panjang English School and RI, remembered him having problems purchasing his Scout's uniform. Goh's family was still coping with the death of his father in 1951, a loss which was among Goh's most enduring and painful childhood memories.

When he was 10, he saw his father, Goh Kah Khoon, being carried on his second uncle's back from his second-floor bedroom to a smaller room on the ground floor of their rented house in Pasir Panjang, in rural western Singapore. Tuberculosis had ravaged the man, and the move was to prepare for his death. His family knew his time was almost up, but kept it from his five children. Chok Tong, his eldest child, was none the wiser. "He was always skinny and so we didn't suspect anything," he said. Kah Khoon initially complained about some pain and weakness, but the family did not know what to do. "At that time, people were superstitious. They didn't want to be admitted to Singapore General Hospital," said Kah Khoon's sister, Goh Shu Er. "They said, 'If you go in, you can't come out.' There were very few doctors. We didn't know where to find one even if we had wanted to." At his deathbed, the emaciated man asked to see Chok Tong. The boy was summoned back from school. Kah Khoon told his son in Hokkien: "When I die, look after your mother, look after your sisters, look after your brother, study hard." That night, on July 18, 1951, he died. He was only 36.

The passing left a deep mark on Chok Tong. "I cried, seeing my father that way," he recalled. "Later on, when I grew up, I understood the significance of his words and I tried to live up to them. The impact was embedded. It shaped my life. I learnt responsibility at a very young age." The blow of his father's premature death hit the young boy hard, said Lee Keow Siong. "It devastated him. It was a very difficult period for him and his family. But he pulled himself together quickly," he said. The death also lodged in Chok Tong a lifelong concern and interest in education and healthcare, priorities which he held onto through his career in politics. As his fellow Cabinet colleague, Lim Chee Onn, who also lost his father at a young age, observed, such a blow creates an empathy which sticks. "When someone tells me his father lost a job, I know how he feels," he said. "Chok Tong and I came from the poor, we know what it is like. If you haven't gone through it yourself, you can imagine it, but you don't know what it is really like."

Conditions at home for Chok Tong would get worse before they improved. The death left the family floundering, coming only five years after Chok Tong's grandfather, Goh Boon Siew, had also passed away. It was a double blow since both men were the breadwinners of the household. "My mother couldn't stop crying," said Shu Er in Hokkien. "First she lost her husband, then she lost her son too." The family could not even afford to hold a funeral for Kah Khoon. "We were very poor," she added. "We just had enough to feed ourselves." Thankfully, two close friends of the deceased, Orh Pu and Ching Piao, stepped in and he was given a proper burial.

The Gohs were not always in such a desperate state. Boon Siew left their hometown in Yongchun county in China's southern Fujian province for Singapore, part of a wave of new immigrant workers seeking better lives in Southeast Asia in the early 1900s. He succeeded fairly quickly and set up a provision shop in China Street, an area in downtown Singapore notorious for gambling dens and secret societies. He named his business Guan Huat, which means "origins of prosperity" in Hokkien, the Minnan dialect of Fujian. The choice was fairly apt — albeit for only a short while. Business grew quickly and soon, he was not only able to have a wife back home in Yongchun, but could also make trips back to China and start a family, with a son — Kah Khoon. After a few years, he sent for his family to join him in Singapore. "According to my second uncle, the bandits were kidnapping young boys in Yongchun for ransom," said Chok Tong. "My father hid in a rafter. He was seven years old and, together with another boy, they were hidden in the rafter. When the bandits came, they looked through the village and did not find my father. After that, his father — that is my grandfather — immediately decided to bring him over."

However, the prosperity did not last and during the decades of the world wars, the global turbulence was mirrored by the lives of the Gohs. A failed venture by Boon Siew led to the loss of Guan Huat and even the Gohs' home. "We lost everything. Then we went to rent a small attap house to stay in. There was no electricity, no water," said Shu Er. Boon Siew became a trading agent, acquiring goods such as rubber, rattan and jelutong from Malaya on behalf of businesses in Singapore. The work, which was known as the "98 per cent trade," or "*gao buay hang*" in Hokkien, saw agents enjoying a 2 per cent cut for each deal. The commission was not enough to sustain the family. To supplement the household income, Kah Khoon, who was only in his teens, had to leave home for Kuala Lumpur, to sell shoes in the Malayan capital. When he returned, he joined his father as a trading agent and set up a new business named Khoon Guan.

Through a matchmaker, Kah Khoon was introduced to a teacher in Johor, southern Malaya, named Quah Kwee Hwa. Despite initial resistance to an arranged marriage, Quah eventually acquiesced. Soon, the couple gave birth to their first child on May 20, 1941, in an unused factory in Tanglin which Boon Siew had converted into makeshift rented residences. As was the case with most overseas Chinese during that era, naming conventions followed the clan's genealogy book. For the Goh clan, the first given name of that generation had to be 作 (*zuo*), romanised in Hokkien as "*Chok*." The couple decided to pair it with 栋 (*dong*) or "*Tong*" in Hokkien for their newborn son. They gave their boy an alias too — a popular habit then, selecting 振梁 (*zhenliang*). Taken together, the two names describe a person who can carry the heavy load of a nation. It is a fair bet that Kah Khoon and Kwee Hwa had no idea how accurate their aspirational name choice would turn out to be. "He was a very cute baby," said Shu Er, with a grin, relishing using such an adjective on a man who later became a Prime Minister. "Everyone treated him like a gem. When he cried, his grandmother would scold us."

Yet, the cheer of a new addition in the family was short-lived. Seven months after Chok Tong was born, the Japanese dropped their first bombs on Singapore in December 1941, a precursor to an invasion of Malaya and Singapore. One of the bombs landed close to the Gohs' homes in Alexandra Road and the attacks worried Boon Siew. He was concerned that Singapore lacked food supplies and that the menfolk in the house, especially Kah Khoon, could be killed by the invaders. He reckoned the vast rural hinterland of Malaya could provide better refuge and moved the family to stay with relatives in Batu Pahat in southern Johor. "He was also afraid the kids would starve," recalled Shu Er. "He said 'If there was nothing to eat, at least we could plant crops in Malaya'." Soon after, the Gohs, with baby Chok Tong in tow, moved further up north to Pahang, where they lived in Kuala Krau, a village by a tributary of Pahang River, through most of the Japanese Occupation. Despite regular checks by the Japanese military, the Gohs managed to avoid trouble. Chok Tong played his part. "When the Japanese came to check, we would carry him to hide in the sampans," said Shu Er. "He was so obedient. We told him not to move or talk and he always stayed quiet."

When the war was over, the Gohs returned to Singapore and settled in a rented house in Pasir Panjang, with no electricity and modern sanitation. Another family, the Lims, were co-tenants. A year later, Boon Siew died. Five years later, the household lost its second head when Kah Khoon passed away, too. The rest of the family had to step up to fill the void. After the Lims moved out, Chok Tong's grandmother carved the house into smaller units and sublet them for rent. The compound behind the house was converted into a mini farm, with pigs, chickens, ducks and geese. His second uncle worked in a biscuit factory and a third uncle took on a job as a newspaper vendor. His mother returned to teaching in a Chinese school at West Coast, and to cut down on travelling, she lived in the school.

Chok Tong was left in the care of his grandmother. "I never felt the lack of love," he shared. "My grandmother was the head of the household. My aunt (second uncle's wife) treated me like her son. She cooked for us and we ate the same thing. So we never felt the loss or disruption to the family." But there was also no strong supervision, or even pressure, for him to take his education seriously. Most children in the area were not keen on studies. Yet, he showed discipline in school and did well in Pasir Panjang English School, which was located adjacent to his home, and qualified for RI. "Nobody told me to do it. I just did my own schoolwork and revision. I was not the top student. I was only an above-average student," he said. "My position was maybe around the 10th. The best was the last year when I got the best progress prize — from 10th to 3rd. Maybe it was my father's words — 'study hard' — so I did. The neighbours' children all could not study. Not that they were bad kids but they just could not study."

To his friends in RI, it was soon clear that he was the studious one among them. "We were always running around and kicking anything round," said Tan Cheng Bock. "Chok didn't join us but he had a very nice personality. He would participate by watching. You could see the difference between his room and ours. Ours like *kiam chye*, and his neat.[1] His books were beyond us, Russian books, high-end books — he loved literature. We knew he was an intellectual." When Goh left RI in 1960, his principal lauded him as "the ideal student" who excelled

---

[1] *Kiam chye* literally translates as "salted vegetables" in Hokkien, but in this context, it means "a mess."

not only in his academic work but also in his extra-curricular activities. "He had the greatest of respect for all his teachers, was polite and unassuming and, in return, won the admiration and confidence of all his teachers," wrote Wee Seong Kang in Goh's testimonial in 1960. "I have no hesitation to recommending Goh Chok Tong to anyone who may require his services. He will most certainly be a credit to himself, his school and to all who venture to place their trust in him." His strong track record would eventually be his family's ticket out of poverty.

After six years in RI, he earned a place in the then University of Singapore. However, the practical needs of his family nearly derailed the education. His mother said that she could not afford the university fees and had preferred him to go to polytechnic instead — the shorter route to employment. "She said polytechnic took three years after O levels and I would graduate," he recalled. "Then I could start working and help to support the family. I said no. I wanted to go to university. She then suggested that I study dentistry. Why? Because you could make money! We went to the dentist a few times when we were young and she could see that it was a job that could make money. But I had no interest in dentistry." His RI friend Othman Haron Eusofe said Goh was always "concerned about salaries" even after he started working, and fretted over whether he could afford a better home for his family.

Goh eventually chose economics. He was granted a government bursary of $1,500 a year — a princely sum at that time. It helped assuage his mother's financial concerns, especially since the bursary came with a five-year bond to work in the civil service upon graduation. Employment was guaranteed. "I was very happy to take on the bond," said Goh. "It was not an issue. To be able to afford my university fees was my bigger concern. The bursary was more than what I could ask for. A bond was never a concern." The decision to take the bursary and the bond would lead him on to an incredible journey in government and politics.

Q: *What were your earliest memories?*

A: My first memory is of Pahang in Malaya, when I was four or five, during the war. My mother was bathing me by the river and I remember seeing buffaloes. When the war ended, we took a lorry back to Singapore. The womenfolk and children sat at the back, together with green bananas. Halfway, the lorry stopped and the adults were talking about why they had to stop. In Hokkien, they said *wu sua ngiao ci* — mountain rats. I did not know what that meant, but later on, I found out they were referring to communist guerrillas.

Q: Was Hokkien the main language you used at home?

A: It was completely Hokkien. My grandmother used only Hokkien, my aunt spoke Hokkien, my cousins all used Hokkien. My other aunts were educated in the Chinese stream. They tried to practise English with me but I never tried to practise Chinese with them. It is unfortunate I never picked up Chinese, but they picked up some English.

Q: What were your nicknames at home and in schools?

A: No nicknames at home. But Chinese like to use 'Ah' before your name, so I was 'Ah Tong' growing up at home. But among my friends in school, I had a few nicknames. I went by *Panjang*.[2] I went by Long. This was how friends teased me, but I never took any offence. One friend called me Shorty. Close friends called me Chok.

Q: So you would respond to Panjang?

A: I turned around and it was obviously me. Who else was so *panjang*?

Q: Were you tall since primary school?

A: Oh, I was. When I was in Primary 6, I was 68 inches tall, I remember. I was very tall.

---

[2] *Panjang* is a Malay word which means long.

Q: *Were your parents tall too?*

A: My father was tall. He had a bit of a hunch, so we were probably about the same height. My mum too. For a woman, she was on the tall side. She was not exceptionally tall but above average. But the 'long bean' strain came from my father's side because it is also reflected in my second uncle's children and grandchildren. So when I went to Yongchun after I stepped down as PM, I was expecting to see very tall cousins! But they were not very tall. My generation of Gohs in Yongchun were not tall. Some even looked quite short to me. Maybe it had to do with nourishment.

Q: *What food did you have at home?*

A: The food was ordinary — just *chye sim, tao gay, tao kwa, kangkong* and those greens.[3] And if we have a fish, it was usually *ikan kuning*. Nowadays, they say it is for cats! And, of course, pork and eggs occasionally. Chicken would be a treat. Most of the time, when there was chicken, it was from my grandmother's poultry farming because we had a compound at the back and she would rear some chickens, and some ducks and geese there as well. My grandmother was quite enterprising. She also reared pigs. So, as a boy, I would occasionally help feed the pigs and clean the sty. The pigs were sold to the market. So you made ends meet and there was always food to eat. What was tight was when you had to see doctors. You would not see doctors until you had no choice.

---

[3] *Chye sim* is also referred to as choy sum; *tao gay* is Hokkien for beansprout; *tao kwa* is fried bean curd; *kangkong* is known in English as water spinach; and *ikan kuning* is yellowstripe fish.

Q: How would you describe a typical day in your childhood?

A: My activity was swimming. This was because the sea was opposite my house. The house where I lived is opposite the current Pasir Panjang MRT station. So I learnt to swim, self-taught. It was first in a monsoon drain behind my house when high tide came. Later, we would normally swim in the sea. Then I joined the Tiger Swimming Club and I was in the club's junior team. I also swam for the school. The Pasir Panjang School swimming team won most of the inter-school swimming prizes. In RI, I was a school swimming captain.

Q: How many extra-curricular activities did you have?

A: In RI, quite a lot. I was chairman of the Historical Society, I was secretary of the Geographical Society. I was student representative of the Tuck Shop Committee. The teacher trusted me and I was invited by the teachers to be the student rep. I was a school prefect, and a class monitor. I was a Scout troop leader. I was a school swimmer — captain. I was also editor of the school magazine. So quite a fair bit.

Q: Surely you were tapped to represent the school for basketball or volleyball since these sports require height?

A: They encouraged me to play basketball but I did not take it up for two reasons. One, basketball would be held in the evenings, around five or six o'clock. I would normally go home after school by cycling back to my house in Pasir Panjang. Yes, you could study in school and stay until five or six o'clock. But it was different. You would have to eat outside. But if I cycled home, my aunt would have kept some food for lunch for me. I would finish the lunch and nap for a while, then I would bathe and study. I would not want to cycle all the way back to school for basketball. It did not make sense to me. The second reason was that I was self-conscious at that time. I was the tallest, but I was not a gifted basketball player and I was wearing thick spectacles. So, I would not want to go to the basketball court. People would expect me to be the shooter and when I couldn't make the shots, it would be embarrassing.

Q: *When did you move out of Pasir Panjang?*

A: When I was in university, my mother bought a three-room flat in Tanglin Halt, Queenstown. I went with her to choose the flat. Queenstown was a new place. It was the nearest estate to my university. It was adjacent to the railway track. I chose the block because there would be no new flats coming up on the other side. It was Commonwealth Drive, Block 55, unit 53E, on the sixth floor. I chose a floor with a lift; the lift did not stop at every floor. The last I heard, it was slated to be knocked down. En bloc. I went to take some photographs before they knock it down. They are tearing it down so there are no preservation problems, like the Oxley Road house. Otherwise, there may be a debate in Parliament! (laughs)

Q: *What are your memories of your time in Queenstown?*

A: I just marvelled at the modern sanitation. You just flush and it would all go away. Because, for years, living in Pasir Panjang, it was the bucket system. The second part was the wind. At that time, we bought, like everybody did, linoleum to cover the cement floor. So, in the early days, the linoleum would be flapping in the wind. But, later on, as you walked more on it, it became stuck to the floor. So these were some simple pleasures. It was also the first time I slept in a bed. In Pasir Panjang, I slept on a straw mat on the floor.

Outside, there was a small carpark. You saw people rushing to park their cars. Later on, when I had a small car, I was also trying to choose the best place to park so that I could get out. Otherwise, I would get stuck behind some other cars and so on. And living in a housing estate was quite noisy. Especially during Chinese New Year. At that time, they had not banned firecrackers. So, there was a lot of noise and firecrackers were thrown from the top floor.

Q: *Was that the first time you and siblings were living together?*

A: No, we lived together until my father died. Then my mother stayed in her school with my three younger siblings. In Queenstown, we all squeezed into the three-room flat. We could manage. Today, some would consider it overcrowded.

Q: Because people don't wonder about modern sanitation anymore.

A: That's the trouble.

Q: What were your political leanings at that age?

A: I leaned towards the left. I was influenced by my fifth uncle, Kah Peck, who studied in Chung Cheng High, and Chinese school students at that point were more politically aware than those in English schools like myself. My uncle was only four years older than me. He pointed me in the direction of some leftist literature in English and I bought some Russian books. I was introduced to Maxim Gorky, Turgenev — I read those. And I came across this word — proletariat. It was a nice-sounding word and very impactful. So when I was in Pre-U 1, I wrote an article about dialectic materialism.

Q: Your essay was on dialectic materialism? That could have gotten you into serious trouble!

A: I didn't know. I thought I was going to impress. Proletariat, dialectic materialism — very big words! The teacher did not scold me. He just advised me and explained a few things. And I said, ah, maybe I was just arguing from one side. But he sort of explained that I did not quite get it right and I did not pursue.

I don't think my fifth uncle, Kah Peck, was consciously influencing me, but he and my aunts were all in the Chinese stream. When there were student demonstrations, they were all caught up and participated. My uncle even took me to the Hock Lee depot where the bus workers were striking. I was there that night, just before the riots took place. We walked from Pasir Panjang to Alexandra Hock Lee bus depot. That was probably about two or three miles. We walked there and we listened. The bus drivers were on strike and one man got up to speak. He never said a single word. He just stood up and stood there for a few minutes without saying a word, but you could feel the tension in the air. The policemen were nearby. Fortunately, my uncle was quite a wise person. He must have sensed something. Had the man spoken, we would have listened to him. The next day, I read in *The Straits Times* that riots took place. My uncle also took me to Kallang Airport to welcome the return of the ministers who went to the UK as part of the talks for independence.

My third uncle was also left-inclined. He was a newspaper vendor — on the bicycle distributing newspapers. One day, he just told his mother he was going to China and he left without anything. He returned for a visit only years later, after China had opened up, but he could not come back for good. I learnt later on that he was actually a cadre in the Chinese Communist Party in Guangxi. He stayed in Nanning.[4]

As an aside, at my interview to be a PAP candidate, I think quite by chance, Lee Kuan Yew asked me if I knew any communists. I said no. Then later on, I thought that was not quite true!

---

[4] Guangxi is a southern region in China, with Nanning as its regional capital.

Q: You witnessed some of these events that are very significant to Singapore. What was your political thinking at that time?

A: I felt that there was a sense of change. In other words, I was intuitively, maybe intellectually, supporting Lee Kuan Yew's side. Not the communists' side. But at that time, I had no strong feelings about anti-colonialism. You were too young to have that strong feeling, but you just felt that change would take place and that the PAP was on the right side.

Q: Did you attend any PAP rallies?

A: I followed my uncle to one in Bukit Timah in 1955 and I also attended one in Pasir Panjang in 1959. That was the first time I saw LKY when he was campaigning for Othman Wok. At the Pasir Panjang rally, I saw him coming from the back. That was his style — he walked from the back, and then he would pause there and listened to the speakers. He would sense the mood before he spoke. He watched there for a while, wearing all white, and he walked to the stage and spoke in Hokkien. People started laughing. His Hokkien was not very good. The pronunciation was not that accurate. When you were young, you had no idea he was trying very hard to learn and that he was not Hokkien. But you just stood there laughing at his Hokkien.

Goh was one of the star students in the university, said several who were at the same school then. "Goh Chok Tong was like one of the sure things. If you were looking to bet your money on who would surely get a first class, it was him," said Chan Heng Chee, who was reading political science. He did not disappoint the campus punters. In 1964, he graduated from university with a first-class honours degree in economics. His schoolmates expected big things of him. "The word 'leader' was not used, but he had all the good qualities — he was a good guy, had good character and you expected him to do well in life," added Chan.

He wanted to pursue a career in academia, but his request to serve his bond as a research fellow in the university was rejected by the government. "I just shrugged it off," he said. "I knew I was on a bond and that, from the very start, the transfer might be difficult, but the university was happy to push for me. But it could not do it, so I said 'Okay' and I went to serve the government." The Public Service Commission placed him in the elite Administrative Service and sent him to the Economic Planning Unit (EPU) in the Prime Minister's Office in City Hall.

When he obtained his first pay packet of $830, it was immediately taken away from him by his grandmother. She used it to pay back Orh Pu and Ching Piao — the two kind family friends who had paid for Goh's father's funeral and burial 13 years earlier.

Chapter 2

The Corporate Bureaucrat

"He basically turned the company around."

Lua Cheng Eng, former managing director of NOL, on Goh Chok Tong's
legacy in Singapore's national shipping line.[5]

I t was April 27, 1973, when a small group of Singapore political
elite and shipping leaders had gathered in the Finnish port of Turku
to celebrate the completion of a semi-containership. It was named
the Neptune Sapphire, taking after its owner, the Neptune Orient Lines
(NOL), Singapore's five-year-old national shipping company. To bless
the expensive $25 million vessel custom built by the famous Wartsila
Shipyard in Finland, a bottle of champagne was smashed against the
ship's bow, as was, and still is, the maritime norm. But the bubbly did
not break. A hush fell over the crowd. "*Suay*," whispered someone in
Hokkien, meaning "bad luck" in English. It is an industry superstition
that a failed christening ritual portends of upcoming misfortune. A
second attempt was made and this time, the bottle was smashed. But
the damage, some believed, was done.

---

[5] Rahita Elias and Leong Ching, *Beyond Boundaries: The First 35 Years of the NOL Story* (Singapore:
NOL Limited, 2004), p. 39.

Less than four months later, when the Sapphire set sail on its maiden voyage, disaster struck. The Suez Canal was closed and the new ship from Finland had to route through Africa to reach Singapore. Midway through its journey, the new ship was hit by stormy weather off the eastern cape of South Africa. "The captain didn't slow down," said Soe Aung, a naval engineer with NOL. The Sapphire was buffeted by 60-foot waves and the turbulence rattled the 35-strong crew, who were all Singaporeans except for the German captain. "That night, none of us could sleep," said Sapphire's second engineer, Chia Che Kiang, in the book *Beyond Boundaries: The First 35 Years of the NOL Story*. "The weather was very bad. The cabin was hot and humid and the ship was pitching badly." Then, the crew heard a muffled thud and they realised there was trouble. "It was very frightening. No one knew what was happening," said seaman Tay Hock Chiang to the *New Nation* newspaper. Sapphire's bow, where the champagne bottle had failed to break, had ripped away from the rest of the hulking 23,000 tonne freighter. "One minute the bow was there — the next it was gone in the night as it drifted past us," added Tay.

When news reached NOL's headquarters in Singapore, its executive director, Eric Khoo, called his finance director, Goh Chok Tong. He told Goh: "The Sapphire had broken up off the coast of South Africa." Goh was stunned. "What do you mean 'broken up'?" he asked. "Broken up — split in two," replied Khoo. Goh could hardly believe what he was hearing. "How could it happen? It was unbelievable. Yes, there was a big storm, but how could a new ship just break up in a storm? I felt shock and disbelief," he recalled in *Beyond Boundaries*. His immediate concern was with the crew. Thankfully, none of the seaman was at the bow at the time of the crash and all were rescued from the crippled Sapphire. Goh, together with other senior management of NOL, later flew to Finland to inspect the damage and discuss repairs with Wartsila. After many months of negotiation and arbitration, they managed to get the builders to accept culpability for the disaster, ensuring NOL kept its fledgling reputation intact. A few months later, in a move unrelated to the accident, Goh was made managing director of the company — the top position in the national shipping line.

The Sapphire crash was more drama than Goh had bargained for when he had requested for a job out of the civil service. Before joining NOL, Goh had been posted to the Economic Planning Unit (EPU) in 1964. However, after a few months, he was bored and craved, in his own words, "more action." The tiny unit, which was tasked to look at statistics and charts, was hardly the most exciting. "What did I learn? My boss taught me how to file the documents," he said. "He would get the paper and puncher and he punched two holes. Then he went to the file, put in number 1, 2, 3, 4. I learnt about filing. What did we do? We cut articles and pasted them on vanguard sheets, put them on the board. No intellectual work in the beginning. It was very mundane."

The arrival of J. Y. Pillay, who subsequently became one of Singapore's top and most famous civil servants, brought the level of work at EPU up a notch. It helped that separation from Malaysia came a year later, thrusting upon the Unit and its bureaucrats like Goh a greater urgency to chart the economic development of newly-independent Singapore. They wrote papers to help the government plan its growth, one which could no longer depend on a hinterland. "My work got more interesting," said Goh. "We got to write the papers, which were included in the second development plan." Pillay began to notice him. "He was a very quiet guy, didn't throw his weight around," he said. "Well disciplined, well mannered, bright guy."

Goh did well, albeit a little too well at times. Once, he wrote a paper on the state of Singapore's economy — the first such report on the domestic economy — and it contained growth figures. Then Deputy Prime Minister Goh Keng Swee liked the report so much that he gave it to the press, which published it. The next day, the young Goh got a note from Prime Minister Lee Kuan Yew. "He said this economic growth figure was normally released by the PM," said Goh, laughing as he recalled his youthful ignorance. "It was not a scolding, but he was asking who gave me permission to release it to the press? So, of course, I told Dr Goh about it. He said he would tell the Prime Minister that he had asked me to."

Despite excelling at the job, Goh's desire for more frontline action was still not quenched. He wanted to leave the civil service for global oil and gas giant Shell and, in 1965, obtained a position after clearing the firm's famous selection process. Despite having resigned from the government, his exit was thwarted by Goh Keng Swee who blocked his move and put pressure on Shell to cease the pursuit. But more on this later. Thankfully, a year later, in 1966, Goh Chok Tong finally caught a break. Pillay suggested that he apply to pursue a Masters in Development Economics in Williams College in Massachusetts, United States. He received a Ford Foundation fellowship. That meant signing another bond, sending Goh back to the civil service and the Economic Development Divison (EDD), the successor of the EPU, on his return from Williams. This time, he was determined to do more than writing papers and get himself some "oomph."

Fortuitously, a new company set up by the Singapore Government borrowed a small room from the EDD on the mezzanine floor of the Fullerton Building, which is today a swanky hotel near the mouth of the Singapore River. That company was NOL — Singapore's new national shipping line, wholly owned by the government. "They borrowed the address, a small room and my clerk typist — that was how NOL started," said Goh. "I got to know the managing director, M. J. Sayeed, and the executive director, Eric Khoo. So when I was thinking of going out to join a new company, I thought of them. I asked them and they said yes." He was successfully seconded from the civil service to NOL, and was appointed its planning and projects manager. "I planned for the company and did certain projects," he said, revealing a time when job titles tended to be, well, literal. "There was more action than what I was doing at EDD." It wasn't much, but it was enough.

The move was by no means unique. Goh, like many promising young civil servants of the post-independence era, was part of a generation of genre-bending bureaucrats in Singapore who were also in business — a seeming oxymoron. While he moved into shipping, there were other civil servants who also ventured into new state-owned enterprises. Pillay took charge of the national carrier Singapore Airlines; S. Dhanabalan helped set up DBS Bank; Sim Kee Boon left his imprint on Intraco, the state-owned trading firm, and Keppel Shipyard; and

Philip Yeo made his mark in defence industries companies which became the Singapore Technologies group. These businesses were largely the brainchild of Goh Keng Swee, who created a phalanx of government-linked companies (GLCs), designed not only to pursue profits but also to secure Singapore's strategic future without an over-reliance on multi-national corporations.

NOL was a good example. While its goal was to be a profitable business, Goh Keng Swee also had strategic objectives for the company. He wanted it to break the cartel, Far East Freight Conference (FEFC), which he felt was responsible for high freight rates that could strangle Singapore's trade. At the same time, building Singapore's own shipping line would be useful during war. "In time of war, many of the shipping lines which were commercial might not want to carry your cargo," explained Goh Chok Tong. "But if you have your own shipping line, you could carry your own. It was wrong thinking at that time and we did not know. We learnt, later on, that if we were prepared to pay a price, high insurance premium, there would always be ships which were prepared to go to the war zone. But at that time, it was a strategic thinking."

To succeed, Goh Keng Swee was prepared to let young bureaucrats like Goh Chok Tong take on leadership roles in these GLCs, even though they had no experience in the industry. "When you are young, you find that you can learn anything," said Goh Chok Tong. "It was not only myself who was new. Most of the people had no idea of ship operations. They took in a few people from shipping agencies, so they knew about getting cargo. But owning and running a ship — they had no experience. The only one who had experience was the managing director. But then, he never really ran a company. He was running ships. He was a ship captain. He knew about running ships, but the company was quite different." The entire NOL was largely filled with young people, recalled Lim Boon Heng, a naval architect who represented the firm in a Danish shipyard when he was only 23. Once, shared Lim, when one of NOL's new ships docked in California, an American went on board and remarked: "My God, they've got a bunch of Boy Scouts running this ship!"

Goh was not sent on courses or training. There were no such privileges or luxuries. Instead, he had to learn about shipping through books. As unbelievable as it may sound today, the man who became the top honcho of the national shipping line was a self-taught novice who relied on 1960s versions of "For Dummies" how-to texts. "I bought two books: one was on how to run a shipping company and the other was on tankers. Those were just level-one kind of books, a primer — 101," he said. The company was not afraid to put good people in charge, said Lim. "Once basic qualifications were obtained, people were promoted," he shared.

To immerse himself in the trade, Goh was put on the Neptune Taurus, an old petroleum tanker, and tasked to learn about cargo operations as the ship sailed from Singapore to the Middle East. He quickly realised that the action he had craved for was not quite coming to life, even out in the seas. "I got onto the tanker. Wow, it was very slow," he said. "The crew was from Hong Kong and all of them spoke Cantonese, which I could not speak a single word of. But the ship's chief officer was an Indian, so, fortunately, I could speak to him in English. He was also quite bored, so he would take me to see the tanker pipes and the colour coding — like how this colour was for pumping out, this was for pumping in and how things worked. He also took me down to the engine room. So, I learnt a bit. I stayed in the owner's suite. It was a small room and there was a deck where I could sun myself. It was quite nice the first time you went up. The breeze was very good, but after a while, you felt very bored. I took along my tanker book and tried to relate it to the actual thing. But when we arrived in Port Klang at night, I had already felt bored."

He got out at the Malaysian port and watched the berthing and loading, after which the ship moved up north to Penang where the cargo was discharged. "By then, I was totally bored," he said. He plotted a quick escape and came back to Singapore from Penang, explaining to his bosses that he had seen the full operations of the tanker, and actually helped the firm save money by not going all the way to the Middle East.

The excitement of hands-on experience building a shipping firm helped Goh overcome the boredom of Taurus. He soon realised NOL had no idea how much each voyage of its ships on the FEFC route would make. To fix the problem, he introduced a "management information system," where earnings and costs were calculated after the last port of loading. The findings shocked NOL. Almost every voyage was a loss, even when the ships were 80 per cent full.

Goh concluded that they were carrying the wrong kinds of cargo, like timber and rubber, which commanded low rates and yet, took up a lot of space. "We were scratching our heads," he said. "Then, I read this book about optimal cargo and learnt that you had to maximise the use of space and high-value cargo, which is heavy. I worked it out and said to go for tin ore — tin ingots, actually — from Malaysia. These were high freight, heavy and small volume. But you cannot have all tin ingots because the ship would sink. So, it was some tin ingots, rubber, and other manufactured goods. Bulky timber should be the last resort as the freight rate was low and handling costs high."

He was making a difference in NOL and was rewarded in 1973, four years after he first joined and soon after the Sapphire accident, with a promotion to the top position as Managing Director. He was only 32. Pillay, who was on the NOL board and among those who chose Goh for the No. 1 position, said he edged out Khoo who was more experienced. "I could see Chok Tong would make a more suitable CEO. There was nothing wrong with Eric, but you felt that Chok Tong was steadier, very constant and straightforward. He didn't say very much and so you didn't pay too much attention to him," said Pillay with a chuckle. "But he was a very competent officer."

The appointment came with a big commitment from Goh. He would make NOL, which was still a loss-making business, profitable in three years. "I told the chairman, give me three years and I would try my best. If I could not turn around the company, then they would have to look for somebody else," he said, before breaking out into a grin. "I was giving him notice that I needed three years to turn the company around, in case they expected me to turn it around in two years or one year!" He relooked the firm's financial strategy, insurance policies and most of all, its fundamental business ethos.

The liner had a bad reputation. "Its reliability was very low," said Lim Boon Heng. When NOL heard of additional cargo which could be picked up en route, it frequently redirected its ships to these ports so as to earn extra money. But this meant the ships were frequently delayed on their voyages, upsetting clients. Goh put a stop to these diversions and slowly changed the liner's reputation. Long-time NOL employee Teo Yak Long said that the company was a little-known player in the maritime world in the early 1970s. "The company was a small player. By end-70s, we were a brand name, the big shipping boys took note of us and respected us, we were respected in the shipping circle," he said. "A lot of it was due to decisions made by Mr Goh."

A key call made by Goh was to move NOL into the era of container shipping, catching the new wave of the maritime industry then. The company had its first purpose-built container ship, the Neptune Pearl, under his leadership, said former NOL marine engineer, Kenneth Kee. "We were definitely one of the pioneers and it was Mr Goh who kickstarted it," he said. "He was not a shipping man, but he is smart and sharp. He could see where shipping was going." At the same time, Goh restructured the company and, instead of relying on middlemen, NOL posted young officers overseas to Japan, Germany and London.

"We were much closer to the ground, our info and intel more reliable," said Teo. "In shipping, you don't learn from textbooks. You learn being out there on the ground, and you make decisions based on what you see and hear and observe." To become a force in container shipping, Goh also instructed his people to gatecrash a meeting in Hong

Kong so as to force its way into a new consortium — Asia Container Europe (ACE). "We waited for days in our hotel to join the meeting," said Lim. "Joining the consortium was critical to NOL. We learnt a lot from our partners. That was how NOL turned around."

Internally, Goh made sure the young team was managed with the right touch in the fairly rough maritime world. In an early glimpse into his shrewd use of talent and his adroit touch with people which became evident later in politics, he made small, but tangible, changes to improve staff welfare and morale. For instance, he introduced a happy hour at work where drinks were on the company. "How do you get the people to bond as a team? Drinking was something most people enjoyed at that time in shipping," he said. "When the ship officers were in town, I said to come and join in, drink and go back to work, because most of them worked overtime. Anybody, even the secretaries, could go up and have a drink. That was not in the book but I think it was just common sense, to bond the people."

It was part of an early iteration of his participatory style of management, where there is a conscious effort to understand the needs of others and put their interests first. "He was the boss but he rarely told people off," recalled Kee. "He would listen to everyone's views and because of this, people dared to speak up and offer feedback and ideas. Of course, you'd have to know what you're talking about. But this was Mr Goh's style — he would take in the feedback and then tell you 'Okay, this is what we are going to do'." By the time the rest of Singapore became familiar with Goh's way, the NOL old boys could afford a smile that they had a sneak preview ahead of others. "The consultative government that he talked about, we saw it first in NOL," said Teo, with a broad grin.

Goh noticed that NOL ship captains, on arriving back in Singapore, had to walk from the ship to the main road because taxis could not drive into the port. "The captain normally would be the last to leave because there were so many papers to sign. And this was the home port. When people come home to Singapore, they want to spend the maximum time with their family and do their own thing," he said. "So, I said, why not, to raise the morale, get a station wagon to take the captain and senior officers home? Otherwise, at least bring them out to the main gate — that would save them 20 to 30 minutes. It was a move that was very appreciated. Again, it was common sense."

The move was also motivated by incidents of sabotage. He had observed that some crew member would deliberately damage the ship so that the vessel needed more time at the dock for repairs. "This would allow the crew to enjoy themselves (on land) because they had been out at sea for two to four weeks," he added. "When your captain is back in home port, make sure he is taken care of. It was nothing brilliant, just that you have interest in people. You've got to run the company and you must show interest in the people. Human relations must come first."

A major part of his man management was also about setting an example, including basics like good manners, said Kee. "In the mornings, he would wish everyone in the lift good morning, didn't matter who you were — a staff, a cleaner... so, because he was like this, people would greet him too," he said, with a laugh. "In the past, if you see your boss in the lift, you wouldn't make a dash for it. You'd just wait for the next lift. But you wouldn't feel that way with Mr Goh."

And while it was common for top management of shipping lines to fly first class, Goh insisted on economy since NOL was still not profitable. "The company was not doing well so how could I travel first class? If I travelled first class, my senior managers would want to go first class too and I could not deny them. And then my ship captains, senior officers would want to go first class," he explained. When others told him that flying economy would reflect poorly on NOL and deter potential clients, he demurred. "Nobody had ever asked me which class I came by," he said. "They asked about the hotel I was staying, so for hotels, yes, I would have to choose a reasonable one. I could not go to a cheap hotel to save money. That was how I knew about Royal Gardens in London. Not the top but quite near the top. It was prestigious. But nobody asked me how I travelled to London."

Despite the temptations of the shipping industry, where a flashy culture of bling and booze intoxicated, Goh was a young man who resisted the lures. Part of it was an external restraint, he said. The reputation of a clean and incorruptible Singapore, even in those early days, was already fairly well known around the world. "The other side knew how Singapore worked. They knew Lee Kuan Yew and how we worked," he said. "There was no need to tempt us. I negotiated on ship purchases, shipping prices and so on — they were all quite transparent. The other side must have come to the conclusion that working with Singapore, there was no need to tempt them. That is my assessment. So, I have never been offered anything." His incorruptibility caught the eyes of the political masters. Lee would describe Goh years later, in 1988: "His ability undoubted, his integrity proven. In NOL, you rub shoulders with shipowners, people like Y. K. Pao, the Tungs, the Hong Kong millionaires, the multi-millionaires. When they exchange gifts, they don't exchange T-shirts! He's totally untouched and unspoilt. So, financially, you can't buy and sell him, which is important."

There was a self-discipline about Goh which belied his age and the social mores of that era. "I got the impression as a young executive in shipping, to get on with your counterparts, the shipowners and so on, you have to learn to smoke a cigar and drink," he shared. "Once, after a dinner at the Raffles Hotel, one of the chaps wanted a cigar and Raffles Hotel offered cigars, so I also asked for one to try. But one, two puffs later, my stomach was churning. I think it was the wine plus the smoke. I asked to be excused and I went to the bathroom. After that, I did not try and learn this kind of stuff. I was never a smoker and even today, socially, I do not smoke. I drink a little socially though. You had to be careful. They (the shipping counterparts) watched you, to see if you liked this or enjoyed going to bars; if so, they would slowly bring you in."

He was acutely aware that the job was not simply about building a private company and making profits. The strategic nation-building thinking of Goh Keng Swee behind the GLCs strongly influenced him and that generation of younger civil servants. Just as it has often been said that Singapore was fortunate to have a founding generation of Old Guard leaders who were not only brilliant but also incorruptible and united, it is also uncanny that the country had a second generation who bought into the same ideology and practices. In the case of Goh

Chok Tong, he repeated several times that NOL was "a national shipping line." "You had a job here. This is your country and you just felt it. I wasn't the only one. We were all young people with the same kind of thinking. We could sense we were part of the new generation that would be helping Singapore," he said. "You were running a shipping line for the country, so the motivation for ourselves was different. You were doing it for the country. The shipping line was for the country. If it was private, then I do not know. Luckily, it was a national shipping line."

Q: *Soon after starting work at the civil service, you nearly joined Shell. Why did you want to leave the government?*

A: Well, my salary at the civil service was $830, with an increment of $35 a year. The first promotion, for the best officer, was after five years. Five years before I could become assistant secretary. So that means my salary would be $1,005 in five years. I saw an advertisement by Shell for a job. The salary was $1,100. Wow.

Q: *But it would mean that you would have to break your bond?*

A: Well, it was $1,100. If I had to break my bond at that time, there was no hullabaloo about bond breaking. So, I just paid back — $3,600. It was a very big sum and I did not have the money. I borrowed from Shell.

Q: *What was the job you got at Shell?*

A: I don't know! (laughs) I didn't know exactly what it was — they called it an executive. At that time, an executive was considered a very big position. It was a nice-sounding title. $1,100 was so attractive.

Q: *So you resigned from EPU to join Shell?*

A: I resigned. At the EPU, they gave me a farewell party. And my boss, Francis Lim, was very envious of me leaving. I remember what he said: 'You are very lucky, you are doing the right thing. Because, later on, you would be driving a Jaguar.' Shell was the best paymaster in Singapore and it was not easy to get into the company. So, if you get into Shell, you have made it. But I was not interested in the Jaguar. I was interested in the $1,100. And the increment every year was about $100. Wouldn't you have done the same? I was getting married, you see. I had to support my family.

Q: *How did you meet your wife?*

A: Call it fate or whatever it is. She was a Malaysian. She went to the UK to study and could not quite adjust to the cold, so she came back. She joined RI in the second year. It was pre-university two at that point. I was seated at the back of the class, as I was the tallest. Normally, it was two by two, but I was sitting alone. She came into the class, the teacher brought her in and told us that she was a new student joining our class. She looked around and there were no seats left in front, so she went right to the back and sat next to me. We did not hit it off immediately. We had to share a book because she had no book.

Towards the end of the year, two friends and I decided to do a tour of Malaysia, or Malaya at that time, as we called it. I had just won $200 in an essay writing competition organised by a local newspaper. We were looking for a place to stay. So, we said jokingly: 'Oh, you are from Kuala Lumpur. Can we somehow stay at your place?' So, the three of us actually stayed in her place.

We were young and didn't know anything. The three of us stayed in a room. It was only later, after I had known Choo Leng well, that I discovered that that was her parents' room. The parents moved out to a small utility room; she stayed with her sister in another room.

Q: She must have liked you a lot for the special treatment.

A: I did not know. I thought her place was quite big. But it was not. It was government quarters. Her father was a school educationist. That was the beginning of the interest. From there, we started dating, more or less. I think before that, we did go out for lunch once in a while. We walked around the areas near the school, to Odeon and so on.[6]

Q: Was she your first girlfriend?

A: She was my first girlfriend. We dated and it went on. And in university, we just carried on and so forth. And after that, we got married.

Q: Was there a fancy proposal?

A: No. At that time, the way I was brought up, it is not like today's kids, where the proposal is very fanciful, very imaginative. No, it was just one step at a time. I don't think there was any formal proposal. I certainly never went down on my knees. I could hardly afford the wedding at that time. My second uncle insisted that I had a dinner. I told him I could not afford it and neither could my mother. But he said, no, I was the eldest of my generation and I must have a wedding dinner. So, he decided to pay for the dinner. He also borrowed his boss' car. He was working for Siong Hoe biscuit factory. We decided to marry before I started

---

6 Odeon Cinema was a famous landmark in downtown Singapore, adjacent to the Bugis campus of Raffles Institution.

work in Shell as I thought I would not be able to take leave in the first year. You didn't normally take leave in the first year when you started work then.

We went to Malaysia for our honeymoon, and I was in Kuala Lumpur when I got a telegram from Shell — 'Please come back urgently.' I came back to see them and they said: 'I am sorry. Dr Goh Keng Swee did not release you. The government will not release you from the civil service.' Dr Goh did not know me personally at that point. I found out much later they (the Old Guard) had an interest in, shall we say, officials with potential. I was one of the few with a first-class honours in economics. There were other good students but they were not in economics. Dr Goh must have paid special attention to me because, by then, EPU was in the Finance Ministry.

Shell told me that we had already signed the contract. If I wished to continue with it, they would honour the contract. But from the way they put it, they would honour the contract but they would not be very happy about it. Because they would not know what punishment Shell would get from Dr Goh. They had gotten the pioneer certificate from the government, which meant tax incentives. I said: 'No problem, I understand, I will go back.' So, I went back. This time, EPU did not give me a welcoming-back party! I just laughed. Francis Lim laughed and laughed.

Q: But were you upset?

A: No. Things that were beyond control — there was no point getting angry.

Q: But there goes your Jaguar... and your thousand-dollar salary.

A: The salary was more important (laughs). Two of us in Singapore got the job in Shell. The other was a Malcolm Goh, by coincidence. I don't know who this person was or what he was doing. Maybe he is driving a Jaguar.

Q: Did the government give you a pay increment when you returned?

A: No, there was no such thing. I went back to my old place with my old pay. You had a bond, you were under bond, so there was a sense that you happily took the bond, took the bursary, so you had to accept it. You were not in control of your life at this stage. I was grateful, which was one of the reasons I gave for serving in the government and joining the PAP. I was grateful because, without the bursary, I would not have gone into university. What life would be like if I didn't have a bond, I don't know. I probably would have joined *The Straits Times* because that was my thought when I was doing arts at 'A' levels — to be a journalist. I never let things which I cannot control to cause me to be unhappy. When I could not continue the research fellowship in university, I just shrugged and went on. And when I went to Shell and I was supposed to get in, but never stepped in, I just accepted it.

Q: *You did leave the civil service soon after that, with a fellowship to study in Williams College. How was the experience?*

A: When I got admitted to Williams College, they wrote me a letter and told me to go to Ford Foundation to apply for funding. And the Ford Foundation was very good. It was based in KL — they gave me an air ticket to fly to KL for the interview. So, at the age of 25, I sat for the first time in an aeroplane. It was such a joyous ride. Looking at the clouds, wow. I was fascinated. Then taking off and landing — it was tremendous fascination for me.

At Williams College, the positive experience for me was getting used to and knowing my classmates who were mainly young officials from emerging economies. It was a class of 20, from 16 countries. There were two each from the Philippines, India, Pakistan and Mexico, and one each from Malaysia, Yugoslavia, Egypt, Ethiopia, Tanzania, Kenya, Uganda, Liberia, Colombia, Honduras, Bolivia. Why did I remember? Because when I came back, and years after that, I kept on asking myself — what made a country grow, what made it tick? Most of the countries I mentioned had broken down, and several broken up.

In 1966, we were all from emerging economies. It was the same starting line — all of us were trying to do what we could for our countries. Some countries like Singapore and Malaysia had developed and some countries had gone backwards, like Ethiopia, Uganda. So, I asked myself, what is the real factor that enables developing countries to progress? Resources? My conclusion was that it was the way a country was led and organised. In other words, good leadership.

The Africans were easy to get along with. I liked them. When I became prime minister and went to Zimbabwe for my first Commonwealth meeting, from Day One I was comfortable with the African leaders. Apart from that, the general atmosphere at Williams College — it was in a beautiful town, but I spent more time studying. I was active in the first few weeks, and went to the club and swam and joined some activities. But then after that, I thought I had better study.

Q: *Did you let your hair down when you were overseas?*

A: My wife was with me! If she had not gone, I might have explored a few things and a few places. So fortunately, I was still quite clear that I had to come back and work. I was under a bond and the scholarship would be taken away from me if I did not do well there. I would not have let my hair down. It might have grown a little longer to save some money.

Q: *Did you at any point imagine that you would return to Williams College one day and be honoured as a Prime Minister?*[7]

A: No. At that time, first of all, I never thought I would become Prime Minister. I never had politics in mind. No, never. And to prove to you, I would describe how I planned my trip to Williams

---

[7] In 1995, when Goh was Prime Minister, he was awarded an honorary doctorate by Williams College. The move led to much controversy when a Williams College lecturer organised a protest against Singapore's human rights record and the *New York Times'* columnist William Safire supported it.

College. The return trip was pre-booked in Singapore. I thought I would never have a second chance to visit any of these places. So, I went to Hong Kong. I had a friend in Hong Kong — he was an old classmate from school. I stopped there for one day and he took me around Hong Kong. Then from Hong Kong, I went to Tokyo. I thought I might never pass there in future. Then from Tokyo, I hopped to Hawaii. We were young, so we did not know the term "jetlag." We spent a lot of time just sleeping in Honolulu. It was one day, one night, just to visit Hawaii. We did not go anywhere. We stayed near Waikiki Beach and went around the beach.

We nearly missed the plane because we were so tired. Next stop was San Francisco. By then, we had more or less recovered from the jetlag, and we enjoyed San Francisco. We went around, looking at places. From there, we went to New York. There, I had a friend — he was one year my senior at university and who attended my wedding dinner. He was working for Mobil and he had a small apartment. He put us up — my wife and I — in his apartment. It was very good of him. We slept on his bed and he slept on the couch. And he took us around in his car. It was a very big American car, with automatic transmission. I had never sat in an automatic car before. He drove me in New York to look around. I was very happy.

So, the thing is, I never thought what my life would be in the future. I didn't know whether I would be travelling again or not. After my graduation, I went to Montreal because there was an exposition. From there, I flew to London and spent a few days there. Then I went to Paris. I was supposed to go to Cairo. But this was 1967 and there was a war.[8] So, I cancelled my plan to go to Cairo. From Paris, I flew to Rome. We flew back home from Rome. This is to tell you that I never planned for anything at that time. I was a young man who thought I would never pass this way again, so I had better make use of the ticket and see as many places as I could.

Q: *You pretty much went around the world!*

A: I did, and all on economy. Then I came back. In other words, as a young man — and I don't know about today's young men — you did not think so far ahead. You could not plan. I was working on the basis that I might never have the chance to go around the world. As a civil servant, what chance did we have? How would I have known that life turned out this way?

---

[8] In 1967, Arab states and Israel fought a war which is commonly referred to as the Six-Day War.

His life would take more twists in the years ahead. Soon after returning from Williams College in 1967, he was called up to see PM Lee Kuan Yew at his office at City Hall. It was the first time Goh had met Lee after their encounter at the RI Historical Society talk. When Lee saw Goh, he said: "I am looking for a general factotum." Goh was puzzled and Lee explained: "You know, an errand boy."

Lee went on to elaborate what the job would entail — secretarial work, running around, getting papers. At the end of the quick job interview, Lee was satisfied and asked Goh to report for work in a couple of weeks as his private secretary. When Goh told Pillay about his new posting, Pillay was annoyed. "I did not send you to Williams College just for him to take you to be his private secretary," he said, according to Goh with a laugh. After Pillay spoke to the Minister for Finance, he was retained in the EPU.

But if Lee's proposal was somewhat unexpected, the next offer from a Cabinet Minister would stun him in a completely different way. After he managed to turn NOL around in three years as promised in 1976, he received a call from Hon Sui Sen, the Finance Minister. Goh believed the meeting was about his going back to the civil service, and thought that he could be offered a job as the Permanent Secretary of the Finance Ministry. Instead, Hon had other plans. He had told Lee that Goh was a possible successor as Finance Minister. In a conversation which Lee recounted in 1988, Hon said to Lee: "I've got a good man. He can take my place and I can retire." Lee replied: "Find him." Hon did. He told Goh he was wanted in politics. He was wanted by the PAP, an outfit which Goh Keng Swee had once famously described as "a holy order."

The
Holy Order

Part 2

I did not have much idea
what politics was.
I had no political inclination.

Chapter 3

"Marine Palade"

"He had a winning factor: he could talk to anybody."

*Veteran Marine Parade PAP activist and grassroots leader S. Puhaindran,
in an interview for this book.*

When Goh Chok Tong was tasked in 1976 to head to Marine Parade, a newly-carved out constituency by the eastern coast of Singapore, he was full of confidence for the job ahead. Despite being a new candidate from the ruling PAP, the rookie politician knew he was representing an all-conquering outfit. The party had not experienced defeat in elections since Singapore's independence in 1965, and the general election of 1976 was not expected to change that winning trend. Like most Singaporeans, he had imagined the PAP as a formidable army with battalions of activists, ready to fight at a moment's notice. Instead, what greeted him in Marine Parade was the complete opposite. "There was nothing," he said.

The barren scene weeks before the polls freaked out the prospective Member of Parliament (MP). "I was quite panicky," he said. "There was nobody and no branch, how would I fight the election?" When Goh Keng Swee, who was tasked by Lee Kuan Yew to keep an eye on the newbie, called him up, the tips were not exactly reassuring. "He told me not to worry. 'Just put a table and a chair in a void deck and people will come to you'," he recalled with a laugh. But Goh Keng Swee was right. True enough, after Goh Chok Tong put up some furniture in a void deck in Marine Parade, supporters and party members in the area began to appear. One supporter was S. Puhaindran, a former teacher from RI, who was urged by old boys to help out Goh, a fellow alumnus. It was clear Goh needed assistance. "He was on his own, he was not a politician, he had no place to go and you could see that he wasn't quite sure of himself," said Puhaindran.

The hawkers started to turn up too, bringing with them the most basic of supplies needed for an election campaign: staples, glue and cardboard for posters and pamphlets. They were strangers to Goh and vice versa. "I did not know them, but they turned up. They were mainly stallholders — pork sellers, fishmongers, egg sellers," said Goh. Soon, the campaign obtained a makeshift headquarters — a grand description for a barren room above a coffee shop most well known in Marine Parade for its "Lao Lee" Teochew porridge. "It was a good place for our headquarters — very easy to buy coffee and food," said Puhaindran with a chuckle. "The porridge was very good."

It was an unlikely introduction into the world of Singapore politics for Goh Chok Tong, more accustomed to the corporate world of global shipping or the organised and orderly structures of the civil service. While he was familiar with the workings of the government, party politics on the ground was alien to him. "I did not have much idea what politics was," he admitted candidly. "I had no political inclination."

Yet, when he was asked by Hon Sui Sen to join the PAP, he agreed to consider the offer. He consulted his wife and also his best friend Lee Keow Siong, who urged him to take it up. "He was a bit shocked and he asked me what to do," said Lee Keow Siong. "I told him he had been chosen and that it was a significant job and he had to do it."

After three days thinking it over, Goh agreed. Two reasons were cited — one national and the other personal. First, he felt that the party and by extension the government were clearly in need of people if they had asked him. "I did not know about leadership renewal," he said. "I thought they had good people. So if they asked me, that meant they did need help." Second, it was a job which he felt he could and should do, having benefited from a government bursary in university. But he was thinking only of the governing side of the work. "Hon said he was looking for a successor, and it was a job I would be comfortable in. I had worked in the finance ministry," he said. "I had seen how the Minister for Finance worked. I knew Goh Keng Swee, I had seen Hon Sui Sen. So, I was prepared to do that part. The thinking was not so much to be a politician. To me, a Prime Minister would be a political person. I thought the Finance Minister was another technocrat — Hon was a technocrat. I never regarded him as a politician. So, I said that I might be in the mould of Hon, and I could do the job." What he failed to account for was the political portion of the job, in particular winning elections. As he would share on hindsight: "Politics — I did not know what it was, like how to win elections, conduct Meet-the-People sessions."

He would have to learn on the job, navigating the new Marine

Parade public housing estate which he never knew existed until he was told he would be contesting in it. "I had no idea an HDB estate had been built in Marine Parade because I lived on the western side of Singapore. I had been to Katong as a school boy to visit a friend who lived in Marine Parade, in a house fronting a beach there. The house is now preserved as a national heritage," he said. "Once I knew I was going to Marine Parade, I drove there and found that it was such a beautiful place. I had seen HDB flats in Queenstown. I knew about Toa Payoh. But I never knew of such a beautiful estate. I liked it immediately." His experience living with his mother and siblings in the public housing estate of Queenstown helped him familiarise with Marine Parade quickly.

"I lived in Queenstown for a couple of years, moving around, buying things from the provision shop, going to the market, cutting my hair," he said. "When I went to Marine Parade, the environment was similar. It was not like somebody who lived in a landed property in Bukit Timah and went to HDB for the first time, losing your way. I might not have known the layout of Marine Parade clearly, but when I moved around, I was familiar with the set-up. The shops, the stallholders, the way they were designed — they were quite similar. There was also a mix of Malays, Indians and Chinese, like in Queenstown, so it was not totally alien to me."

Even though veteran MP Fong Sip Chee had asked to be deployed to Marine Parade, Lee Kuan Yew insisted that the new constituency, which had a high proportion of English-educated residents, was a better fit for the monolingual Goh. Lee was right. The ease and comfort which

Goh had with Marine Parade were critical given the short lead time and skeletal crew he had in the race to win an election. Despite being a fresh face on the ground, he connected easily with the voters. Veteran PAP politician Ch'ng Jit Koon observed that Goh had the right personality in politics. "He was *qin min*," he said, using a Chinese phrase which translates as being "sensitive to people's needs." "You could tell his interactions with people came very naturally to him. He couldn't speak Mandarin, but he used Hokkien. And he liked to crack a joke, teased people a little. Before you know it, the ice was broken and the residents were laughing."

Goh's fellow second-generation leader Lim Chee Onn made similar observations. "If I were a resident, and I have a problem, I would not hesitate to approach him, because I could see that I would not be fobbed away or given a cursory reply," he said. "His response would be quite earnest, quite genuine, quite friendly. He has that grassroots touch. He was a jovial person who could see the funny side of things." Goh shared that he had "No reservations whatsoever" walking the ground. "Talking to the hawkers, bantering with them and shaking hands with pork sellers — these were not a problem," he said. "I was comfortable and I used Hokkien. I went around to meet the residents and the mood at that time was quite good. Most people were polite and friendly. They would say, 'yes, we would support the PAP'."

Although Goh was supposed to get help from neighbouring ward Joo Chiat's activists, the support was not forthcoming. Joo Chiat was facing an electoral battle itself and its volunteers made only a couple of appearances in Marine Parade. "After that, I never saw them because they had to fight in Joo Chiat. Yeoh Ghim Seng could not help and did not help," said Goh, referring to the then Joo Chiat MP and Speaker of Parliament.

Thankfully, Fong stepped forward to lend Goh some much-needed assistance. Despite not being sent to Marine Parade, Fong bore no grudge. His new ward Kampong Chai Chee was near Marine Parade, and he was made in charge of PAP candidates in the eastern region. He asked Goh what he needed. The reply? Manpower and money. "I had no money. I did not have a single dollar from the party to fight," said Goh. "Fong Sip Chee was very good. He said: 'I will give you $2,000'. He said his Chai Chee branch had the money. Party headquarters never offered and Yeoh Ghim Seng was supposed to look after me, but never offered." For manpower, Fong assigned a few of his men who lived in Marine Parade to help Goh, offering the new candidate some precious firepower.

The haphazard ways of the PAP surprised Goh, who realised that the party had been set up to fight elections as a guerrilla force. "Every candidate was his own guerrilla leader, whether he was seasoned or not. You are a guerrilla leader — you fight, which is a strong point," he said. "The guerrillas were not organised centrally. It was just Lee Kuan Yew who held all these commanders together. It was much later, when I became PAP's organising secretary, that I turned it into a conventional army. Then, the party began to control everything — 'You do not say this, you say that, you go to this rally'."

But despite the uncoordinated efforts on the ground, the ruling party benefited from a strong national brand and weak opposition candidates in the 1970s. Every contest centred on the margin of victory, with the results a foregone conclusion. No one expected the opposition to win even a seat. The extent of the PAP's win would indicate the support it had from the people for its policies. It was no different in Marine Parade. Even though Goh was a rookie with hardly a public profile, victory was taken for granted. Ch'ng explained that the people had a great amount of trust in the party. "At that time, the people had seen the results of the PAP government and their lives had improved," he said. "They knew the PAP wanted to do the right things for the people. They believed Lee Kuan Yew would find good people. So even though they did not know the new candidates, it was okay, they would still support the PAP." The rookies knew the score too. Lim, who joined politics in 1977, said: "Let's be candid, nobody voted for Goh Chok Tong or Lim Chee Onn at that time. They all voted for PAP and LKY and the leadership, that's all."

When Goh's opponent turned out to be a relatively unknown Mansor Rahman from United Front, a small splinter party of the larger Workers' Party, his confidence received another boost. "Well, I felt I had a good chance. First, the party was not very well known compared with the PAP. So, I felt it was a sure win," said Goh. "Then I saw the poster of Mansor Rahman. His poster was smaller than mine. And he had spelt the constituency as 'Marine Palade — P-A-L-A-D-E'. I said, if he could not even spell, then what chance would he have? In Marine Parade, many residents were English-educated and they would ask how they could support this other candidate. And then you look at the qualifications: Mine were much better than his. So, if you look at it rationally, there was no doubt who people would vote for."

The attention turned towards the margin. Most of his volunteers believed they could garner 85 to 90 per cent of the valid votes. Goh estimated it would be around 80 per cent. On polling day, he won with 78.6 per cent. It was more than four points above the national average of 74.1 per cent. As expected, the PAP swept every single one of the 69 seats. "I was quite happy," said Goh. "Many branch members were disappointed — they said it should have been 90 per cent. But how could that be possible?" He had cleared his first hurdle as a politician and was now an elected representative.

But a sobering lesson was not far away. Two months after the election, the new Parliament sat for the first time in February 1977. Lee Kuan Yew gave one of his most memorable speeches, one which lasted nearly four hours. At the end of the speech, he offered a riddle on psephology — the study of election results. He compared two new constituencies — Marine Parade and Buona Vista. While Marine Parade won 78.6 per cent of the valid votes cast, Buona Vista did better with 82.8 per cent. The results were incongruent, said Lee. Marine Parade had the "mostest" five-room and four-room flats and no one-room flats. In comparison, Buona Vista had 1,300 one-room flats. In other words, Marine Parade residents were more well off and should be more supportive of the ruling party. "On all counts, and at every stage, the Member for Marine Parade had the better constituency," said Lee. "By the seaside, you get sea breeze. What more can you ask for? Higher income." Both PAP men also faced "unknown candidates," he added. Why then were their results four points apart, asked Lee.

He offered two possibilities. Was it because Ang Kok Peng, the Buona Vista MP, was a second-term MP who shifted from another constituency and hence more well known? Or was it because the MPs from neighbouring wards made a difference in the years before the new constituencies were carved out — Ulu Pandan in the case of Buona Vista and Joo Chiat for Marine Parade? Lee did not offer any answers. But he made this challenge: "Can somebody solve it? The team who can sit down and solve the riddle has got one of the qualifications to succeed us. Only one of the qualifications — solve it."

The young Goh sat in the back row, spellbound by the speech. But the new MP had more pressing concerns then, as he recalled in a Facebook post in 2015: "After his speech ended, there was a rush to the washroom. My bladder was about to burst. There was no time to think of the answer." Later, when the calls of nature had subsided, Goh came up with his answer to the riddle. The crux lies with race, he believed. Both the opposition candidates in the two wards were Malay. But Marine Parade had many more Malay voters compared to Buona Vista, observed Goh. While his ward had about 15 per cent Malays — mostly resettled from Kampong Chai Chee and Kaki Bukit — it was only about 2 per cent in Buona Vista. His conclusion was that race played a part in voting patterns. "You look at the population demography right away and it slapped me in my face," said Goh in an interview for this book. "A different demography. So, I just looked at it and realised it must be that. The answer is racial."

His guess is most likely correct. Ch'ng, who worked closely with Lee on the ground, said that Lee was particularly concerned with rising race-based voting in Singapore after the 1976 election. It would eventually give rise to the Group Representation Constituency (GRC) concept to ensure minority representation in politics. Goh, it seems, had one of the qualifications to succeed the Old Guard, although he never checked with Lee if his answer was accurate. Once he reached his conclusion, he made a stronger and sustained effort to reach out to the Malay residents in Marine Parade, attending their events as often as he could and consulting experienced Malay MPs for tips to reach out to the community.

He had picked up his first political lesson. "Do not just assume on a rational basis that because you are more qualified than the other person, your party is better known, that you would get very high votes," he said. "We were expecting more — we were expecting 80 plus. But we got a bit less. That was the first lesson — do not assume. And this was proven later on. Do not assume you have done so much for the people and they will support you. It would depend on so many other factors."

Q: *Were you regarded as the top high-flyer in the 1976 general election and seen as one of the potential new Cabinet ministers?*

A: I would not say so. At that time, nobody expected you to be anybody. Succession was still not quite yet flaunted or talked about. How did you know the others would not be high fliers? Nobody speculated that you would be an office holder and there was no point in speculating because the old ministers then were still quite young. It was too early to say. Your bigwigs in politics were there — Toh Chin Chye, Ong Pang Boon, Chua Sian Chin, Jek Yeun Thong, S. Rajaratnam, E. W. Barker. They were in their late 40s, at most 50s. I was 35.

Q: *So your entry into politics was fairly low profile?*

A: Yes, it was. There was no introduction of candidates. I think somebody from *The Straits Times* came at night to my house after the list of candidates was released. He wanted to interview me but I said only one or two sentences.

Q: *Was it communicated to you during the interview process to be a candidate that they wanted you to be a Cabinet minister?*

A: No, no, no. At the interviews, they never promised anything.

Q: So, there was a chance that you could have joined and remained as a backbencher and stayed in NOL?

A: Of course. But Hon Sui Sen did tell me that he was looking for a successor when he invited me to stand for elections. However, he was not in the party's Central Executive Committee.

Q: There was no bargaining or negotiation?

A: Oh, no. If you bargained, you could be sure you would not be selected. But I know what you are trying to say. I was giving up so much. I could have well said 'Oh I have so much, what are you offering me?'. But had I done it, they would have said, no, this chap is too materialistic, he is looking for himself, he is looking at this as a career. In my case, Hon said he was looking for a successor, so I knew he was looking for a Minister. And it was a job I would be comfortable in. I had worked in the Finance Ministry. Instead of becoming a permanent secretary, which I was also prepared to do, he wanted me to be the Finance Minister. Of course, a minister is a different level.

Put it this way: If a Minister for National Development asked me, I would probably think through. I'm not sure I would have said yes because I'm not familiar. What is national development? What do I do? Or if the Minister for Culture was looking for a successor, I would say I'm not somebody into music or art. I would have said no. But finance was something I was familiar with and which I felt that I could do. And one question which stood out came at the end of the interview: 'What is your ambition?' It was asked by Lee Kuan Yew. My straightforward answer was: 'I will serve. I do not have any special ambition in mind. Wherever I am, I will just serve to my best.' And I explained why: That I had a bursary, so when I am asked to serve, I serve.

Q: *In September 1977, nine months after the general election, you were appointed Senior Minister of State (SMS) for Finance. How were you groomed by Hon to succeed him?*

A: When I was SMS for Finance and working with Hon Sui Sen, he asked me to attend many meetings with him. He also asked me to present the Budget. If you look back in history, I am the first non-Finance Minister to present three Budgets.[9] The first was in 1979. Mr Hon had sent the whole file to LKY with a scribbled note: 'This is the Budget prepared by SMS.' He had not made a single correction. It came back approved. Lee Kuan Yew made about two, three small editorial corrections — that was all. So, I presented the Budget as SMS.

Then I got promoted to Minister for Trade and Industry and I presented the Budget again in 1980 and 1981. Hon Sui Sen was still the Finance Minister but I presented. In other words, as Trade and Industry Minister, if I could do the Budget, then I could take over as Finance Minister after that. But I never became Finance Minister.

---

[9] Tony Tan was the only other non-Finance Minister to have presented the Budget in Singapore. In 1982 and 1983, he read the Budget speech as the Trade and Industry Minister. In 2007, Tharman Shanmugaratnam presented the Budget as Second Finance Minister.

Q: *What happened to all the talk about finding a successor?*

A: Hon had to plan for retirement. So he wanted somebody in the ministry. I presented three Budgets, answered questions in Parliament, so that when the time came for him to retire, there would be somebody ready. But when Hon died in office in 1983, there was somebody else who could do the job. By then, Tony Tan had already come in. He was the right person, and I went to do other things.

Life is like that. In some ways, you can say I'm a failure in my career (laughs). I wanted to be an academic — I failed. I wanted to be a Shell senior executive, but I failed to get it. NOL, I succeeded, but could not stay there for long. Then Finance Minister — they wanted to groom me for that. But I never became one. I presented three Budgets but never became Finance Minister.

Q: *Back to the 1979 Budget — so you wrote the Budget statement? But the discussion on what to do and all that, you must have worked with Hon Sui Sen?*

A: No. I did it on my own, with help from one officer and inputs from the Finance Ministry. Basically, I wrote everything but with strong staff support.

Q: *This is incredulous. You mean there was no discussion with Hon Sui Sen?*

A: No. If I discussed with him, then it was Hon Sui Sen's work. So, when I finished and I gave it to him, he sent that to LKY. Mine was a straightforward budgeting exercise. You decided, from the ministries, what to give and not to give, what projects to approve — they were all straightforward. And those projects, to be frank, would already have been processed by the internal project evaluation committee. You just put in the Budget, so it was simpler. I must add that I had helped Goh Keng Swee prepare his Budgets when I was a young Ministry of Finance official. So, I was familiar with the process and the format.

Q: *Looks like it was still a very lean and mean government in 1979?*

A: Lean, yes, not mean!

Q: *At this point, when you just stepped into politics, how did you balance your ministry work with your constituency and party work?*

A: It was all one piece of work. How did I balance? I did not get into the nitty-gritty of many things — those were the jobs of civil servants. I did not try to become the super perm sec. You looked at it, took decisions and moved on. Of course, when civil servants reported to you, you had to understand how things work. But I did not go down to the last decimal point of statistics given by the civil servants. But from time to time, you knew how to keep them on their toes. You checked for some errors. So, you glanced through and you pointed out a typing error here and there. Then the civil servant would go 'Oh, he can even spot a typing error'. These are tricks of the trade. You must look for some mistakes here and there. But this is a trivial example.

A more important example would be spotting contradictions in the arguments. They argued for something here, but towards the end, they did not quite straighten the point. You found that there was a contradiction — those were more important. Of course, other more important things were whether you agreed with the policies that were being recommended or with their fleshing out of your thoughts. Ministers must have thoughts — we give them ideas and they flesh them into policies and programmes — and you have to help them shape them.

I had to be able to manage my time or I could not do my work. I was in charge of the ministry and I had a big staff to help me. On the party side, I had no staff to help. The PAP HQ then had only two administrative persons working — plus one chap looking after the HQ, cleaning and so on; and there was another doing despatch on a bicycle, and later a motorcycle. That was all.

Q: *What were some of the earliest things which you tried out in Marine Parade?*

A: Marine Parade was one of the first places to have a Residents' Committee (RC). After the 1976 election, the party set up a task force under the chairmanship of Hwang Soo Jin and I was a part of it. There was a paper put up to the task force for discussion. It was on forming block working committees, using policemen, who had priority to get their HDB flats, as the nucleus. At that time, petty crime was quite rife in the many new housing estates, so the idea was to use the police. They were given priority in buying their flats, so they would anchor a block and, from there, form a block working committee.

When I saw the proposal, I was alarmed. I said you could not do that and my reason was: some people already labelled us as a police state. If you had policemen forming the core of this block working committee, then you would confirm that perception. It is not quite the same meaning, but in the literal sense, we would be seen as a nation watched by policemen.

Hwang Soo Jin recognised my point and asked what I would do. I said the alternative was to form a precinct residents' committee. The police should still be drawn in — those who owned their flats — but the leaders must be non-policemen. He said it was a good idea. But how would you identify the leaders — these were new housing estates, not just in Marine Parade but all over Singapore? I said to do surveys, send out forms — about how they perceived problems in the estates and what were their ideas to improve the estates — and from there, we could see the potential RC members.

He said it was a good idea and he reported, of course, to Lee Kuan Yew. All the task force's meetings' minutes — the main ideas — would be reported to him. Then Lee Kuan Yew said yes, go ahead. The first three places to try out the pilot RC were Marine Parade, Mr Lee's Tanjong Pagar and Bedok. I said I would need resources and People's Association support for surveys, forms, analysis and so on. Tan Kin Lian, my branch secretary, and myself worked out the questionnaire.[10]

Q: *What kind of results did you get?*

A: Around 10 to 12 per cent of the questionnaires were returned, which was not bad. We went through the returns and those who took the trouble to give suggestions on open-ended questions — which were by design — these could join the RCs as members.

Q: *What was the purpose of RCs? You mentioned petty crime earlier.*

A: The original purpose of the block working committee was to, of course, get the block's residents to know one another and to bond. Plus, also security — to look out for petty crimes, corridor thefts and so on. There were all kinds of petty stuff at that time. The larger purpose would be to get people to know one another. I did it on a precinct basis and the objective would be to bond neighbours, to build a more cohesive neighbourhood. People from all over Singapore were moving into new places — the relocation from *kampungs*.[11] How do you quickly build up a new

---

[10] Tan Kin Lian was the first PAP branch secretary of Marine Parade. He became a long-time CEO of NTUC Income, one of Singapore's largest insurers. He was also an unsuccessful candidate for Singapore's presidency in 2011.

[11] *Kampung* is a Malay word for village.

kampung? Everybody was new, on loose ends and asking, where are my friends?

Q: *Some have said that the RCs were the PAP's versions of "demo-cratic united fronts" against the communists. So was there a larger political purpose?*

A: To bond people is in itself political. But the aim of RCs was not with the purpose of winning elections. It was not directly political. Today, we made it very clear that grassroots leaders are not necessarily PAP members — they do not have to be. They do not have to come out during elections to support the party. And the rules are very clear. For example, we cannot wear white and white to go into the community centres or RC centres during elections because the uniform is the party's and the premises are the government's. We are quite clear.

As a fact, in my case during election time, many of them said they were grassroots leaders and asked not to campaign. They wanted to be nice to their neighbours. They did not want to be criticised by the neighbours, which is very real. Of course, the branch people would get very angry and wonder why they did not come and help. I said no, we make a distinction.

My intention behind RCs was to do good. Most people would want to know their neighbours. So, how did we do this? We used very simple ideas at that time. For one thing, we collected old newspapers. Every month, we went around to collect old newspapers and sell them to the *karung guni* man and the receipts would go to the RC and they could use the money for their own expenses. A little extra for *makan* here and there.[12] It was hard work. The RC members asked why we were doing this. We said it gave them an excuse to knock on doors. Otherwise, they would have no reason. Another way was the monthly cleaning of the precinct. I would join them and clean the corridors together with the cleaners. As we cleaned, we got together and knew each other.

Q: How did you know that this pilot was a success?

A: Well, because after that, they said to form RCs all over Singapore! As far as I am concerned, the big boss said it was a success. The fact that Lee Kuan Yew gave the okay to the others meant he could see some benefits. The benefits are in the general sense for Singapore, and not for the PAP. Now, RCs have grown. They organise many activities to forge neighbourliness — pot luck, children's party, block party and so on. There are also health activities, such as health screenings and looking after the vulnerable people in the estate.

---

[12] *Karung guni* is a Malay phrase for rag-and-bone man. *Makan* is Malay for eating.

Q: _Few people know that you are behind it. Is the creation of RCs something which you are proud of?_

A: Yes, of course. I was not given enough credit (laughs). In life, every good deed done goes to the top. That is the system. And everything that goes wrong, the underlings must accept responsibility. But a good boss will say he is responsible. A good boss would say no, it was not the subordinate's fault and I would take the responsibility.

Q: _Looking back, do you think this idea of RCs and its success was one reason you were then earmarked for bigger things?_

A: It was probably one reason. Of course, you did not know you were being tested. But it was not me alone. Mr Lee was, like what the current PM is doing, just giving the new ministers a lot of political work to do and to see how we fared. One or two of these chaps could do it and maybe so-and-so would be better than the other.

His success on the ground in Marine Parade quickly led to more responsibilities at the party level and a speedy leap into the Cabinet, uncommon in post-independence Singapore. To Ahmad Mattar, a fellow RI-boy-turned-politician, it was obvious Goh was slated for bigger things. "We saw him as someone who would move up the ladder very quickly," he said. "But not as PM!" Indeed, after 18 months as Senior Minister of State for Finance, he was made full minister when a new ministry was carved out of Finance in 1979. "I had the luxury of choosing the name," said Goh. "LKY asked me what name I wanted to call it. I chose the Ministry of Trade and Industry." It was clear that he was a young and promising politician, slated for bigger things in the government and the PAP.

But, as Goh would discover, a strong beginning in the exacting world of the PAP could often become merely a false start. It was a long runway to the top, especially in an all-dominant party where the founding leaders remained young, agile and sharp. Talk of succession from the Old Guard, both out in the public and within the party, remained at its infancy. Lee Kuan Yew and his comrades had more tests ahead for the young Turks and Goh would feel the full force of the challenges as the early frontrunner of the pack.

Chapter 4

The Magnificent Seven

*"They were only seven — but they fought
like seven hundred!"*

Taken from the 1960 movie "The Magnificent Seven".

Days after his hard-fought victory in the 1976 general election, Hwang Soo Jin was summoned to see Lee Kuan Yew. The MP for Jalan Kayu, a farming ward in north-eastern Singapore which had borne the brunt of the British military pullout in 1971, had just endured a rough battle in the polls. His winning margin of 61.57 per cent over Workers' Party M. P. D. Nair was the second lowest in the PAP and nearly 13 points below the ruling party's national average. But given the difficulties on the ground in Jalan Kayu, which also used to be a stronghold of the Barisan Sosialis — a splinter party of the PAP — Hwang was regarded to have done a good job to secure a win. Lee recognised as much. "He held his ground… and he's quite shrewd," he said in *Men in White*, a book on the history of the PAP. The reward for Hwang, as was the norm in an action-oriented party, was more work. Lee wanted him to set up and head a task force to monitor the 11 new candidates fielded by the PAP. One of them was Goh Chok Tong, a man whom Hwang's committee would first identify as the next Prime Minister.

Hwang gathered a team of seven MPs in his group and dished out assignments to the new politicians, a cohort which slowly expanded as by-elections were called in the late 1970s to bring in more newbies. Some, like Goh, were told to draft a new party constitution, others were assigned to look at branch finances, and another group had to overhaul the PAP's kindergartens. The aim was to familiarise the rookies with party politics, said Hwang. "The PM said 'Well, you people might as well look at these new members and help them to develop their grassroots connection'," he said. "To politicise them… because most of them arrived by helicopter, not from the grassroots." Lee wanted them appraised on their character, ability, reliability and strength to connect and influence people on the ground. It soon became clear that there were seven who stood out: shipping boss Goh, banking high-flyers Tony Tan and S. Dhanabalan, academic Ahmad Mattar, civil servants Lim Chee Onn and Bernard Chen, and architect Ong Teng Cheong. They were branded "The Magnificent Seven" by the public, after the iconic American Western film of 1960.

The identification of the septet was the clearest indication of an acceleration of leadership renewal in the PAP, a process which first kicked off in 1970. Lee said the PAP had to be proactive in the talent hunt. "For a long time, we believed it would happen automatically, by osmosis," he said in 1988. "You know, party branches' activities, elections, people will come forward and automatically the good ones will emerge. Then we discovered — no, this is dreadful." After a few missteps in the early years of the decade, when an emphasis on selecting candidates with PhDs failed to pay off, Lee switched his focus.[13]

Beginning in 1976, the talent search pivoted to technocrats who blurred the lines of business and bureaucracy, usually with proven track records of success. Goh, for instance, had already made a name for himself transforming NOL into a profitable outfit. On hindsight, the timing of their entries into politics was near perfect. They were entering a political cocoon of sorts, buffered from the usual vagaries and viciousness of politics in the developing world. Lee and his Old Guard had banked more than 10 years of goodwill with the people after independence, delivering unbroken economic growth. The abdication of Barisan in 1966 had also handicapped the opposition's momentum, clearing the deck of strong adversaries to the PAP. The conditions were optimal.

And it needed to be for this peculiar batch of rookie politicians. While most political systems drew their leaders from among the rank and file, the PAP's second echelon leaders were, to use Hwang's words, parachuted in by helicopters. They were not party activists who rose from the branches and most were clueless about politics. As Lim admitted candidly: "When I stood for my first election, what did I know about politics? Nothing. I was slightly better than a lamp post, that's all." But these technocrats, bland and stiff as they might be on the surface, came with fresh ideas and a new style in politics and governance that were exactly what the PAP was looking for.

---

[13] "We soon discovered that they (the PhD holders) needed to have other qualities besides a disciplined mind able to marshal facts and figures, write a thesis for a PhD or be a professional. Leadership is more than just ability." Lee Kuan Yew, *From Third World to First — The Singapore Story: 1965 to 2000* (Singapore: Times Media, 2000), p. 736.

Party ideologue S. Rajaratnam wrote in an article in 1969 that the party's new role must be to find new leaders who can cope with the new world. "The party must become a workshop for forging bold new ideas to meet the requirements of a rapidly changing society and a rapidly changing world... ." To do so, it had to renew itself. "One of the most difficult tasks of politics is not how to acquire power but how to transfer it to a new generation of leaders. More difficult still is for leaders to deliberately create new and able leaders to systematically take over from the older when the time comes."

Lee would deliver the same message more emphatically. "My colleagues and I can keep on solving problems until we are dead," he said in 1980. "One day, one by one, we shall cease to be able to solve Singapore's problems. This is for sure... we have to bring together the best team possible in Singapore... men who can meet new, startling and unexpected problems, think out the possible answers... ." The renewal took on greater urgency when three of Lee's most trusted lieutenants all fell ill at about the same time in 1983. Hon Sui Sen and Goh Keng Swee were hospitalised together, staying in rooms adjacent to each other. Rajaratnam had a heart attack in the United States.

The Magnificent Seven would, largely, prove to be more suitable for politics than the batch of PhD holders before them. To the Hwang task force, it became clear fairly quickly that there was one among the pack who was the sharpest gunslinger. His stature helped. "Goh Chok Tong stood out, there was no doubt about it," said Hwang. "First of all, he was very imposing physically because of his height. Then, his qualifications. He got a first class in economics and he had industry experience with NOL. Singapore was at a stage where economic development was the top priority. Third, his personality. He was very approachable and prepared to go down to the grassroots. He appeared very gentle, but you could also see that he was full of confidence. And despite the gentleness, I think there was certain firmness in him. He's got all the attributes. He impressed us from the word 'go'." By 1979, the *Far Eastern Economic Review* was calling him the "young managing director of Singapore Incorporated."

It helped that Goh was more hardworking and obliging than his peers when it came to clocking up mileage, literally. When the PAP started weekly walkabouts for the young ministers in the early 1980s, he was the most willing and eager to pound the streets, said veteran MP Ch'ng Jit Koon, the organiser of the visits. "Some of the others would find excuses to turn me down, but Chok Tong always said yes," he recalled with a laugh. "And if I couldn't find a young minister at the last minute, I would always turn to him because he would agree and was happy to do it." It was tough work, recalled Goh. The walkabouts covered the entire day and ended only at night. "We had to walk the corners of the whole constituency. I started off by wearing one shirt. Then second time, I became wise and carried extra shirts. I was completely drenched," he said with a grin, raising his eyebrows at the recollection of his mini learning journey.

But he relished the visits because they offered him opportunities to get to know all parts of Singapore — an exercise which the Old Guard, particularly Lee, had when they campaigned for merger with Malaya. "I got to know the geography of the constituencies — a temple here, a Malay village there, and a feel of the residents," he said. "I also got to know the grassroots leaders and they got to know me. They would size me up and maybe, hopefully, it was positive and therefore they would support us, the younger leaders."

While others in his batch began to falter, as the initial enthusiasm in politics fizzled out, Goh continued on a steady pace, rising through the ranks in the government and also impressing on the ground with party work. "There were quite a few who clearly turned out to be more opportunistic than anything else," said Hwang, referring to the 18 new candidates of 1976. "They were just seeking to further themselves, and not really dedicated to serving the people. We were really concerned about a few of the other members and had to intensify our watch over them. I even had to interview the wife of one particular individual just to make sure whether he was crazy himself or if he was dominated or controlled by the wife!" But Goh never gave Hwang and his team problems. "Chok Tong was never a concern to the committee. We didn't actually find him wanting in anything at all."

The feedback from the ground was shared with the PAP leaders and as Goh's creation of the Residents' Committee began to take off, it became apparent that the party elders agreed with the appraisals. When the PAP called for by-elections in seven wards in 1979, Lee put Goh and Lim in charge of campaigning — a pair of novices with combined political experience of five years. It was a test. But it was also testimony to the measure by which Goh was regarded by Lee and the Old Guard that he was given such a key task within three years of joining politics. Goh, typically, downplayed the significance. "It was a job. I got to get them elected, which was not difficult. What was more difficult would be taking them through the process, the various steps to Nomination Day — that was No. 1 — because if that had gone wrong, they would have been disqualified and my head would have been chopped," he said, gesturing with his palm.

In the midst of the hustings, Lee announced to Singaporeans that four members of the Magnificent Seven had moved into the PAP's central executive committee (CEC). Ahmad was made second assistant treasurer; Lim, first assistant treasurer; Ong, second vice-chairman; and Goh, second assistant secretary-general. Goh's position was the highest among the young leaders. It was the first public sign that he was leading in the race to be the next Prime Minister of Singapore, although it was still very early days. Chan Heng Chee, a young political observer then, said there was little reading of political succession tea leaves at that point. "In those days, because there were so many of the Old Guard who were still around, it was not so critical for people who was going to take over. It was like long innings," she recalled. The 1979 by-election went well for the PAP and it swept all seven seats with nary a hitch. Goh, it could be said, had passed his first test.

But despite the stellar work he had achieved both on the ground with the party and in the government, there were kinks which the Old Guard observed in the young tall man compared to his peers. For one thing, his public speaking skills were poor. His voice coach, Sue Greenwood, was not surprised Goh was stiff. Unlike Lee who was a street fighter, Goh "never really had to sell in public," she observed. Goh was aware of his own weakness. "I think they (his peers) were probably better," he said. "Chee Onn was quite good; Tony was very scripted but he was very clear; Dhanabalan was quite a natural; and Ong Teng Cheong was good. I was stilted in the early years and trying to explain through facts and figures, which was not political. You must convince people. I was used to using facts and figures to convince people."

Rajaratnam began to pay closer attention to Goh's speeches and turned up at several events where Goh was speaking. "He would sit there and listen, like a Cheshire cat," said Goh. "At the end, he would give feedback about delivering speeches in a persuasive way. He would say don't give so many figures, people are not interested in figures unless I gave some startling numbers, out of the blue figures. Otherwise, the figures would be inconsequential. Giving numbers was what I was fond of doing. Because when you write a speech, what do you do? You look for figures and analyse. In the beginning, my speeches were very analytical, academic types and giving facts. So, he said do not do that."

There was also feedback from the ground that he came across on TV as aloof. *Asia Magazine* wrote in 1989: "He was considered ambitious, arrogant, aloof, even pompous. He was perceived as trying to be another Lee Kuan Yew and projected a cold and condescending image."

The negative feedback took him by surprise. "I'm not an arrogant person and I asked people around me if I were. They said no," he shared. After drilling deeper, he discovered the perception could have been shaped by his height, made worse when he delivered speeches from a podium. "I was seen as literally talking down to people," he said. His right-hand man in Marine Parade, S. Puhaindran, observed that most Singaporeans had never met Goh in person then, and mass media coverage of him was limited. "They didn't realise how tall he was," he said. "And mind you, this was the late 1970s. Singaporeans were just not used to tall people!" Goh discussed his problem with Lee Kuan Yew who suggested that he ask the state broadcaster to bring along a short ladder when filming Goh. It would allow the camera to roll at eye level with him.

But while that was easily solved, it was more difficult to improve Goh's uptight demeanour on air. He admitted he froze once the lights came on: "Off air, I was very relaxed. Once the TV camera was on me, I just could not speak or think. I was so aware and conscious that I was on TV." Again, Rajaratnam stepped in to help. "He told me that when we speak to an audience, you have to assume their mental ages have dropped," he said. "It is like watching TV. When you watch TV, your mental age is not your present age but it drops to that of a teenager. In other words, it was the entertainment value and sound bites and not a very well-scripted academic speech that would connect. It was very sound advice."

While these flaws were minor, the Old Guard took issue with the Magnificent Seven on a sharper and more important weakness. "In the early years, the biggest criticism against us was a lack of passion. Kim San, who was frank enough and who said, 'You all can do your job, but there is no passion'," said Goh, referring to housing czar Lim Kim San. "I think Rajaratnam put it as no fire in the belly. We came in, we were all technocrats. But to govern and to lead, you must have passion or fire in the bellies. This is not just doing a job. It was a criticism, but it was correct."

It was how Goh had approached his early life as a politician. Instead of volunteering, or even fighting, for the job, he was *asked* to enter an arena which he was completely unfamiliar with and had showed little inclination for. The manner of his entry, which is dissimilar to the Old Guard, but replicated among his peers and those who came after, shaped a certain mindset in him. As Greenwood observed: "If you see something as an obligation and as a duty, how does it make you behave?" A telling example for Goh came during his interviews to be a PAP candidate. He said with a laugh: "They asked many questions to know more about me. But for one question, I wanted to give a stupid answer: 'Why do you want to become an MP?'. I wanted to say: 'But you asked me!'."

This attitude carried through to his early years in the party and government. He would say repeatedly in his interviews for this book that in his first few years after 1976, "it was just a job." Lim Chee Onn explained that the way they were recruited played a part in shaping how they approached politics initially. "That was how LKY convinced me, and I suspect he did the same with Chok Tong, and Dhana and the whole lot — there was a job for you to do," he said. "Create a better Singapore for Singaporeans, that's the job. So we saw a job to be done, because LKY convinced us that was the job to be done. He is a very persuasive man! If he had not approached me, I would never have volunteered. Why? Because it's not in my blood!"

But Lim stressed that it was not true that the second generation lacked passion. It was simply in a different form. "We didn't have that earth shaking urge to go and change the world, because we are not built that way," he said. "But if you tell me 'Oh, you better go and get it done because Singapore needs it', I think we were as passionate as anyone else." For Goh, the fire in his belly took some time to heat up. "Organising secretary (in the PAP) — I organised. Ministry job — I did it. But later, you understood. To move people, to get them to follow you, you must have that passion for the job, to do something," he said. "When we were put more and more in charge, some of us developed that passion. I certainly developed more passion than in the first few years. It came slowly. Mine must have been a slow ember, not a spark. And you grew into it and realised it was not just an ordinary job. The team itself, collectively, we began to show more understanding for politics."

The way the team entered politics also had an unintended positive effect which was almost unique, setting it apart from politics practised elsewhere: they did not fight for power. Tony Tan attributed it to a sense of duty. "There was no jostling for power and no one was trying to climb on top of each other," he said. "All of us were very concerned about Singapore; about the duty we had, which was to ensure a smooth transition from the first-generation leaders, and that the Singapore story should continue even after the passing of the first-generation leaders. It was a sense of duty for all of us. So, it was a very collegial environment and we all knew we had a common purpose and we worked well. There was no fighting for power, unlike other countries. I think we were a bit unusual… very unusual. In most other countries, this would not be the case." Lim agreed. He said: "We were there to do something that is good for the country. If I can work with you, it'll be faster. Why would I fight with you?"

Dhanabalan explained that while most people go into politics in other countries for personal ambitions or a strong conviction that the government of the day was on the wrong track, it was not the case for him and his peers. "We never said we wanted to be leaders because of the high standing in society or we wanted to change the system, that this or that policy was wrong and we had to change it," he said. "We all came in because we agreed to the reading of the then leadership: that successful people, in business or civil service, if they did not come forward to enter politics, then the wrong people would come in, those with an axe to grind, people who had a personal ambition to achieve; and that would be disastrous for Singapore. So, we actually responded to a need, a call. And having done that, the priority was to work together — but not so much to position ourselves to become leaders. So, there was no jockeying for position or power."

To instil passion into the Magnificent Seven, Lee impressed on them the urgency of leadership renewal. And very often, he used his own mortality as a morbid example. "He would always ask us 'What happens if a lorry ran over me, then what would you do?'," said Goh. But Lee did not bargain for the wry, and somewhat cheeky, observations of Goh. "Regarding the lorry, I said it was going to be very difficult to run him over because there were always security officers around him! Then he changed and said 'What happens if it's an aircraft?'. In other words, he was saying, prepare for the improbable which may happen to us. We understood the urgency not immediately, but over time."

Q: *How was the political contestation during the early years of your political life?*

A: Not severe at all. The opposition was weak, the economy was doing well and the people were not looking for checks and balances. They trusted the PAP government.

Q: *You could say that these were almost ideal conditions for testing new blood like yourself, technocrats who had no political experience at all. If the political landscape had been different, if there was very strong opposition and people were very political, it might not have worked?*

A: Yes. Given the conditions, LKY could then bring in people who could govern, who knew about government. It was not just about winning elections, but about getting a government into place. That was his key point. He believed we could learn politics. If you could not, it was hopeless. He made some speeches that if you cannot tackle the Jeyaretnams and so on, you would not be able to lead. There was no doubt we could govern, but could we win elections? He knew we could not at the start. But he believed we could learn and subsequently do it. So, he created the conditions to bring us in, and gave us tests. 1979 by-election — we learnt to fight elections but there was not much of a fight. 1980 general election, again I learnt. Later, the fight became more and more severe. Today, it has become very severe. So, things would be different.

We can be speculative. Supposing the fight with the

opposition was very severe in the 1970s, what would Lee Kuan Yew have done? He would probably have brought in fewer technocrats. And let us have a longer runway to learn more about politics. And he would probably look for people who were good, trustworthy rabble rousers. They may not be able to run a ministry but they would help the PAP win elections first. In other words, have more backbenchers. Your minister types like Howe Yoon Chong — they would still be brought in but at a later age, when they have established a stronger reputation. But he would have more fighters — he who can rally the ground and fight, so you win. Then they form the government and people like us can be appointed ministers.

In the end, you come back to the basic thing. You must be able to win elections. But you must have technocrats to run the government. The best example is Donald Trump. He is a very good politician but he still needs able people to run the government. Unless he brings in good people and listens to them, he can't run the government. Nelson Mandela told me he could win elections and he knew politics, but he did not know economics or how to run a government. Thabo Mbeki would run the government.

Q: *While there may not have been strong opposition outside of the party, it has been well documented that there was fairly strong opposition to you guys the technocrats from within the party. How did you cope with that?*

A: After some time, we began to be more sensitive about the so-called vibe within the leadership. Toh Chin Chye, Ong Pang Boon and that camp never got involved with us. Goh Keng Swee — that was Lee Kuan Yew's camp — Rajaratnam, Lim Kim San, Hon Sui Sen and so on, they were supportive of renewal. I began to understand the differences from the way the two camps were interacting with us younger ministers.

Q: *What kind of reaction did you get from the camp who was resistant to succession?*

A: They were friendly. They resisted on principle. They were not against us personally, but felt that the pace of preparing us for succession was too fast. I made a point before that Toh Chin Chye was not against political succession or self-renewal per se; he was against the speed of change. They were in their 50s, late 50s, and still had many years to serve. And they were asked to leave for succession! They had no doubt that we could do it, but we lacked the political nous. So, why not let us come in, learn and then we could take over from them later? Why was it so fast? Within one year, in 1977, I became Senior Minister of State. Within three years, I became the Minister for Trade and Industry. The others felt they were being edged out by Lee Kuan Yew.

Q: Did Toh Chin Chye make things difficult for you in Parliament with his speeches, taking you on?

A: No, I think he spoke his mind. He was not making things difficult on purpose. But outside of Parliament, I had been to his functions because I was organising secretary of the PAP. I was asked by his Rochor branch people to go and I went. And there, he would criticise. And this was how I knew about his view on the pace of self-renewal, about why it was so fast. Of course, I was there and people looked at me. But he was not attacking me. I knew he was making the speech against Lee Kuan Yew. He said yes, we had very bright people — and he had no doubt they could do this — but why should it be so fast? They had not had experience and were quite raw in politics, so the chaps thought he was criticising me.

Of course, I was being regarded as one of the raw ones. It was so uncomfortable because you were sitting there, but I understood him and never took it out against him. He was against the speed of change whereas Lee Kuan Yew said Toh was against political succession.

Q: What about grassroots leaders and party activists? What was the reaction to you and your peers?

A: The older ones were against it. At one party conference, one cadre stood up. He was one of the older ones and he spoke in Mandarin. Of course, he qualified by saying that he was not against this change, but why were old people being discarded like a pair of used shoes. That one I remembered. He asked why were old cadres shunted aside when they had fought with the PAP for many, many elections. I think there was a lot of applause. So, you knew that the older ones — and not just the ministers who were being replaced — but also on the ground, had these feelings. When younger ministers came in, they brought in their own people.

Let me jump forward here a bit. Before the 1984 general election, I had the most awkward experience of my political career. I was running the elections and Mr Lee wanted to retire many of the older MPs, and also move some of the ministers to the backbench — Ong Pang Boon, E. W. Barker. I prepared the manuals and reading materials for the MPs who were contesting — what they needed to do on Nomination Day etc.

We were having a meeting with the PAP MPs, so I asked Mr Lee if I should hand out the materials to all the MPs or to only those who would be standing for elections because this was very close to Nomination Day. I knew who were being replaced. He said to give to all. So, I gave the manuals to all and I could see the relief on the faces of those who thought they were going to be replaced. They were very happy.

Within a week, the list of candidates from PAP had come out. I had to go to those MPs who were dropped to ask them to return the manual. That was my most awkward, most difficult moment. It was not that the MPs were against stepping down, but they had gone back to tell their branches that very night that they received the manual that they were standing for election. The branch people cheered, of course. Then within a week or so, I took the manual back. It was a loss of face for them.

Q: When you took back the manual, what did they say to you?

A: The look on their faces was enough, they did not have to say anything. If they had said anything, it would have been swear words. It was not that they were stepping down, it was a loss of face. Somebody asked why I did not tell him when I gave it to him earlier. Others also asked why they were not told earlier — they had brought it back to their branches and now they had lost face. I said Mr Lee Kuan Yew asked me to hand out to all of them first and take them back later.

Q: So why did LKY ask you to give it to all of them?

A: That is the nub of the story. If you let them know too early, Toh Chin Chye, Ong Pang Boon and a few others might organise a protest.[14] They might leave the party and fight us. In other words, LKY was not sure whether they would do it or not. They were all politicians. 'You want to retire me as minister and so on? I get all these disgruntled people who are going to be retired, we go out and fight you.' This was politics, you know. Lee Kuan Yew was worried.

---

[14] Toh Chin Chye had stepped down from the Cabinet earlier, in 1981. He remained an MP until his retirement from politics in 1988.

Q: *He genuinely believed that Toh Chin Chye and Ong Pang Boon could go out and set up a new party to challenge the PAP?*

A: If you knew Lee Kuan Yew, you knew what he had gone through when Barisan split from the PAP. After that, he did not trust anyone fully in politics. Not even me. To be fair, this is politics and also because he learnt from experience. He trusted nobody fully in politics because he learnt it the hard way. Chan Sun Wing — his parliamentary secretary — and others just turned against him.[15] From that experience, when he was making these big changes, he knew anything could happen. Trust but verify — that was what he would say. And from my own experience, when I told him something, I found that later, he verified. In other words, when I gave him sensitive political information, he verified. Why? To him, I was a player. So, if I gave a comment on ABC, was I advancing my own career? Was I truthful? He verified. So, trust but verify.

Q: *Why do you think Toh Chin Chye and Ong Pang Boon did not come out and set up a new party?*

A: They were for Singapore and not for themselves. And they knew what Lee Kuan Yew wanted to do was correct. Toh Chin Chye had told Lee Kuan Yew the branch had so many activists and they could become MPs. Lee Kuan Yew would just laugh — a few could become MPs and among those few, how many could

---

15 Chan Sun Wing was a former PAP MP and parliamentary secretary to then Prime Minister Lee Kuan Yew. He broke away from the PAP in 1961 to form the Barisan Sosialis. After the 1963 polls, he fled to Indonesia and later joined the Malayan Communist Party as an armed guerrilla.

become ministers or office holders? And I would totally support Lee Kuan Yew's view, having been in the branches at that time and getting to know the people. You did not have enough people to become office holders. MPs maybe, because they were very good ground workers. Then you would be like UMNO, just groundwork and getting votes and so on.[16] Toh Chin Chye genuinely believed that there were so many people in the branches who could take over from them. That was his argument basically.

Q: *It must be very rare that there is this loyalty among the Old Guard that they would not split up to form a splinter party.*

A: Correct. Despite all this, they did not split up the party. Ong Pang Boon came from Malaysia to join Singapore, and for what? It was a fight, first to be part of Malaysia, then later independence and to make the place work. So, they had larger causes. They were fighting for larger issues. So, this succession — they knew it was the right thing to do, but it was the speed that they were against. And you do not just split the party for that because that becomes personal. But if it had been ideological, they probably would have split.[17]

---

[16] UMNO is the acronym for the United Malays National Organisation, the biggest and most powerful component party of Barisan Nasional, the ruling coalition of Malaysia from 1957 to 2018.

[17] Toh Chin Chye had said in 2004: "There was no jostling for power. Our aim was the same and, if there were any differences, they were not so great." Sonny Yap, Richard Lim and Leong Weng Kam, *Men in White: The Untold Story of Singapore's Ruling Political Party* (Singapore: Singapore Press Holdings, 2009), p. 361.

Goh's early political career was moving as swiftly as it was smooth. By the end of the 1980 general election, he was not only the Minister for Trade and Industry, but also trusted to do the heavy lifting in the PAP. He had successfully organised both the 1979 by-elections and the 1980 polls, with the latter proving to be an easy fight for the ruling party. Once again, the PAP had a clean sweep of the seats — all 75 wards, and even improved its shares of the votes from 74.1 per cent in 1976 to 77.7 per cent.

Goh was on the ascendancy and seemingly could do no wrong. But gravity can be annoyingly persistent, especially in politics. When the PAP announced its new CEC weeks after the general election, it was widely expected that his position as first among equals among the Magnificent Seven would be cemented. Instead, Tony Tan was moved above him, in a move which surprised many. Goh remained as second assistant secretary-general, while Tan — who joined politics only a year earlier — was catapulted to the post of first assistant secretary-general. "LKY told me he wanted to make Tony the first assistant sec-gen, so I said okay," recounted Goh. "It has always been my attitude: okay, no problem. The good thing is I never aimed for the top post." Lee asked Goh if he minded but did not tell him why he was pushing Tan ahead of him.

Goh found his own answers: "My guess was this: Maybe Lee Kuan Yew might be coming to the conclusion that politically, I was better and I could do it. But Tony was never tested," he said. "Tony, in his view, could be a person who could govern better. And he gave the reason (later). Tony was very thorough and meticulous; he would know the subjects in-depth; and once he made up his mind, he would not shift. In my case, I like to talk to people and sometimes change my decision. I was a bit more flexible. So, he might have come to the conclusion that it was safer to test out somebody else politically. I think it was quite wise of him — do not place all your bets on one person. Test out somebody else who could do the job. If he could do it, you might have a better man."

But Goh remained quietly confident that he had the support of the party grassroots. After organising two elections and spending extensive time on the ground in many constituencies, he was the more well-known and popular choice of the cadres. What he did not expect was that he was about to be dealt the most dramatic challenge of his young political career. Political gravity would soon drag him back down to ground and through some rough debris.

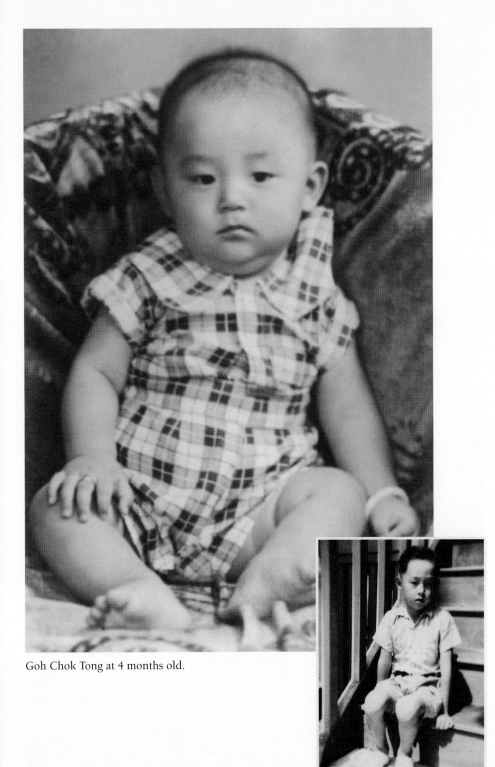

Goh Chok Tong at 4 months old.

Goh on the steps of his family home in Pasir Panjang.

Goh (first from left), 7, with his parents and two younger siblings.

Goh (left, away from group) stands in front of his family home at 744 Pasir Panjang Road.

Goh (last row, first from left), with his Standard 5 class from Pasir Panjang English School.

Goh, during a 2014 visit to his former primary school with classmates Cheng Heng Kock (left) and Lee Keow Siong. The compound, which has remained largely unchanged, is now Breakthrough Missions, a halfway house.

Goh (fourth from left, standing), 18, with Raffles Institution's (RI) water polo team.

Goh (fourth from right, last row), 18, with RI's prefectorial board.

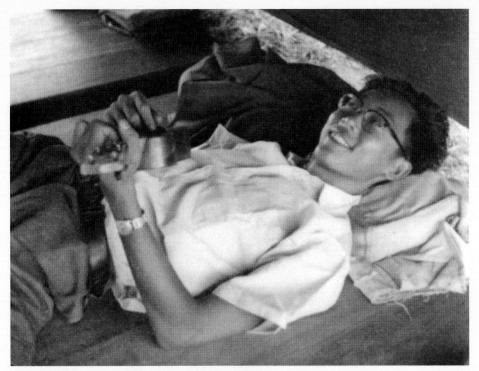

Goh, 16, plays with a ukelele at a Scout troop camp in Jurong Park in 1957.

Top: Goh, 15, on his bicycle in front of his Pasir Panjang home.

Right: Goh (first from right), 16, with fellow Scouts and RI schoolmates in 1957. Tan Cheng Bock is next to Goh.

Lee Kuan Yew gives a talk on democracy to RI students on the invitation of Goh. Goh (onstage, not in photo), was then the chairman of the school's Historical Society.

Goh (first from right), 18, with RI schoolmates Lee Keow Siong (left) and Chan Kwong at Pulau Semakau in 1959.

26 · 1 · 60

Dear Bock,

Good friends we have been
Good friends shall we remain
Forever and ever.

Yours sincerely,
Goh Chok Tong.
(chok)

A graduation note from Goh to Tan Cheng Bock in 1960. [Photo credit: Courtesy of Tan Cheng Bock]

Goh (seated), 19, with future wife Tan Choo Leng at her home in Kuala Lumpur in 1960. With them are Wong Chow Siong (left) and Yaacob Yem.

Goh visits his family's first purchased home at Commonwealth Drive in 2014, after learning that the block is slated for redevelopment. He lived there with his mother and siblings in the early 1960s.

Goh (second from left), 23, at the University of Singapore's graduation ceremony in 1964. Chan Heng Chee (second from right), leads the Bachelor of Arts' First Class Honours graduands.

Goh receives his degree from the Chancellor of the University of Singapore Lee Kong Chian.

Goh returns to his Pasir Panjang home for the wedding tea ceremony in 1965. His grandmother, the matriarch of the family, is seated second from right. His second uncle, who took care of Goh after his father's death, is seated first from left. Goh's mother sits next to bride Choo Leng, while Goh's best man Lee Keow Siong is next to him.

Goh and Choo Leng on their wedding day in their rented room in Balestier in 1965.

Goh experiences his first snowfall in Williams College, Massachusetts, in the winter of 1966.

Goh (on extreme left) with his Class of 1967 studying Development Economics in Williams College. He is one of 20 young officials from 16 emerging economies.

Goh with his twins Jin Theng
(left) and Jin Hian at their
home in Moonbeam View
in 1973.

Goh with son Jin Hian in 1978.

Goh, along with shipping executives, partying in Vienna after attending an international shipping conference in 1973. Tung Chee-hwa (second from left) became the first Chief Executive of Hong Kong in 1997.

At the opening of a $6.5-million complex belonging to Container Warehousing and Transportation Pte Ltd in Jurong Town in 1975. Goh, then managing director of Neptune Orient Lines, is with Woon Wah Siang (first from left), chairman of Jurong Town Corporation, and other officials.
[Photo credit: MITA Collection/NAS]

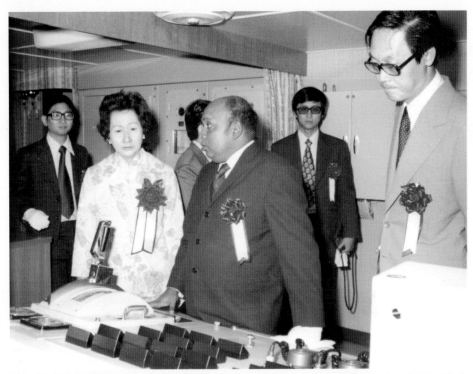

Goh, at the christening of Neptune Pearl, NOL's first purpose-built containership, by Mrs Yeoh Ghim Seng in 1976. Second from the right is Lim Boon Heng, who oversaw the construction of the ship.

A Shinto priest conducts the keel-laying ceremony for ANRO Temasek, a roll-on roll-off ship, at the Kawasaki Kobe shipyard in 1977, as Goh looks on.

Goh, a new face in the People's Action Party, arrives at Chai Chee Secondary School to file his nomination papers at the 1976 General Election. [Photo credit: The Straits Times © Singapore Press Holdings Limited. Reprinted with permission]

Goh speaks at his first rally at the 1976 General Election. [Photo credit: MITA Collection/NAS]

UNITED FRONT 統一陣綫

馬林百列區候選人

曼梳拉曼，現年廿八，已婚，服務公司書記
，在本坡魯曼混合中學畢業，曾當過記者，一
九七一年參加政治活動，並任正義黨副祕書長
，兼組織祕書，一九七四年，加入統一陣綫被
黨推選任當副主席，現任統一陣綫副祕書長，
曼梳拉曼，年青有為，學識過人，是本坡國一
位積極工運者，現任「森那美工友會」工友推
選為該會主席，本屆大選將參加馬林百列區競
選。

曼梳拉曼
MANSOR BIN RAHMAN

UNITED FRONT CANDIDATE FOR MARINE PALADE

Married, aged 28, Shipping Clerk.

He was educated in Jalan Daud School and Dunman
Intergrated Secondary School.

Ex-reporter of Fantasia. He involved in politic
in 1971, and was former Organising Secretary and
Assistant Secretary General of Singapore Justice Party.

Join United Front in 1974, and was Elected as
Vice Chairman and later became Asst. Secretary General
of the Party.

A Branch Chairman of Sime Darby Employees' Union
in 1976.

曼梳拉曼
MANSOR BIN RAHMAN

VOTE P.A.P.

**YOUR FUTURE IS SAFE WITH P.A.P.
MASADEPAN ANDA ADALAH
SELAMAT DENGAN P.A.P.
有了行动党前途就有保障**

Polling card of opposition candidate Mansor Rahman. The United Front candidate misspelled Marine Parade.

Goh's debut election polling card to Marine Parade residents.

Jubilant supporters celebrate Goh's election victory in the 1976 General Election. Hoisting Goh are local market stallholders. [Photo credit: Marine Parade PAP Branch]

An aerial view of Marine Parade Estate under construction in 1973. It is the first housing estate built entirely on reclaimed land. [Photo credit: Courtesy of Housing & Development Board]

Goh, now a Senior Minister of State for Finance, waters a sapling in Marine Parade on Tree Planting Day in 1977. [Photo credit: Marine Parade Community Centre Collection/NAS]

Goh officially opens Marine Parade's Residents' Committee (RC) centre. He pioneered the formation of RCs in 1978. [Photo credit: MITA Collection/NAS]

The Old Guard with the New Guard, as second-generation leaders (back row) join the pioneers of PAP (seated in the front row) in the party's central executive committee in 1979.
[Photo credit: Ong Teng Cheong Collection/NAS]

Goh leads the PAP campaign during the 1979 by-election, the first of several elections which he would take charge of as a second-generation leader. Candidates Devan Nair (on Goh's right) and Tony Tan (his left) became the third and seventh President of Singapore, respectively. The PAP also brought in Howe Yoon Chong (first from right) and Teh Cheang Wan in this by-election. Consequently, both were appointed ministers.
[Photo credit: MITA Collection/NAS]

PAP candidate Devan Nair being lifted by supporters after winning the Anson seat at the 1979 by-election. Goh, who led the campaign as PAP's organising secretary, watches on. The party would retain the seat in the general election a year later, before suffering a shock defeat in Anson in 1981 when Nair vacated it to be the country's president.
[Photo credit: MITA Collection/NAS]

Five of the Magnificent Seven on an official trip with Lee Kuan Yew in Bonn, the capital of West Germany, in 1979. From left: S. Dhanabalan, Lim Chee Onn, Bernard Chen, Goh and Tony Tan. [Photo credit: Courtesy of Lim Chee Onn]

PAP's second-generation leaders frequently gathered for meals outside of work, with Ong Teng Cheong a regular host at his home as shown here in 1983. From left: Ong (partial), Goh, Lim Chee Onn, Tony Tan, S. Jayakumar and S. Dhanabalan (back facing camera). [Photo credit: Ong Teng Cheong Collection/NAS]

Goh chats with a resident while touring the Buona Vista constituency in 1983, part of a series of monthly constituency visits organised for the second-generation leaders to gain a better feel of the ground and understand grassroots politics. [Photo credit: MITA Collection/NAS]

Goh interacts with residents during his walkabout in Bukit Merah Estate in 1984. Lim Chee Onn, Member of Parliament for Bukit Merah, looks on (first from right).

Goh on an official trip to China with Lee Kuan Yew in 1980.

Goh in Kunming, Yunnan province, during an official trip to China in 1980. Singapore delegates (from left): Ahmad Mattar (Minister for Social Affairs), Goh, Lim Chye Heng (Internal Security Department director) and Eddie Teo (Security and Intelligence Division director).
[Photo credit: Courtesy of Eddie Teo]

Goh and PAP candidate Pang Kim Hin speak to the media after the 1981 Anson by-election. It was the PAP's first electoral loss since independence. [Photo credit: Sin Chew Daily (Singapore) © Singapore Press Holdings Limited. Reprinted with permission]

J. B. Jeyaretnam celebrates with aide Wong Hong Toy at the 1981 Anson by-election counting centre as PAP branch secretary Ong Ah Heng consoles PAP candidate Pang Kim Hin.
[Photo credit: The Straits Times © Singapore Press Holdings Limited. Reprinted with permission]

Newly-minted Health Minister Goh at the re-opening of the Singapore General Hospital in 1981, by Lee Kuan Yew. [Photo credit: Courtesy of Singapore General Hospital]

Goh, Defence Minister from 1982 to 1991, loads a mortar during a visit to the 22nd Battalion Singapore Artillery in 1982. [Photo credit: Courtesy of the Ministry of Defence]

Goh stresses the importance of camaraderie when chatting with soldiers from the 22nd Battalion Singapore Artillery in 1982. [Photo credit: Courtesy of the Ministry of Defence]

Goh being congratulated by fellow second-generation leaders (from left) Ong Teng Cheong, Tony Tan and S. Jayakumar after it was announced in 1985 that he would be the First Deputy Prime Minister and presumed successor to Lee Kuan Yew. S. Dhanabalan is in the background on the right. [Photo credit: The Straits Times © Singapore Press Holdings Limited. Reprinted with permission]

The Marxist Conspiracy, where 22 people were arrested and detained without trial, was the first major domestic security challenge that Goh had to manage. [Photo credit: The Straits Times © Singapore Press Holdings Limited. Reprinted with permission]

Goh meets with German Chancellor Helmut Kohl in Bonn in 1986. The former West Germany was one of many countries Goh visited as First DPM, getting to know global leaders as he prepared for the top job. [Photo credit: The Straits Times © Singapore Press Holdings Limited. Reprinted with permission]

Goh, then the First DPM, calls on China's leader Deng Xiaoping at the Great Hall of the People in Beijing in 1987. [Photo credit: The Straits Times © Singapore Press Holdings Limited. Reprinted with permission]

Lee Kuan Yew hosts British Prime Minister Margaret Thatcher at a dinner in Singapore in 1988. Thatcher would coincidentally resign as PM on the same day Goh became Singapore's PM: November 28, 1990. [Photo credit: The Straits Times © Singapore Press Holdings Limited. Reprinted with permission]

Goh introduces new PAP candidates at the 1988 General Election, under his campaign slogan: More Good Years. Lee Kuan Yew was initially not in favour of the phrase, revealed Goh, for fear of overpromising and not being able to deliver. [Photo credit: MITA Collection/NAS]

Rare photo in 1988 of Lee Hsien Loong, Goh and Lee Kuan Yew together in a pensive moment after the General Election — three generations of Singapore Prime Ministers, or sometimes referred to cheekily as "Father, Son and the Holy Goh". [Photo credit: The Straits Times © Singapore Press Holdings Limited. Reprinted with permission]

Goh with Lee Kuan Yew after the 1988 General Election, which came weeks after the latter told Singaporeans Goh was not his first choice as successor. [Photo credit: The Straits Times © Singapore Press Holdings Limited. Reprinted with permission]

Goh waves to cheering Singaporeans outside the City Hall after being sworn in as the country's second Prime Minister. His new Cabinet, including Lee Kuan Yew as Senior Minister, is in the background. [Photo credit: The Straits Times © Singapore Press Holdings Limited. Reprinted with permission]

The Nutgraf team and *The Straits Times* editor-at-large Han Fook Kwang with Goh. From left: Aaron Low, Sue-Ann Chia, Peh Shing Huei, Goh, Han and Pearl Lee. [Photo credit: Sean Lee]

The Nutgraf team interviewing Goh at his Istana office. To Goh's left is Han Fook Kwang, followed by special assistant Bernard Toh, press secretary Heng Aik Yeow (partial view), Lee, Low, Chia and Peh. [Photo credit: Courtesy of Ministry of Communications and Information]

Photographs from Goh Chok Tong except where otherwise indicated.

Chapter 5

Anson

"Never."

*Lim Chee Onn on whether he expected the PAP to lose the Anson 1981
by-election, in an interview for this book.*

As the results started streaming in from different parts of the large multi-seat ward in Marine Parade during the general election of 2011, Goh Chok Tong's mood darkened considerably. The numbers he was hearing were not what he had been used to. His PAP team of five candidates was up against the National Solidarity Party (NSP) and while the ruling party incumbents were leading, the margins were narrower than expected. Even in a country where the ruling party enjoys an overwhelming majority in most polls, Marine Parade had usually stood out for its higher-than-average scores. It was seen as such a stronghold of Goh that no opposition gave it a fight in three consecutive general elections — 1997, 2001 and 2006. The last time it saw a contest was in a by-election in 1992, when Goh's team secured 72.9 per cent of the vote in a four-way fight. They did even better a year earlier at the 1991 general election, winning a 77.2 per cent majority. But 2011 was different.

Goh's team had included a rookie, Tin Pei Ling, 27, who became emblematic of the electorate's displeasure towards the ruling party during the polls. She was slammed for lacking maturity and being out of touch with the people, with a photograph of her posing with a Kate Spade box widely circulated online and lampooned. By the time of the election, a Facebook page "I do not want Tin Pei Ling in Parliament" had chalked up more than 44,000 "likes" — more than Goh's Facebook page "MParader."

To make things worse for the PAP, NSP's team in Marine Parade GRC had an even younger fresh-faced woman newbie who was seemingly everything Tin was not. Nicole Seah, a 24-year-old advertising executive, was charming, articulate and far more popular than Tin immediately. Goh acknowledged as much after the election. "She communicated very well, spoke very persuasively to younger people... I could sense that quite a few people supported her," he told the media. He was right. The Tin-Seah contrast hijacked the Marine Parade GRC contest and when the results of the election were announced, it shocked many. Goh's team scored 56.6 per cent, below the national average of 60.1 per cent — which was already the lowest in the PAP's history.

It was a bruising conclusion for Goh, and at that moment, his thoughts went back to an epochal event in Singapore politics almost exactly 30 years earlier. "In 2011, Anson came to my mind," he said in an interview for this book. He was referring to the by-election of 1981. "2011 reinforced a lesson I first learnt in Anson — never take things for granted, no matter how good the past result was. In everything, you must expect the unexpected to happen. I did not think that I, as a former Prime Minister, would lose the GRC. But Tin Pei Ling and Nicole Seah came… and the votes came down to 56 per cent. It is not how popular you are, how good you are or how much you can do for the people. You get a new face, people just attack you. The election became a Tin-Seah contest. But that is politics."

The mother of Goh's political lesson came in 1981 in a working-class district called Anson by the southern shore of Singapore. It was adjacent to Tanjong Pagar, Lee Kuan Yew's stronghold. While Anson has long been scrubbed off electoral maps, its name lives on as an iconic reminder for both the ruling party and the opposition of the unforeseen possibilities even in the relatively staid and mundane world of Singapore electoral politics. Most of the history about the Anson by-election, predictably, has focused on the underdog winner, the late J. B. Jeyaretnam of the Workers' Party (WP). JBJ, as he is commonly referred to, was after all the person who ended the PAP's complete dominance of the Parliament since independence. In contrast, less attention has been shone on the losers, particularly Goh's role in the defeat. His involvement in Anson has long faded from public memories in the last four decades.

Yet, by his own admission, the contest played a pivotal role not only in his political career but also in the shaping of his political inclination and sensibilities. "When you talk about how you are shaped, you are often not conscious of it," he said as the creases between his eyebrows tightened. "It is like growing up — at what stage do you become a man? You do not know exactly at what stage you go from a teenager to a man. But you find that suddenly, your thinking is very different. There are certain events you can attribute it to. Anson accelerated and shaped my mind to be where and who I am. It is one of a few such events in my life."

No one could have predicted Anson's impact on Goh — it was another by-election with no obvious signs of anything unique or untoward which should draw the concern of the ruling party. "The mood was one of calmness," he said. "We would win, no problem." For an all-conquering PAP, by-elections in the era were largely risk free and called so as to allow leadership renewal and gauge ground sentiments. Anson was no different. Its popular incumbent MP, Devan Nair, was nominated as president of the country, and resigned from not only his parliamentary seat, but also his leadership of the labour movement — the National Trades Union Congress (NTUC). Lim Chee Onn would take over Nair's place in NTUC. "It was part of the self-renewal," said Goh. In other words, the by-election was like the four called in the 1970s and nothing extraordinary.

Goh was put in charge of Anson, with Pang Kim Hin chosen as the new PAP candidate. Although Tony Tan had leapfrogged Goh as the first assistant secretary-general in the PAP's leadership, Goh was surprisingly still tasked by Lee Kuan Yew to lead and organise the by-election. He was assisted by Lim Chee Onn again, reprising a successful partnership first forged in the 1979 by-election and repeated in the 1980 general election. The duo started the campaign with utmost confidence, gunning for a hat-trick of successes. Nair had won 84.1 per cent in the 1980 elections, above PAP's national margin of 77.7 per cent. "After 1980, we won quite handsomely, so there was no sense of any potential danger," said Goh, who was then the Health Minister. "And since the MP for Anson, Devan Nair, would be the president, all of us felt rationally that the people of Anson would be very proud that their MP was becoming the president. So there was no sense of any disquiet or danger to the by-election. I took it as my task to organise and win. Not just to organise, but I had to organise and win. But I was very comforted that there was a huge buffer of 34 per cent." Lim shared Goh's belief. "Never expected," he replied, when asked if he had an inkling what was to come. "Never."

Once campaigning began, Goh and Lim noticed that all was not right on the ground. "I will be frank — I had no feel of the ground until Nomination Day, when all the little bits came in," said Goh. The problems cut close, into the base of the PAP. Its branch was in disarray. When Nair became MP of Anson in 1979, unionists close to him joined him at the ward. Most of the older activists at the party branch moved out. Two years later, when Nair departed for the Istana, his supporters left Anson too, creating a vacuum at the party branch. Branch secretary Ong Ah Heng had to rally the older members back to help. "But the enthusiasm was not quite the same anymore," said Goh, with a sigh. "They did not know Pang Kim Hin, who also brought in his own supporters. In other words, we discovered that the branch was not quite unified to fight the election."

To make matters worse, it soon became apparent that PAP's candidate, Pang, had difficulties connecting with the ground. He came with a big reputation as the nephew of Old Guard minister Lim Kim San. And despite reservations by Lim himself, the PAP decided to field young Pang, who was a 32-year-old manager. "Lim Kim San was a little sceptical about Pang Kim Hin. He said he was a rich man's son — *ah siah kia*," said Goh, using a Hokkien phrase. "Could he be fielded? All these were discussed. But secretary-general Lee Kuan Yew thought he was suitable." The candidate was "quite personable, confident of himself and articulate" during the interviews, recalled Goh. He had also served national service and Lee wanted to field a candidate with such an experience, a sign of the party's support of National Servicemen or conscripts.

But once the campaigning started, Pang suffered from an early image problem — not unlike Tin in 2011 — and struggled to relate with the mostly working-class voters of Anson. "Pang would come in a fairly big car and the way he dressed, it was different. You are a rich man's son, you walked a bit differently," said Goh, with a rueful smile. Pang brought in his friends to help and they were mostly well-heeled professionals. "They came in Jaguars," said Ong Ah Heng. While the PAP team in Anson was in flux, they faced a formidable opponent in Jeyaretnam, leader of the WP. Like Seah in Marine Parade 30 years later, JBJ was a powerful communicator. "When I saw Nicole Seah, she reminded me of JBJ — very articulate," said Goh. "And Tin Pei Ling reminded me of Pang Kim Hin."

Although the by-election was a three-cornered fight, the third candidate Harbans Singh was widely dismissed from the start. It was clear that the main opposition fighter would be JBJ, the London-educated lawyer and one-time judge. He had contested two elections in neighbouring Telok Blangah in the previous two years, and came close to victory. In the 1980 election, he scored nearly 47 per cent against the PAP — the best performance by an opposition candidate.

By the time he entered the race in Anson, he was a seasoned campaigner, albeit of five failed campaigns, and was by far the most famous opposition politician on the island. Goh said he was a factor behind the eventual result. "He was able to show that he could champion their (voters') disaffection," he said. But at the start of the hustings, neither Jeyaretnam nor Goh foresaw the impact he could make in Anson. In fact, Jeyaretnam's supporters begged him not to run, arguing that the seat was a PAP stronghold and impossible to win. Goh felt the same way. He told a press conference: "I don't think there is any way Mr Jeyaretnam can win."

Two critical issues during the nine days of campaigning played a role in overturning Goh's prediction: housing and transport. First, there were anxieties about housing across Anson. Ground Zero was in a place called Blair Plain, where there were nine purpose-built Port of Singapore Authority (PSA) housing blocks. More than 1,000 PSA and other workers lived there on temporary tenancies and they were earlier served eviction notices as the blocks were to be torn down to make way for a new container complex. They wanted priority in getting new flats, but were denied. Instead, they were told to join a long queue of 100,000 applicants for public HDB flats. "They were most unhappy," said Ong. "1,000 workers plus their spouses. That means about 2,000 votes." It translated into about 13 per cent of the voter share. Lim Chee Onn said that the Blair Plain hotspot was given fuel by Pang's kinship to Lim Kim San, who was the chairman of PSA then. The thinking of the port workers was: "I'm not happy because you are moving me, and on top of that you send the candidate of the chairman of PSA," he said. "My goodness, this is a good opportunity for me to show my displeasure."

In other parts of Anson, there were also concerns about housing. New residents resettled from Duxton Plain, which was in Lee Kuan Yew's ward, had paid higher prices for their new flats because of rising costs, some by as much as 35 per cent. Goh explained: "In the old days, we had a date for increasing the prices of HDB flats across the island. It was bureaucratic and not by market forces. So bureaucratically, you decided you had to increase the price for all the flats." Still, some in PAP had believed that these new residents would be votes in the bag, said Ch'ng Jit Koon, MP of neighbouring Tiong Bahru. "They thought these residents were still in a honeymoon phase of living in their new homes and since they were strong supporters of Lee in Tanjong Pagar, they would also vote for PAP in Anson," he said. "But they bought their flats at a high price and the candidate they were voting was no longer Lee Kuan Yew!"

Second, in the midst of campaigning, *The Straits Times* ran a front page report on impending bus fare hikes. It was a scoop by the national newspaper's transport reporter, based on sources within the Singapore Bus Service. The government denied it, but the damage was done. The reported increase dovetailed with a narrative building among the Anson voters that the cost of living had been increasing and it irked the electorate. "Of course, we jumped," said Goh. "We checked — there was no plan for bus fares to go up. So, they (*The Straits Times*) were playing politics. They said, 'Oh, they heard bus fares were going up'.

You can't report that you heard bus fares going up, so bus fares going up became the headline. So, we got angry. But at that time, there was no point telling Lee Kuan Yew. It was not Chee Onn's and my style — you asked us to be in charge, so we were in charge. We had to tell people that it was not true. Then there was a correction. But it was too late. The correction was in small print, the smallest font you can find." Former *Straits Times* editor Cheong Yip Seng partially disputed the account in his memoirs *OB Markers*. "Later, in his (Lee Kuan Yew) analysis of the defeat, the PM disclosed that SBS did intend to increase fares, but was stopped from doing so," he wrote. "Our reporter was not completely wrong... ."

Despite what seemed a perfect storm against the PAP, Goh still did not think the PAP would lose. The party was living a Panglossian paradise of extreme optimism, where all is for the best in the endless victory parades of the PAP. Midway through the campaigning, he discussed with Lim Chee Onn, Ong and Ch'ng, on their readings of the ground sentiments. All four felt that vote share for the PAP would dip sharply from Nair's 84 per cent, but the party would still win. Goh and Lim put it at between 55 per cent to 60 per cent. Ch'ng estimated it would be above 55 per cent. Ong was the most pessimistic, saying it would dip below 55 per cent. "But even he, towards the end, when I asked, would we win? He would think over and say, yes," said Goh. No one expected defeat. Said Lim: "We did not think it was so serious that we would lose it, because my feeling at that time was that the people were still voting for the party, they were not voting for Mr Pang." The feedback was delivered to Lee by Goh. "He checked with me and

I said that there were problems here and there," said Goh. "He just asked 'Would we win?'. So I said yes. 'Are you sure?'. I said yes. It wasn't just my view. I told him I had checked with the rest. He said okay, as long as we win."

PAP's campaign spiralled further downwards quickly. The cold and distant reactions of the residents morphed into outright displeasure and even dissent. "There were doors slammed at our faces," recalled Lim. "Both Chok Tong and I got it." During a PAP rally, litter was thrown from adjacent blocks of flats, said Goh. "In the middle of making a speech, I heard '*brang*' — someone threw a packet of *kway teow* and also a tin can down," he said, referring to a popular local rice noodle. "Someone threw down empty biscuit tins. It was a little grim." The rallies were poorly attended. "I think many were our own friends," said Goh candidly. "I went to the stage from the side on purpose — I followed Lee Kuan Yew's style. I would go a bit late and come from the back and walk by to get a sense of the crowd. Then I found many people squatting, talking among themselves, not listening to the speakers."

By polling day on October 31, any remaining strain of optimism had been flushed out of the white camp. "We felt the chance of losing was there, because when you walked by (the polling centres), people did not look you in the eye, they walked away very fast. You picked up all these things here and there," he recalled. "By then, we thought maybe it would be 50-50. At best, it would be a narrow win for us." Lee was getting the same intelligence, but not from Goh. He called Ong at about noon and asked him to speak the truth. "I told him honestly it was 50-50 and the margin would be less than 1,000 votes," said Ong, who gathered the information from bookies at Jalan Bukit Merah. "He asked me if it was possible to turn things around and I said I would try my best." The checks by Lee did not catch Goh off guard. "I'm not surprised that he would also have caught up with Ah Heng and Jit Koon," he said. "As I have said, trust but verify. He would verify."

Regardless, it was too late. Goh led a small PAP contingent to the packed counting centre at Gan Eng Seng Secondary along Anson Road at night. They were outnumbered by the WP supporters three to one. Ch'ng recalled it was a nervous occasion. "There could have been bloodshed if WP didn't win," he said. "Their supporters' flag poles were sharpened. It could have easily turned violent." Goh said the night was incredibly tense. "There were very few PAP supporters because it was a by-election. We were at the back, at the periphery while they were in the front." Without mobile phones then, the supporters on both sides could only wait till the results were announced. "We had no clue what was going on inside," said Goh. "It was not like today when you have mobile phones and you can WhatsApp and SMS."

At 10.53pm, returning officer Richard Lau announced the result:

Harbans Singh: 131 votes.
Jeyaretnam: 7,012 votes.
Pang: 6,359 votes.

The roar of the crowd drowned out the announcement. History had been made. In just 10 months, the PAP suffered a 37-point swing in the same ward, the most dramatic electoral reversal in independent Singapore's history. When Pang tried to give a speech, he was booed off stage and the first PAP losing candidate since 1965 stomped off the grounds. The scene at Gan Eng Seng haunted Goh for years. "Oh, jubilation, but not on our part," he said, tilting his head back at the memory. "The whole crowd was shouting 'Jeya, Jeya'. And each time a bus passed by, somebody would run after the buses and shout 'Jeya, Jeya, Jeya won'. It was excitement. And the buses would sound their horns. Some cars were going by and when they heard this, they also honked." When asked how he felt seeing such happiness from the people at a defeat of the PAP, he replied: "Well, grim was the word."

His ordeal wasn't over. He was told by his security officer that Lee wanted to speak to him. But without mobiles phones and with shops nearby having closed, Goh had to walk more than a kilometre to the Anson PAP branch. He walked fast, with only one thing on his mind: "What should I tell Mr Lee?" When the call was made, Lee asked him what happened. "My answer was that we lost," he said. "I gave some reasons why I thought we lost. I said we did not expect the loss and it was worse than we thought. There was no point giving all kinds of excuses — I never blamed anybody; just that we lost. I did not say the candidate was poor — that was the wrong time. It was not Pang Kim Hin's fault. Below the surface, there was discontent and unhappiness that we were not aware of. Mr Lee said okay. He asked about Pang Kim Hin and I said they were inside and they seemed to be all right. He wasn't angry. That was when you learnt about being a leader — it had happened, but what do we do now? You look forward."

Q: What was the discussion with Lee Kuan Yew after the result?

A: There was a post-mortem. And that was how you learnt again. It was a quick post-mortem, but we all knew the reasons. But it was also looking forward. So, you learnt that what had gone, had gone. We called a meeting of all MPs and the question was: What do we do now in Anson? Do we continue to run the community centre (CC) in Anson or do we pass it on to JBJ? I felt that we should pass on the CC to JBJ. And many of the young ones felt so. I thought we should be fair — he had won, so pass on everything to him. The CC was part of Anson and we should pass it on. British parliamentary rules — accept it and shake his hand. Write him a congratulatory letter and so on. That was the thinking of the younger ones, the MPs.

LKY never scolded us but he asked the older ones. And they said, no, we do not pass on. We keep it, this is our base. You pass it on to him, he would be entrenched and we would never win Anson back again. This cannot be done. So, you learn. Yet, what is the reason to justify keeping it? This is part of government facility. CC is part of the government — you do not pass on part of the government to the other side. We young naïve ones thought the CC was part of the constituency's institutions and we had to pass it on. The older ones said, no.

Q: *And that extended to all People's Association (PA) outfits as well, such as RCs, Citizens' Consultative Committees (CCC)?*

A: Yes, they are all part of the government. But you must be fair. Anybody who is prepared to promote government policies and progress, you can use our RC and CC. But you cannot use it for party politics. No opposition party would go and promote government programmes. We would. So, the rules became clearer because, in the beginning, we all wore white and went to the CCs. But once there was an opposition, we observed our rules. We had a code of fair conduct. So, no one was allowed to wear white and white and go to a CC. I was very angry initially. I kept telling them that I was going to get an RI boy to go in and see what happened! So, PA had to impose the rules, much to our inconvenience and unhappiness.

Q: *So that was the beginning of the separation of PA and the PAP and since then it has become the norm.*

A: Yes, we began to separate it out. We were justified that the CC cannot be given to JBJ because it was part of the government. Therefore, it should not be given to the PAP too — you could not. It must be even-handed.

Q: *And you saw no desire to change that later on when you became PM?*

A: No, you cannot change it because the justification is that it is a government facility. You are government staff, so therefore you must scrupulously observe the rules, so that you cannot be faulted by the other side. Are you aware that we are not allowed to use MP in our banners in our grassroots activities — we can use only 'adviser to grassroots organisations'? Because if an MP can use all these facilities, then at Hougang, they can also use it.[18] And we said no, so we said only adviser. You say it is unfair, but I say it is very fair.

Q: *Would you say that in doing this, you actually have no concept of a loyal opposition?*

A: We have, but how can we allow them to take over a government facility? It is not a political entity; it is government.

Q: *I think the other point of view is that a Member of Parliament, whether opposition or for the ruling party, is part of a system. The country benefits from having Members of Parliament from different parties. They are as much a part of the system as the ruling party. So when they win an election, you should accord them the same sort of privileges, because they are good for the country.*

A: You fight fairly to win and the spoils — if you can keep them, you do. But if you cannot keep them, you give them away legally. Had we given away the CC at Anson, then we would have had to give away the HDB area office; and when we lost more wards

---

[18] Hougang is a constituency in north-eastern Singapore which the Workers' Party won in 1991 and has held on to since.

later, we would have to give more and more to the other side — Aljunied and Hougang.[19] But the key is to be consistent and fair. For the town council, we did give away. You cannot say that the town council is the government. For the town council, the other side would take over if they win. And we know they used the town councils to build themselves up and employ people. The employees became staunch party supporters because had their party lost, they might lose their jobs. It is double-edged. So, the employees of the opposition town councils are more hard-headed in supporting the Workers' Party than ours in supporting the PAP.

Q: *That is a very hard-headed approach to politics. Was it part of your political education?*

A: Yes, you learn all this. At first, you were a bit naïve, in the sense that was what you learnt in textbooks. You wanted to implement textbook knowledge. But on the ground, it was entirely different. But, at the end, like I said, you must be fair in terms of contest-ability. Of course, we have an advantage as an incumbent — that cannot be helped. We have ministers in GRCs — that is our advantage. People say it is not fair. If you do not have ministers, is it my fault? And we look at the loss of Aljunied GRC positively — we did not like it, but we can argue that the GRC was not meant for the PAP only. The opposition can win. That was what

---

[19] Aljunied is a mega constituency in north-eastern Singapore which the Workers' Party won in 2011.

we had been saying. Ministers or not, the opposition can win. The GRC is not a hindrance to them.

Q: *How else did Anson change the PAP?*

A: The way Lee Kuan Yew put it, the loss was not in the seat. Losing one seat was neither here nor there. We had all the seats at that time. It was a loss of the perception of PAP's invincibility. That was the loss for us. Up till then, we were invincible. Anything which the government wanted to do, popular or not, if we had to do it, we decided and we did it. Invincible. Whatever we did, the people would support. There was total faith in the PAP — invincible. People thought the PAP was invincible. And therefore, after this loss, you must expect more losses.

How do you prevent more losses? The PAP MPs must speak up frankly in Parliament. Otherwise, JBJ was playing that role. So, all of us had to play the role of the opposition as well, and intelligently. This was so that all the difficult issues were raised by the PAP MPs, and not just by one opposition MP. So, we became more opposition-minded, until some of us think that we are, in fact, the opposition, and stand against the PAP for presidency.[20]

---

[20] In the 2011 election for the state presidency, former PAP MP Tan Cheng Bock, a close friend of Goh Chok Tong, contested against the PAP-backed candidate Tony Tan.

Q: How was it watching Mr Lee in the boxing ring with JBJ when the latter got into Parliament?

A: I felt very uncomfortable. There was one battle when both sides used language which was so — shall we say — un-Parliamentary-like.[21] Most of us just felt very awkward. Mr Lee used very strong language, but all within Parliamentary rules. It was very personal, very insulting. And JBJ tried to insult back but he did not have the same vocabulary. In other words, it was intimidation. Take out the gloves, as Mr Lee would say. Either I destroy you or you destroy me. I wanted to get up and say, stop it. For us, it was not the way Parliament should be conducted. That was the way other countries ran their Parliament. I was not used to such a display.

Q: Did you share your views with Mr Lee at that time?

A: He did not ask. If he had asked, I would have said he had gone a bit too far. That was the politics of his generation. You have to fight to win. But our generation would be different and the make-up is different. We would not employ the same language which he would do. Hsien Loong is very articulate but it is a different kind of language he would use, because times have changed. And the other party is different.

So that is the decorum, which the Speaker and ourselves try to uphold. We try not to be too personal to set a tone of debate

---

[21] It occurred during the 1986 Budget debate, when Jeyaretnam challenged Lee to reduce ministerial pay. Lee called Jeyaretnam's allegations "the distorted workings of a sick mind." When Jeyaretnam interrupted Lee repeatedly, Lee called it "the heckles of a street hustler."

for future Parliaments. So if somebody emerges and wants to be like JBJ or LKY and just insult the other side, the Speaker would put a stop to it and people would agree that that is not the kind of Parliament you want. You can have very intense debates, but let's take away that personal animosity. But if you have a very difficult opposition who engages in personal attacks, the PM must have the ability to fight back. If the PM is a gentleman, then get somebody who can. That means you get a hatchet man. Your DPM or Minister for Law — that is the hatchet man, who can fight with you.

Q: Was LKY demonstrating to the younger generation of leaders how you should deal with this sort of political opponent?

A: Yes. He did not tell us to do it his way, but we could see that that is a difficult one and that was the way to deal with JBJ. And when we dealt with Chiam See Tong — you know, it was in a very friendly, disarming way.[22] I did not copy LKY's way in being very personal. You are not Lee Kuan Yew, so do not try to do it.

Q: As you have said, LKY has this almost-personal dislike of JBJ. What about yourself?

A: I did not have the same feeling. I hardly knew him, other than through politics. I knew that he was a little pompous, the way he spoke and so on, but there was no dislike. I was not too friendly. I just put him on the other side. I mean, when I met him,

---

[22] Chiam See Tong is an opposition leader who was in Parliament from 1984 to 2011.

we did speak. But if LKY had seen anyone speaking to him, the person would get asked why he would want to do that, does he know what JBJ was like!

Q: But you would agree with LKY that he is not the sort of opposition desired?

A: Yes, because I watched him. He was appealing to the ruffians. He was talking about criminal law and all those things. He was more or less signalling to his support base that he was championing them. Criminal law and all kinds of police cases — he would handle. Allegations of police abuse — he handled those. That was his base that he wanted. You can read up the questions he asked in Parliament. They were aimed at the down and disaffected types. My conclusion was that this fellow was quite dangerous. You could see it at the rallies. Many of the chaps who turned up to support him were the ruffian types.

You think elections are so straightforward? Now, the police separate the supporters during the announcement of election results. Previously, like in Anson, we were all together in the same place. In other elections, we carried flags and the opposition supporters carried flags too. Ours had our bases sawed flat. The other side had their bases pointed. They planted their flag posts into the ground. But when they took them up, they could be used as a weapon. So, we learnt. You all think elections are so calm? We fixed it to be calm! Make sure the police tell them not to have any sharp objects or poles to carry the flags. Politics is not as simple as you think. It is harmonious today because we fixed it. In the past, it was very rough. The opposition had many ruffians. Ours were all gentlemen types. Lee Kuan Yew told me, go and get some karate people, get them to stand in front. Rough them up first, if necessary, then they would be afraid. Play by rules? Those are the rules. You are tough, so am I.

Q: How did Anson influence you?

A: LKY said that the loss would have to come sooner or later. Rajaratnam also said so. It is not possible in politics that we would win all the seats in every general election. It is not possible. That is not the nature of human beings. Sooner or later. It came sooner than we expected. But the Old Guard said, 'Might as well'. Then we the younger ones could learn how to handle and how to fight elections. So, they turned this into a lesson for us.

The effect on me was in understanding practical politics. It was not just organising. Up to that point, as organising secretary, I could organise very well. But Anson taught me that politics is more than just organising. You have to win. How do you win within the rules? You must be able to understand the ground. You have to build up the supporters and you have to persuade people. But you need to make sure that the policies are right in the first place. If there is genuine discontent, try and get the unhappiness sorted out first before you call the election. If the mood is wrong, do not call a by-election.

In the days after the Anson loss, the murmurings within the PAP were that the game was over for Goh's political career. Lee did not suffer fools lightly and the man in charge of the party's first electoral defeat in 13 years would surely pay the price. "Many MPs thought that was the end for me," said Goh, with a shrug. "When I bumped into them in Parliament, they gave me a quick glance and walked away. I could tell, I was not that insensitive. Some would come and talk to me, like commiserating, saying it was all right. But others thought I was over. This was because we had not lost and that was the first time we lost. And Mr Lee, you know, he never took failures lightly."

Indeed, Lee did not take kindly to the defeat, especially the manner of the loss. He wrote in *From Third World to First*: "I was disturbed, not by the defeat, but because I had had no signal from Goh that we might lose. I worried about his political sensitivity. James Fu, my press secretary, told me that people on the ground resented the over-confident attitude of the party leaders in the campaign." But neither he nor the Old Guard leaders blamed Goh.

Lee saw something in Goh on that election night: he remained calm and accepted responsibilities. Fu, who was at Gan Eng Seng Secondary reported to Lee that Goh had stayed collected and did not cave. "By then, I had understood Mr Lee better," said Goh. "He was not that kind of a person who would blame others for one failure. He was more interested in what kind of a person you are. He wanted to see my reaction. He was testing me. It was a loss, yes, but the man who had lost, can he continue to be a leader of that group? I think that was what he was interested in." In a strange way, although Goh failed the Anson by-election test, he passed the political leadership examination. Lee had bigger challenges lined up for him.

Building
a Brand

Part 3

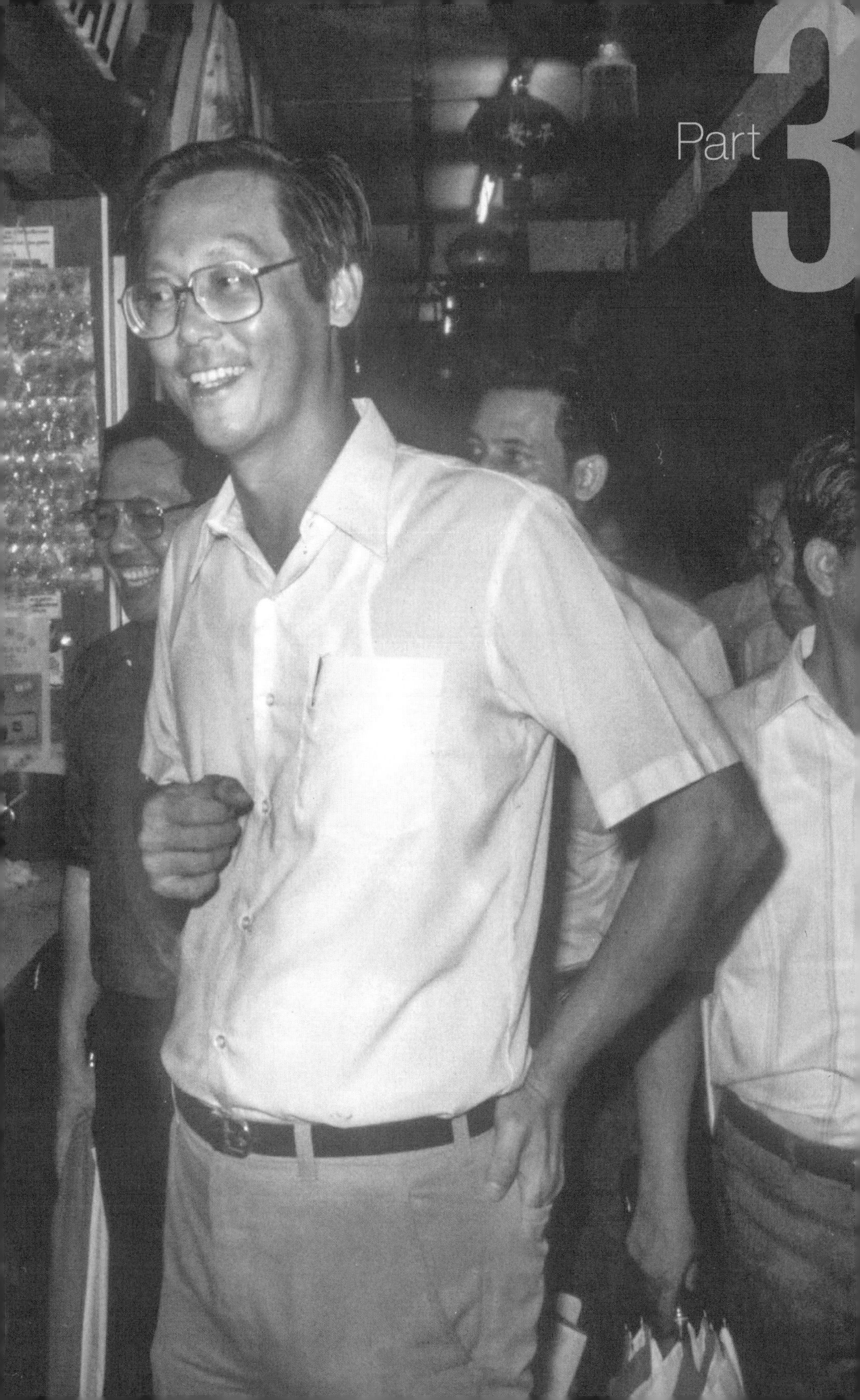

"

I learnt early on that
I wasn't LKY.
You must be practical.
You must do what you can do.

"

Chapter 6

Reformer of Health

"MediSave is one of Goh Chok Tong's legacies which has satisfied everybody."

Health economist Phua Kai Hong from the Lee Kuan Yew School of
Public Policy, in an interview for this book.

L ee Kuan Yew was not one who was used to being stymied and
brushed off. But for six years from 1975, his Old Guard colleague
Toh Chin Chye refused to budge. Lee, the Prime Minister, had
been wrestling with the problem of controlling Singapore's health budget
and he came up with an innovative idea. Instead of relying on taxation
alone to fund healthcare, he also wanted the individual to be personally
responsible for his own medical needs. Lee's plan was to tap on the
Central Provident Fund (CPF), Singapore's national pension scheme.
"My proposal (was) to set aside part of each person's monthly CPF
contribution for co-payment of his medical bill," he wrote in *From Third
World to First*, adding, "Expenses would be charged against an
individual; this would prevent abuse."

But Toh, who was the Health Minister, rejected the proposal
completely. After visiting hospitals in Beijing, he was impressed with
the free healthcare which was provided to all in China. The Old Guard

minister had brought his own socialist bent into his health portfolio, said health economist Phua Kai Hong. "Toh Chin Chye was very strong on ideology," he said. "He wanted a tax-based healthcare system of redistribution. Tax the rich to help the poor. If it were so easily achieved, socialism would have thrived. But the fact is that communism failed." Lee rubbished Toh's Chinese takeaways. "I said I did not believe they had such medical standards for everyone in Beijing, let alone for all in China," said Lee in his biography. The premier pushed for his plan and succeeded in a tepid move in 1977. Every CPF member set aside 1 per cent of his monthly income for medical expenses for himself and his family. But it wasn't enough. Based on the health ministry's calculations, each person needed between 6 and 8 per cent of his CPF contributions to cover his health costs.

In 1981, Lee had had enough after clashes with Toh over numerous issues. He removed Toh as Health Minister and left him out of the Cabinet, a sharp move since Toh was chairman of the PAP. In his place, Lee appointed the fast-rising Goh Chok Tong. The appointment shocked many. At that point, the Ministry of Health (MOH) was not seen as an important ministry. Toh had nicknamed it the "Cinderella Ministry," said Khaw Boon Wan, a young officer at the MOH then, suggesting that it was a ministry taken for granted and largely unrecognised. To some, his transfer to MOH was a demotion, said Goh. For those in the ministry, they had an opposite interpretation. "He was a rising star, so why was he coming to the Cinderella Ministry?" said Khaw. "There was sort of a shocked reaction. Why were we suddenly so important that the big man had to come here?"

But Lee knew what he wanted from the young, and very tall, prince charming Goh. "He understood what I wanted: good health services, with waste and costs kept in check by requiring co-payments from the user," wrote Lee. "Subsidies for healthcare were necessary, but could be extremely wasteful and ruinous for the budget." In three years, Goh would turn Lee's idea into reality, and implemented the world's first national medical savings fund, MediSave.

In some ways, although he was not trained in the medical profession, Goh was the ideal man for the job. As he would share later in his first National Day Rally speech as Prime Minister in 1991, the loss of his father at a young age shaped his views on healthcare for the rest of his life. "I know the meaning to a family of someone dying prematurely," he said. "But if I can help, I will try and save someone from dying prematurely, for his sake and for his family's. I would therefore make sure that every Singaporean can afford essential healthcare." Goh's poor background having grown up in crowded conditions with poor sanitation in Pasir Panjang further sharpened his interest in providing a modern healthcare system, said Phua, who had researched extensively into Goh's years as Health Minister. "For somebody who had gone through that era of pit latrines, there is an appreciation of health and hygiene," said the observer from the Lee Kuan Yew School of Public Policy.

It helped that Goh was not only bringing into the ministry an economist approach to healthcare, but also a private sector bent to extract maximum value and minimise wastage. Productivity and efficiency became buzzwords of the health system. "Singapore was the first country to put its economic imperative in healthcare," said Phua. "You want Singaporeans to be healthy not just for health sake, but to be productive, to be able to contribute to the economy. And you are not going to spend money and waste it. You are going to spend it efficiently. It can only come from an economist!"

Such changes were part of the "transformational thinking" of his generation of leaders, said Goh, several of whom injected a market-driven impetus into policies. "Without discussing, each of us initiated big changes in our own ministries," he said. "This had a collective effect and managed to persuade the older ministers to come along." For instance, National Development Minister S. Dhanabalan introduced differential pricing into public housing, with those on higher floors, having better views and enjoying more convenient locations costing more. Before that, Housing Board flats were priced simply according to the zones they were in. Over at the Ministry of Communications and Information, Yeo Ning Hong switched fixed pricing for telephone calls to time pricing. Such changes fostered a climate of competitiveness and fairness, said Lee Hsien Loong, creating a system where resources were properly allocated. "They were eminently rational and sensible things to do, which were efficient and which would have created the right incentives and covered your costs, and would make the whole economy work better and really be a fairer system," he said.

But it was not easy to make these changes in government, shared Dhanabalan. "We brought a perspective which was not there from the older ministers," he said. Khaw agreed. "At that time, the thinking was very different. There was a fear about the private sector, would they mess things up and so on," he said. "So, it required a lot of convincing and many rounds of debate, which meant convincing Mr Lee himself. That took quite some time."

For Goh, the health sector was the first canvas in politics where he could not only sketch a vision, but also paint the finer details to a colourful — at times literally — and sustainable medical masterpiece. The showpiece of his achievements was MediSave. The thinking behind the scheme was clear: against a backdrop of an ageing population, Singapore needed to move away from a tax-based financing system because the tax revenue was likely to reduce as the workforce shrank. Instead, the solution was in a compulsory personal savings plan for hospitalisation. Such a plan would also detach the quality of healthcare from the vagaries of economic growth. When individuals co-pay for their own medical expenses, the likelihood of abuses and wastage reduces too. "Otherwise, everybody's money becomes no one's responsibility," said Phua.

But selling MediSave to the public was tricky. When Goh first announced the outlines of the scheme in March 1982, it was only five months after the Anson by-election. The mood on the ground was one of increasing rancour towards the government and the first glimpse of a slightly sceptical people after almost two decades of almost unquestioned trust in Lee and the PAP. It did not help that MediSave was the first major dipping into the CPF for non-retirement purposes after housing in 1968. The public was wary, recalled Goh. "We were going to take CPF money for something new," he said. "There were quite a lot of murmurings... what was the plan of the government?

People were quite rightfully suspicious. Was this the first move? What else would you do with my CPF? The money was supposed to be for retirement and, suddenly, MediSave came about."

The policy would draw heavy fire from within the PAP too, particularly from Toh, who went so far as to abstain from voting for the scheme in Parliament. He said in 1983: "The provision of healthcare facilities must be accepted as a social responsibility. It is not that an individual who has the misfortune to be inflicted with some particular disease is solely responsible for searching the facilities to cure his illness. This is a social responsibility which is accepted by governments all over the world. This is part and parcel of the organisation of individuals into societies. It is a measure of the degree of civilisation." On the fear of abuse, he slammed Goh in colourful prose: "I think it is a very dangerous assumption to believe that persons love to fall ill, that they go around shopping for sicknesses in the supermarkets, or that they like to spend their weekend in a hospital as if the hospital is a hotel. Or that the food served in the hospital is *a la carte* or buffet. That is perverse propaganda."

Goh knew from the outset that he needed the wide support of the people if he wanted to push through MediSave. "We, the younger ministers, hadn't got that goodwill," he said. "The trust from the people was for Mr Lee. The people trusted the old government." So he kicked off a year-long consultation exercise, visiting different parts of Singapore to explain the policy and gather feedback. Such an extensive outreach process was pretty much unheard of in Singapore at that time. "Mr Lee would say, 'Why do you want to spend so much time getting feedback?

Just decide and do it'," said Goh with a laugh. "But I learnt early on that I wasn't LKY. You must be practical. You must do what you can do. If you want to do something, you must ask yourself if you can deliver it."

He was very patient on the road, led the campaign and hosted many sessions, said Khaw. "MOH organised many dialogue sessions, big groups, small groups, one-way broadcast, narrowcast, interactive dialogue, radios, TVs, print media. There were no social media then. Everyone chipped in," he recalled. "I myself must have held nearly 100 dialogue sessions. With unions, with grassroots organisations, with professional bodies, with employers, with academics."

Tough questions were posed from the ground. Some feared they may never get to use their MediSave. Once, someone asked Goh if MediSave could be used to buy a coffin after he died. It was a curveball. "The answer was yes," he said. "I told him that after a person passed away, the MediSave still belonged to him. It was his estate. Obviously, the person would not be there to buy his own coffin. Somebody had to buy it for him. But it could be paid out of MediSave, through his estate, later. Everybody clapped."

Others were concerned why they had to co-pay and Goh used the "buffet lunch syndrome" to explain, said Khaw. "This is something which Singaporeans can easily relate to. Having paid for the buffet lunch at a fixed price per head, diners simply fill their plates with more than what they need or can eat, resulting in waste," he said. "The latter means higher operating cost for the restaurants which eventually have to pass on the higher cost to the diners through higher prices. There is no free lunch. Ultimately, the patients have to pay, either as taxpayers or as insurance subscribers."

While the sessions were punishing and tiring, Goh found them useful, allowing him and the officials a good feel of the ground. Khaw said: "I remember he said, 'Every time, we learn something'." The outreach grew so extensive that dialogue participants became increasingly tired of listening to Goh and the health officials. "Many told us frankly: please get on with it!" said Khaw with a laugh. "And as participation rates dwindled — my last dialogue at a grassroots event attracted only two participants! — Goh told me that it was the time to get the scheme implemented! I learnt a very valuable lesson in how to implement a controversial policy and retain trust."

The success of the groundwork for MediSave would translate into a signature policy of Goh when he became Prime Minister later, as he embraced participatory democracy as a key plank of his leadership. He said: "The MediSave experience informed me in the way that when I had another problem, I would go to the ground again and explain, and not have a scripted speech and make a speech and so on." The consultations were not simply a public relations exercise. He took in the concerns of the people and tweaked the proposal for MediSave. Instead of raising CPF contributions by 6 percentage points, and reduce take-home pay in the process, he increased it by only 1 point and diverted the remaining from existing contributions to MediSave. The confidence gathered from the ground also gave him the confidence to take on the intra-party challenges towards MediSave.

Lee was concerned that Goh might not be able to withstand the attacks of Toh in Parliament. "Mr Lee was very good. He asked me if I wanted him to speak, to answer Dr Toh," said Goh. "I mean, Dr Toh would know much more about health — he had been there for many years. I was then a young Minister for Health. Mr Lee was worried I couldn't explain the policy. I said no and I would handle it." He managed comfortably, with a blend of disarming clarity and decency. "His (Toh's) primary thrust is: health is a social responsibility of any government," answered Goh in 1983. "I do not see how we can disagree with that. Healthcare must be the social responsibility not solely, but primarily, of any government. But it does not mean that you discharge your social responsibility by dispensing free medicine or heavily subsidised medicine."

He lobbed Toh a few sharp questions of his own: "Can he guarantee continuous economic growth at 8 per cent per annum? Can he guarantee that Singapore will never face unemployment again? We should not forget that it was not so long ago that we experienced an unemployment rate of over 10 per cent," he said, adding: "All of us know that we are heavily dependent on exports, on the export of goods and services. And if there is a collapse of the international financial system or a deep world economic recession, then where do we collect our payroll tax from? So many people will be unemployed! Can this House guarantee that there will be no profligate Finance Minister ever in Singapore? We can guarantee that for the next 10, 20 years but not forever. One profligate government or Finance Minister and the entire resources of the country will go up in smoke. Where then would there be sufficient funds to look after the health service, to pay for doctors and nurses, to maintain high standards in the hospitals and outpatient dispensaries?"

Toh, to his credit, was not a "troublemaker," said Goh, and did not attempt to demolish the arguments of his successor Health Minister. "He just stated his view on why he was against MediSave," said Goh. "Then when I replied… he left it at that." Predictably, the scheme was passed by the PAP-dominant Parliament. But remarkably, the public embraced MediSave with nary a hint of controversy. By the time the scheme was implemented in government hospitals in April 1984, Goh had already prepared the ground for two years. Khaw praised it as an exemplar of a good policy. "As a result of all this hard and patient work, the implementation was a non-event. That is what a good policy ought to be like," he said. "The worst is being unprepared and, after you implement, people go 'What is that all about' and they start questioning why we are doing this — that would be an example of a bad policy implementation." Phua concurred. He said: "When he implemented MediSave, no fuss! MediSave is one of Goh Chok Tong's legacies which has satisfied everybody. Goh Chok Tong is a health reformer."

Goh's reforms in health extended beyond his signature policy. He introduced an awareness of cost into the healthcare system and bridged the gap between the private practices and the public hospitals in more ways than one. He also initiated the relocation of hospitals from prime land, such as the Middle Road Hospital in downtown Singapore, allowing the hospitals more room to grow and also releasing higher-value land for other uses. By the time he completed his four-year tenure at the Health Ministry in 1984, the medical scene in Singapore had evolved from one with strong socialist leanings into a clear market-based system. The foundations for Singapore's subsequent corporatised public hospitals, where they run as autonomous agencies or as wholly-owned state firms, were established.

In fact, one of Goh's first acts in the ministry was to replicate the management information systems he had first started in NOL, so as to have a better grasp of cost and finances. "How much did it cost to treat a patient in a C class? The civil servants did not know," he said. "How do you charge? They just charged what they thought the public could bear. And how much should the government subsidise? Then how did you decide on an A class rate, compared to a C class rate? You could be subsidising an A class more than a C class. They did not know. They just knew they had to pay more. But how much they were putting in — consultants, air-conditioning and so on — are you sure you are not subsidising more than a C class? No, they had no idea."

More than that, there was a strong division between the public and private sectors in health. The doctors who had left the public hospitals for private practice were seen as having betrayed the health ministry. On their part, these doctors resented being cut adrift and having no access to the government. The split was obvious, remembered Khaw. "The wall between public and private was clear, so you were in or out," he said.

For Toh and earlier Health Ministers, their responsibilities were confined to the doctors in government hospitals. But Goh saw it differently. "The Minister for Health's job was to look after the health of the whole country, not just those who came to the public hospitals," he said. "Healthcare is a concern for the ministry, not just hospitalisation and polyclinics." To end the medical cold war, he called for meetings with doctors on both sides of the divide to discuss and share ideas. "The people from the private sector were very happy. They could give their views and we could try and marry the two," he said. He also encouraged MOH to bring back private consultants to serve in public hospitals, including to teach and train younger doctors, said Khaw. "He was active in nudging MOH to learn and leverage from the expertise and experience of the private sector, and not just from the health sector," he said. "He was instrumental in getting the National University Hospital to set up a Department of Ophthalmology, run by private consultant ophthalmologists... such innovation in blurring the line between the public and the private sectors led to the setting up of the Singapore National Eye Centre in Singapore General Hospital."

Goh was also not above copying good ideas from the private sector. When he noticed that nurses in private hospitals wore colourful and comfortable uniforms, he urged for it to be replicated in the government hospitals. "Ours were very thick cotton and white, you had to starch it and you had to wear a cap," he said. "You had to starch it like a soldier's uniform — everything had to be spick and span and polished. It was very British, it never changed." When he saw baby cots in public hospitals that were made of cast iron and with peeling paint, he asked for it to be changed to transparent plastic. But, as always, there was an economic justification. With the old cots, nurses could not see the babies from afar and would get up from their work stations to check every half an hour. If the cots were see-through, the nurses would be able to check at a glance if the baby was restless or uncomfortable. "So I asked if it would help in productivity," said Goh. "They said yes. It was also cleaner. Then I said change it."

But it was not completely smooth sailing. He had taken on the job with a strong zeal to save lives but was soon educated on the limits of government in matters of life and death. In the initial months as the minister, he came across cases of young people with kidney failure who could not get access to dialysis machines because of its limited numbers. "Why did we have to play God in deciding who could get it and who could not? Why are we not saving a life just because of a lack of dialysis machines? We should save every life," he said. "My father died young and I looked at these young people and I asked why couldn't we save them?"

He did the sums and concluded that the government could afford to get more machines. But his permanent secretary in the ministry, the late Andrew Chew, cautioned him against it. "He said, 'Minister, it is not just kidney failures that we have to worry about. There are other diseases, like cancer, and if you do likewise, you would not have enough money. It is not possible to try and save everybody. You do not have the money. The Finance Minister would not agree'," recalled Goh. "So somehow, we had to decide. It is very sad, but somebody has to play God." The lesson became personal when his closest uncle, the one who brought him to election rallies in the 1960s, died of a heart attack at a young age of 44 in a hospital when Goh was the Health Minister, shared S. Puhaindran. "It affected him very badly that he could do nothing," he said.

Q: *In 1982, you went from being Health Minister to being the Second Health Minister. That was quite an unusual career move. What happened?*

A: It was the PM who wanted to make certain changes in both the defence and health ministries. First, he was not happy with Toh Chin Chye in health. Then, he was also not happy with Howe Yoon Chong who was the Defence Minister. So he put me as Second Defence Minister to understudy him. I was Health Minister and Second Defence Minister. After a while, I suppose the feedback was that I could take over as Defence Minister.

But LKY had to park Howe somewhere. He chose the Health Ministry. But he knew that Howe would be totally demoralised as Health Minister and may undo things which I started. So LKY asked me to stay in health as Second Health Minister. In other words, keep an eye on the Health Ministry. But I was very wise. As Second Minister, I never stepped into the Health Ministry.

Q: *Why is that so?*

A: When Howe was Defence Minister and I was Second, he was able to accept me because I was learning from him. But when he became the Health Minister and I was Second, it was different. I was the previous Health Minister and he knew Lee Kuan Yew was upset with him. If I attended the meetings as Second Health Minister, it would be like spying on him to report to Lee Kuan Yew. I was very wise. I never went. He could scold the doctors — it was up to him — I did not bother. I just watched whether MediSave was in place or be discarded. I never stepped in. But Mr Lee never asked me if I went to the ministry. Howe also never asked why he never saw me in his meetings. If he had asked the question, I would have gone, but he never did.

So that is human relationships. Who taught me that? I do not know. It was common sense. First one in defence, I was there to understudy. And as a young minister, Howe Yoon Chong supported me. He supported self-renewal. I knew him as a permanent secretary. We worked quite well and I think he knew that this was part of the succession. But as Second Minister for Health and to make sure that he did not do crazy things — I think that was very difficult. I don't think I have ever told people that I never stepped into the Health Ministry as Second Minister.

Q: *You figured out that had you remained active in health, you would have problems with Howe?*

A: Yes. The moment I became Second Health Minister, I told myself that I was not going in. And I had good reasons because I had to focus on Defence.

Q: *Did LKY tell you why you were posted to the Defence Ministry?*

A: To lead Singapore, he said, I had to understand defence. So that was one of the early signals that I was one of those who could lead Singapore. That means, I must know the capability of our armed forces. If ever I had to stand eyeball to eyeball with a threatening neighbour, I need to know what we were capable of doing or not. If you are a brown belt and want to take on a black belt — don't, let's not quarrel, negotiate.

Q: *Do the leaders today still believe that you need to know the Defence Ministry before you can become a Prime Minister in Singapore?*

A: I do not know. I am not the PM. You have to understand something about the military. But maybe today, it is less necessary because it is a much better run SAF and many of the ministers came from the SAF. So that is not a problem. Whereas, at my time, nobody in my cohort came from the SAF, except for Hsien Loong later. So, we could all be, let us just say, overconfident against any threat. But you have to understand what you can or cannot do. Do not be a bravado and do not be a coward. You do not have to give way easily — you know what you can do and you have backbone and you have people to back you up. But if you do not know the military, it becomes very difficult. You talk to someone who has big armed forces and can stare you in the face, and you wouldn't know how to react.

Q: *When you moved from being Trade and Industry Minister to Health Minister and Second Defence Minister, there were murmurings that it was a demotion?*

A: I did feel that among some colleagues. They did not say so. However, sometimes, in their reactions, you know that they think you are being demoted. For some people, MTI was much more important at that time. Health was — you give me the money, I look after health, but the doctors were there, I just have to answer questions in Parliament. So, it was perceived as a demotion by some people. But you cannot be listening to murmurs all the time.

Q: *How did you react to that?*

A: As usual. I was self-confident. I did my job. If I were not going to be No. 1, then so what? I did not fight for it. I just did a job. The way Mr Lee put it to me was that something needed to be done in health; and in defence, you had to know some things. So, I know that I was not being shunted aside. In other words, people might think that it was a demotion, but the way he said it, there was a role for me to play. A critical role. And I enjoyed the health part because I was able to go and visit hospitals and introduce changes. That made my work as a Health Minister fulfilling.

Q: *Lee Kuan Yew was the one who moved you to different portfolios, with a brief on what he wanted to be done at the different ministries. How much did he intervene in your work after that?*

A: He knew a lot about micro issues and can get into the details. But he was not a micromanager. When something was not right, he would ask questions. But he was more concerned about the big picture. For the small picture, he could know more if he wanted to. He would ask for the figures and would brush up and know more than you very quickly. He believed in getting the right man for the job and leaving him alone. That was the way he led.

Q: *But when he decides that an issue is important, then he will go deep into it?*

A: Ohhhhh. Let's say terrorism. He would read about radical ideologies and understand it much faster and quicker and deeper than anyone.

Q: *But let's go back to MediSave. It was his idea and yet he didn't intervene in how you put it together?*

A: He had a file, he had some ideas, one of which was to use CPF to pay for your medical costs. He did not know a lot about the issue, but he just left it to me. He gave me a file and that was it. I went through it. At that time, I was also looking for a new and big idea. I was thinking to myself what I could do in the ministry and lo and behold, he gave me the file. I went 'Ah, yes, this is something which I can do, something which I wanted to do'. So this was the big idea and he seeded it.

I remember another example. When I became Minister for Trade and Industry in 1979, Ngiam Tong Dow and Albert Winsemius saw me.[23] Ngiam was the perm sec. They wanted to convince me that the earlier policy of keeping wages down would be detrimental to Singapore's development. With wages kept low, we were attracting a lot of foreign investors. Moreover, our land prices were also kept low. So, we were attracting many investments which were taking advantage of our low cost to produce. As a result, we were producing low-cost goods and the economy was expanding. But many industries were actually hoarding labour and land. They were cheap and if the businesses were going to expand, they hoarded labour and land in anticipation of growth.

So, they convinced me. We had to move out of low-skilled jobs to higher-skilled industries. At that time, as a new minister, I was quite easily convinced. You were a young minister — first time — and I knew Winsemius as an economic expert and consultant, and Ngiam was my senior before, like a Buddha. They were quite convincing. So, I put up a Cabinet paper. I think it was my first Cabinet paper. When we went to Cabinet, Mr Lee looked at me and he asked if I knew that Winsemius and Ngiam Tong Dow had been trying to convince him of this high-wage

---

[23] Winsemius was a Dutch economist and Singapore's long-time economic adviser from 1961 to 1984. He died in 1996.

policy for the last few years! My jaw dropped. They had been trying to convince him for the last three years and he was not convinced! Then he asked if I was convinced and I said yes. I put up the Cabinet paper, so I had to say yes, for the reasons given in the paper.

Then he looked at me and said, if you are convinced, then go ahead. That is a mark of a leader. Whether his mind was changed or not, this minister was in charge and if he was convinced, let him try.

Q: He never argued against you and overruled you?

A: He said he was not convinced earlier but I said I was convinced. His earlier reservation was that you had to attract investments and create jobs. You have high wages and they would not come. High wage policy is taking a risk. If they do not come, then what happens to investments? Once wages go up, they would not come down. So, be careful, you up it, it cannot come down and if investments do not come, then what happens? He could have asked me that, but he did not. That was how he worked and that was how we learnt to work. But I think he himself was beginning to be convinced by this idea after three years.

He didn't press me on it. The reasons were all given in the Cabinet paper. But Ngiam never told me that I would have to persuade the PM and that he was against the idea for the last three years. Those two never told me! Otherwise, I would at least think of ways to persuade the PM. Anyway, what a relief. If he had argued against me, I don't know how I would have defended.

Q: *Did you follow Lee Kuan Yew's example and leave your permanent secretaries to do their work? In other words, you did not operate like a super perm sec?*

A: Nor super minister. That is also my recollection of how the older ministers worked. The ministers would give ideas, ask questions and then the perm secs would implement. The perm secs would report to the ministers and the ministers asked further questions and refined the ideas. But the relationship between the minister and the perm sec has changed quite a bit over the years. Now, they are in the same group, interacting directly and frequently. And in their interactions, the ministers function as super perm secs. Today, I think some ministers would know much more than the perm secs on issues under their charge.

Q: *Were you very conscious of not wanting to micromanage the bureaucracy?*

A: Let me tell you a story. In NOL, I had an administrative manager. He was very good but he wanted to do most work by himself. I felt that he was not delegating enough. So, I told him one day, you are a very good worker and you do so much work. But do you know that if you want to get promoted, you cannot make yourself indispensable? Because nobody else could do his job! In other words, learn to delegate. If you want to get promoted, you have to train people and delegate. Train them, then you are free to do other things.

So, again, from that philosophy, in the government, if you want to do more work, you must be able to delegate. Get good men. Mr Lee Kuan Yew had the same thinking. He did not say delegate. His job was always to get a good person to do the job for you. Once you have a good minister, you leave him alone. Let him do the work. From time to time, just discuss and ask but you leave him alone. Always get the right person for the job.

And the other part he imparted to me was, between an organisation and a man, go for the man first. Do not try and shape an institution, perfect it and find a man for that. Get a good man first. The good man will shape the institution and make it a good one. I share Mr Lee's philosophy. He ran Singapore his way, but he built institutions so that when he departed, the institutions would survive.

He did not get all ministries or all civil servants to report to him, like a strongman. He did not govern Singapore in the way of a dictator, like Saddam Hussein, with all lines and decisions going to him. Otherwise, when he left, we would not be able to take over the lines. You can't do it this way. You cannot manipulate so many lines.

So, in my case, if I made myself indispensable as PM, I cannot leave the job. Mr Lee never made himself indispensable. A good leader makes himself dispensable. So, now I have time to talk to you.

Q: *Has it changed today with ministers who feel that they need to know every detail, partly because of the pressure of social media?*

A: There is no need for a minister to know everything or every detail which the perm sec must know. There is also no need to answer every social media post. I do not bother. He (his press secretary) would send me what he thought I should know, but the rest, I do not bother. I know there must be a lot of brickbats and curses. But if I'm bothered by every chap who curses me, I cannot do my job. And people who praise you — do not try and read all those compliments because they then go into your head. But you must get a sense; otherwise, you are totally ignorant. So, get a sense of the mood, and you behave in a certain way or you try to persuade in a certain way. You cannot be totally ignorant about the mood. But that is not the same as reading every post or comment on your Facebook page.

By the time MediSave was implemented in April 1984, Goh had built up eight years of work and achievements in politics and government. For an unprepared and unlikely politician, it was an impressive body of work. He had organised and led the PAP to victory in one general election and one by-election, with the Anson poll a blip, albeit a significant one. In the government, he had delivered three Budgets, and successfully pushed through important but tricky policies like the High-Wage Policy and MediSave. As *Asia Magazine* wrote in a profile of Goh in 1989: "He was sucked into public service where every job he touched, he transformed."

While his eight-year report card in 1984 was hardly unblemished, it was a glittering one which marked him out clearly as the strongest performer among the second-generation leaders. It is a status which would be officially confirmed by the end of the year. For the first time in Singapore's history, the successor to Lee would be made public to the people.

Chapter 7

Striker Takes Charge

"I shall now play goalkeeper."

Lee Kuan Yew in 1985.

I
t was December 30, 1984 and an unusual fatigue hung over Singapore despite the festive season. Merrymakers shied away from some Yuletide cheer with sales of liquor dipping as much as 30 per cent compared to a year ago. Christmas shopping had been dampened by the heavy monsoon rain, and even the expected craze for Cabbage Patch Kids dolls did not quite take off. After a bullish start to the year, the stock market had been limping for months amid the shocking news of trading firm Chop Hoo Thye's collapse. The new year did not look promising, according to most economists, a prediction echoed by Prime Minister Lee Kuan Yew two days later in his New Year's Day message.

For many in the country, there was also a heavy diet of politics to digest after the general election a week earlier. Those were the days when polls were regularly held in December, a time when most Singaporeans usually stayed at home during school holidays rather than vacationing abroad as is the case today. The results of the election were stunning, with a 12.9 per cent nationwide swing against the PAP and the loss of two wards by the ruling party. There was jubilation on the ground that the mighty PAP was humbled. But there was also concern that voters had overcooked their message to the party. Few, after all, wanted to topple the government. An exasperated PAP was still coming to terms with the numbers. As Sidek Saniff, an MP for Kolam Ayer, had told the media on the night of the election: "I don't know why. I really don't know why. I had even intensified my door-to-door visits." He had seen his vote share plunge from 80 per cent to 57.9 per cent in four years. *The Straits Times* summed it aptly with a headline which said: "Night the winners felt like losers."

Yet, in the midst of such confusion and lethargy in the country and the party, Lee decided a post-mortem of the election could wait. He had a more pressing task. For four years now, he had made known publicly that he would not choose his own successor. He had seen how Winston Churchill failed with his, and later Deng Xiaoping too. Instead, Lee wanted the second-generation leaders to select from among themselves, reasoning that they would then be more likely to support the new leader. Now that the election was over, he wanted a decision, although he had yet to set a date for his own retirement. He hurried Goh Chok Tong to gather the rest. "Mr Lee Kuan Yew was getting impatient," said Goh. "He was chasing us on whether we had come to a decision yet. I was one of the people who could be chosen — how could I go and convene the meeting? So, I pushed it off. I did not convene any meeting to decide who would be the leader."

The job fell to Tony Tan, who felt the urgency, despite chatter within the party that the succession could be delayed in light of the poor election result and weak economy. "It was a period of confusion, with some feeling that we should delay the transition and some people thought we should not," said Tan. "I felt, at the time, we should not delay the transition, despite everything."

On the night of December 30, Tan invited 11 of his fellow young Cabinet ministers to his house in Bukit Timah. The group included himself, Goh Chok Tong, Ong Teng Cheong, S. Dhanabalan, Ahmad Mattar, S. Jayakumar and Yeo Ning Hong — the new Magnificent Seven after Lim Chee Onn and Bernard Chen dropped out. Ministers of State Lee Yock Suan, Tay Eng Soon, Wan Soon Bee and Ch'ng Jit Koon joined the seven, with rookie Lee Hsien Loong, who had just entered politics, the final member of the dozen.

But there was a slight glitch. Goh had a community event at Marine Parade and could only get to Tan's place later. The rest did not wait for him. Dhanabalan remembered that Tan, as the host, chaired the meeting and guided the discussion. Critically, Tan "made it clear that he was not seeking nor did he want to be the next PM," said Dhanabalan. "His reasons were not discussed." After that, over coffee, orange juice and chocolate cake, the group asked who should be the next Deputy Prime Minister, replacing outgoing DPMs Goh Keng Swee and S. Rajaratnam. It was not an explicit choice of the next PM, although the implications were clear to all those involved. "The way the discussion was framed was who should be DPM?" said Lee Hsien Loong. "Should we have DPMs and who should be DPM?"

The decision did not take long, said Tan. "It was quite clear to us that all of us supported Mr Goh Chok Tong to be the next Prime Minister," he said. For Lee, who was new to the scene, it was clear that the frontrunners had already settled on their choice. "Four of them: Tony, Dhana, Teng Cheong, Chok Tong — they had worked together for some time and have worked it out among themselves," he recalled. "And they were happy to support Chok Tong. I had worked with Chok Tong and I was quite happy to support him too. There was no hot contest." Jayakumar, who would be the first to make public the meeting in 1987, said in *Petir*, the PAP's party organ: "A candid discussion took place and we had no problem arriving at a unanimous decision that Chok Tong should be the 1DPM, Ong Teng Cheong 2DPM." Goh Chok Tong, barring any changes later, would be the successor to Lee.

When Goh arrived at Tan's house at about 9.30pm, he was offered a slice of cake. Goh asked: "So okay, what have you decided?" Tan replied with a smile: "You." Goh would joke later, in an interview for this book, that the moral of the story was not to be late for a meeting. "You might end up doing a job that nobody wants to do!" he said. But on that night in 1984, he graciously accepted the group's decision, recalled Jayakumar. "He said he realised the heavy responsibility but was prepared with our support to take on the task and give of his best, according to his own style," said Jayakumar in his *Petir* article. Dhanabalan recalled that "the clear impression" was that Goh was prepared to do the job. "He did not say 'No, I do not want to be'; nor did he give the impression that he was very keen to be the leader," he added.

The outcome was not a surprise to Goh, he admitted. He was already tasked by Lee to draft a new Cabinet line-up after the election and was, in his words, "more or less the one doing a lot of things," including leading the 1984 election campaign. He had also taken charge of "the most hardline and top-down of economic and security portfolios: finance, trade and industry, defence," as observer Cherian George noted in *Singapore: The Air-Conditioned Nation*. Dhanabalan gave three more reasons why they chose him: education, background and cohort. "There was an implicit agreement that… you needed someone who was able to provide leadership in a society that was changing and becoming more English-educated, more exposed to Western concepts, and someone who was seen to be able to tackle economic problems more effectively," he said. "Chok Tong's background was in economics. All of us implicitly saw him as being more of an economic man than anybody else," he said.

And since Goh was among the earlier ones to enter politics compared to the rest, he had an advantage too. "There was an understanding that the ones who came in earlier should be one of the leaders. So, Chok Tong was an obvious choice." More than that, the team trusted Goh, said Dhanabalan. "We focused on who the team had confidence in to make the right decisions, when the right decisions were needed. And there was clear confidence that when it came to policy matters, he would be able to make the right decisions," he said.

Once the decision was made, the New Guard — a moniker which became associated with the second-generation leaders — did not hesitate to share it with Singaporeans. The next day, on New Year's Eve, Goh chaired a press conference at the Istana, flanked by his peers, to announce the new Cabinet. "My colleagues have decided that I should play centre forward," said Goh to the media, taking on the position of First Deputy Prime Minister. "They have asked me to play the role of striker in the new team. It is a heavy responsibility. I accepted the role which they have asked me to play. I shall discharge that role to the best of my ability and with total effort and total dedication." On the role of Lee, who remained as the Prime Minister, Goh continued with the football analogy. "My colleagues and I will play a prominent role. The Prime Minister will take a back-seat, but he will not play the role of the back-seat driver. He will play the role of goalkeeper."

Goh's elevation received instant and spontaneous applause from the PAP MPs when they heard the news at the Istana, a sign of his steady popularity on the ground after years as the organising secretary. They responded with more football references, as analogies ran amok. Tan Soo Khoon, for example, said: "The striker also has got good wings. And we also have a good goalkeeper who won't let in the shots. I think the goalkeeper could also play the role of a sweeper across the field but I doubt such a situation will arise as the team as a whole has good players." But perhaps sensing that the analogies could confound Singaporeans, Ong gave a clear indication of the significance of the new Cabinet line-up. It is "logical to conclude from this that barring any unforeseen circumstances, he (Goh) will be Prime Minister in time to come." For the first time in a quarter of a century, Singapore and the rest of the world could put a definitive face to the second Prime Minister of the country.

But Goh refused to be caught up by the hubris of the moment.

Looking back, he said he never believed, at that point, that he would be the next PM. At most, he conceded that he was a potential PM, but nothing more. The presumptive candidate refused to presume. "I am a realist. I did not go around saying that I would be the next PM," he said. His job, he believed, was to be the leader of the New Guard. "That was 1984. Lee Kuan Yew still had a long runway. You never knew whether he was going to step away in 1988 or 1990. You cannot presume."

There was also the issue of Lee Hsien Loong, whose entry into politics in 1984 led some to speculate that he could succeed his father. Goh acknowledged candidly that it was a thought which entered his mind too. "Lee Kuan Yew was a very Machiavellian leader. After a while, it was possible that Lee Hsien Loong would take over. How would you know?" he asked rhetorically. "Lee Kuan Yew might say that 'Hey, my son is accepted by all the MPs as the one who can lead Singapore, and not Tony Tan or Goh Chok Tong'. You never know." These considerations led Goh to not get ahead of himself and behaved as if he was the new sovereign in town. He was well aware that an overreach by him would have led to his head being chopped. "If I had really thought at that point I was the next PM and started walking ahead of Lee Kuan Yew, behaving like I was the boss, he would have asked me to get out!" he laughed, thrusting his thumb outwards to emphasise his point.

But that was not to say that Goh did not take his new role as *de facto* leader seriously, with a clear delineation of his authority in relation to Lee. In the Istana press conference in 1984, he made it plain that the PM would provide ideas going forward while the new team would make the decisions. "The style of government and the substance of policies will be ours," he said. Unless the issues involved national security and survival of the country, he did not expect Lee to overrule the younger ministers. "We will run this place and we must be left alone to run the country," he said emphatically. Critically, that would involve overturning some of Lee's signature edgy policies which had led to the groundswell of unhappiness during the 1984 election.

The most controversial was the infamous Great Marriage Debate, possibly the most disturbing social engineering project in independent Singapore. In the first half of 1984, Lee introduced schemes which gave better educated women more benefits, and cash grants to the less educated women who agreed to sterilisation. This came after he noticed that graduate women were not marrying or not producing as many children as those who were less educated. The most eye-catching of the package was the Graduate Mothers Scheme, which gave graduate mothers tax breaks and priority admission to schools. The uproar from Singaporeans, including the graduate women, was immediate and fierce. One letter writer to *The Straits Times* memorably likened the PAP to "the storm troopers of Nazi Germany," a reference to the eugenics experiment.

Lee strongly believed that human intelligence is innate and inheritable. In short, smarter people create smarter kids. The policies were vigorously debated in the Cabinet before implementation, with several younger ministers voicing their disagreements. But Goh was on Lee's side. And more than 30 years later, Goh maintained that he agreed with Lee, despite the obvious political incorrectness. "I instinctively supported it," he said, in a rare revelation of his thoughts on this startling social engineering push. "I was more or less on his side. There were others who were not. There were others who were on his side but would not talk too much."

Goh's argument was that nature does play a part in the development of a person. Based on his own observation of people, including those in his extended family, he came to the conclusion that it would be unrealistic to completely dismiss the role which genes play. "I have family members who were better educated — not even graduates — than those who were not. And those who were better educated — their children did better," he said.

The crux then was in the proportion between nature and nurture. Some in the Cabinet said 30 per cent nature, others committed to 50 per cent, said Goh. Lee would produce statistics which gave nature a 70 per cent weightage. But Goh was more ambivalent. He said: "Do you believe Mr Lee was right? Nobody believed that he was 100 per cent right, in terms of the percentage. I mean, we did not quite know. He would produce statistics like 70-30, but none of us would actually believe in all those. But we must believe that nature plays a part. Mr Lee used to say, how is it that when it comes to muscles and other physical attributes, you all believed in nature? But when it comes to the brain, nobody believed in him!"

Goh gave the example of a bodybuilder. The result is because of nurture, chiselling a body for years through exercises and diet. But without the right body type to begin with, the bodybuilder would not have a beautiful shape. "If you ask me, I do not know what percentage," he shared. "I do not bother about all that. I said I assume 50-50. Maximise here, maximise there — why not?" Some in the Cabinet argued, said Goh, to pour resources into nurturing people, rather than to promote selective breeding. Lee agreed, but added that the government should do both. "He said to maximise the nurture — the environment and the education system — but could you say that nature does not play a part?" recalled Goh. "Of course, you could not. So, why not maximise nature as well — graduate and graduate — you maximise that. Intuitively, and just based on observations and logic, I supported and agreed with it that nature plays a part."

Then came the tricky bit on how to have policies which maximise nature and sell it to Singaporeans. Lee wanted to push through the schemes before the election, knowing that he would leave the front seat after the polls. "He told us very frankly that he wanted to clear the deck because these were very important matters, you people would not be able to do it," said Goh. "He was the one who was prepared to go and sell the policy. We could not sell it because we were not as well read as him. He had read and gone in-depth and he could defend himself logically. And, politically, he had the stature and capital to do it."

The robust and negative reactions from Singaporeans led directly to the 12.9 per cent swing against the PAP in the 1984 election. Along with other measures introduced by Lee, such as a proposal to push back the age to withdraw CPF savings from 55 to 60 and eventually 65, the ruling party paid the price in the ballot boxes. In its own post-mortem, headed by Goh, the party admitted it had "tempted fate." "Had it not been for the tremendous depth of support which PAP enjoyed, we would have been voted out of office," said the internal report.

It was clear to Goh, once he was made the heir apparent on December 31, 1984, that the Graduate Mothers Scheme had to go. Even though he was in favour of it, he knew the political costs were too high and a refusal to change course could be fatal to the PAP, especially when the New Guard lacked the political stature and goodwill which Lee and the Old Guard had enjoyed. "It was not sustainable," he said. "By then, even those of us who were in favour of it knew the political costs. It may cost us to lose the election. That was the time when we began to modify. We were all pragmatists on what was doable and what was not." More than that, he believed that policies ought to signal a compassionate meritocracy, where the more well-endowed helps the less fortunate. Tony Tan, as the new Education Minister, was put in charge to dismantle the scheme.

Lee did not resist the rollback by the Cabinet, said Goh. "He was also a practical man. The young ministers did not want to carry through and he left it up to us, that was his style," he said. "He believed in it and that if he were in charge, he would do it. But he was no more in charge. We had to decide if we were to carry on with the policy, could we defend it? It would not be easy. We were not Lee Kuan Yew who could be so forceful. So, we had to shift." The striker has taken charge.

Q: *After the defeat in the Anson by-election, was there an attempt by the PAP to look for a different type of candidate before the 1984 general election to appeal to a changing electorate?*

A: The party was always looking for a diverse slate of candidates. It was whether we could get them or not. It was not that we preferred civil servants or military officers. We were always looking for candidates who might be suitable. We were also focusing very much on those in the private sector. At that time, Mr Lee would ask all the MPs to nominate somebody, but I was the principal scout. So, I read the newspapers and I saw a promotion somewhere and thought that this chap could be a person of interest, and then I would just invite the person for tea. And I would talk to various people and widen the network. Anybody in F&N? SPH?[24] And if we approached somebody and he said he was not interested, then we would ask who he thought would be interested. And we'd chase up.

Q: *How difficult was it to attract candidates then?*

A: Getting MPs was not difficult. The pay was quite reasonable and it was part-time, so it was not difficult. It was getting potential ministers that was difficult because you were looking at a different level. There was uncertainty that they would succeed when they came in. It was a different kind of job. So, you had to look for a person with the conviction and interest and it was

---

[24] F&N refers to Fraser and Neave Limited, a former Singapore-owned food and beverage conglomerate. SPH refers to Singapore Press Holdings Limited, a media organisation with strong ties to the government.

difficult. We were more likely to succeed if we discovered a former civil servant — Dhanabalan and myself. We were former civil servants who went out to the private sector and we did well. Coming back, we knew the system and we were not very motivated by the money outside. We were not chasing the last dollar outside. We were prepared to come in. But those who had been purely in the private sector — that would be very difficult.

Q: *Leading up to the 1984 election, the major talking point was Lee Hsien Loong as a new candidate. Were you prepared for the public interest in him?*

A: Of course. Surely. He is the son of Lee Kuan Yew. Surely people must speculate. The difficulty was for him to convince the public that he was not there because of Lee Kuan Yew. First, he must convince Lee Kuan Yew's colleagues that he was not put in there by Lee Kuan Yew. Second, the ministers must be convinced that Lee Kuan Yew was not building a dynasty.

Lee Hsien Loong — and I have said it before on many occasions — came in because I spotted him. He was a colonel in the general staff office. He was a young man and I was the Defence Minister. At our Monday meetings, he had to make presentations. He was very articulate. I was very impressed by his articulateness, his logical thinking. So, I said, yes, he has the potential. I asked him if he was keen to be involved in politics some time in the future. He said he was. After discussing with his wife, Ming Yang, he confirmed his availability. So I sent him to help computerise NTUC so that he could get some exposure and contacts with the unions. But then, unfortunately, his wife died unexpectedly and we put it aside.[25]

As the next GE approached, I surfaced the idea to Lee Kuan Yew that Hsien Loong would be a good candidate. Mr Lee said, no. He had just lost his wife, he had two young children and one of them is autistic, and was looking around to re-establish a family. No, he would not be interested.

I told Lee Kuan Yew that if Hsien Loong had an interest in politics, 1984 would be the time he should come in. And the reason I offered was that the 1984 cohort would be the biggest, about 24 candidates. And in politics, cohort counts. If he joined this cohort and he became the leader, he would have so many people supporting him the next time. So, he said for me to try and convince Hsien Loong. I spoke to Hsien Loong. He said, no, his family is this and so on and he had no time. I asked him if he was still interested in politics and he said, yes, he was.

I said that if he was interested and instead of postponing to 1988 or later on, then come in now. I gave him the same reason I gave to Lee Kuan Yew. He thought it over and he came back and said he would come in. So, I knew for a fact that I brought in Hsien Loong. It was not the father who told me that his son was in the army and a very bright man. So, you have to under-

---

[25] Lee Hsien Loong's first wife, Wong Ming Yang, passed away in 1982 from a heart attack.

stand the way we work. Lee Kuan Yew never suggested Hsien Loong to me. I brought him in.

Q: *How did you convince the other ministers that he was a good choice?*

A: Once Hsien Loong agreed, Lee Kuan Yew knew that there would be unhappiness among the ministers. And true enough, Toh Chin Chye, Ong Pang Boon were very unhappy because they thought he was trying to establish a dynasty. They were not against Hsien Loong because they knew he was a bright boy, but a dynasty for Singapore would be very bad for the country and the PAP. And they spoke their minds.

So, how would Lee Kuan Yew persuade them? He wrote a letter to Hsien Loong's mathematics professor and this professor sent him a letter which he had written about the potential of the son. So, at the right stage, Lee Kuan Yew would say that he was not pushing for his son, but this is what his professor said of him. So, he asked for the contents of the letter to be read aloud after a Cabinet meeting. It revealed that Hsien Loong gave up an offer to pursue an academic career in Cambridge because he felt that the country needed him. Lee Kuan Yew was a persuader. He was using others' opinions on his son. What you say about the dynasty is another matter. But this son was very highly regarded and had potential. So, it was established that his son was not a dud, but a suitable person. Everybody knew that Hsien Loong was real.

Next — how did you get Hsien Loong in? He went through the process — tea sessions. Now look at this file on Hsien Loong's candidacy. This is to show you that the way we work is not at Lee Kuan Yew's whim and fancy. It is very systematic. Look, Lee Hsien Loong had to submit his CV. Chinese — C4, so he was not straight As! There were people who were better than him, all A1s, but when I interviewed them, they were not very good. He had to give all his results. He was an army officer and the pay was quite high — $7,672. He was a colonel. He put down as his referees Edwin Thumboo and Lim Siong Guan.[26] And he had to write his personal history.

Lee Kuan Yew did not write to the referees. He instructed Rajaratnam to do so. He did not write even though he was the secretary-general of PAP. Had he written, people would say surely, the referees must give a very good report, isn't it? Thumboo said that they were not surprised that one day Lee Hsien Loong would be an MP.

Then there were two interview panels. The first panel was chaired by Lim Kim San. Other members included Ong Pang Boon, Chua Sian Chin, Ong Teng Cheong and myself. Jayakumar and Yeo Ning Hong were in attendance. The assessment was that he was confident and thoughtful and knew what he wanted — this is quite true. The interview took 1 hour 15 minutes. For

---

[26] Edwin Thumboo is an academic and poet, widely regarded as the unofficial poet laureate of Singapore. Lim Siong Guan was a senior civil servant who rose to become the head of the Singapore civil service. He was also a Permanent Secretary of the Ministry of Defence.

the second interview, which took just as long, the panel comprised Rajaratnam as chairman, Teh Cheang Wan, Tony Tan and myself. Yeo Ning Hong took notes. The committee said that he would be an asset, had thought through the invitation and knew what he was in for. So, the panels were not made up entirely of people favourable to Hsien Loong. Ong Pang Boon would be against and Teng Cheong might see Hsien Loong as a threat to him because, at that time, we had not quite decided yet on the second-generation leadership line-up.

Lee Kuan Yew had no say. He did not write to the referees; he did not sit in for the meetings. And it was chaired by somebody else. Lim Kim San chaired the first interview and Rajaratnam the second.

Q: *Let me play the devil's advocate. Maybe Lee Kuan Yew expected you to suggest Lee Hsien Loong because he is of that particular age and he is very bright and almost like an obvious candidate. And, true enough, you did. If he didn't, maybe something would have happened?*

A: Correct. But not that something would have happened. He told Rajaratnam later he was surprised I was not afraid of competition. He looked at it that way — that Goh Chok Tong suggested we look at Lee Hsien Loong. It showed that I was not afraid of competition. This was before the 1984 election. Hsien Loong came in in 1984 as a young man. When would Lee Kuan Yew step down? We did not know yet in 1984. So, if Lee Hsien Loong came in, he could do very well in a matter of two to three years and Lee Kuan Yew might have said, let it be an open competition between him and others.

Instead, Lee Kuan Yew saw it the other way around. If I did not suggest Hsien Loong, then he could have said, 'My god, this fellow is afraid of competition. It was right in front of his eyes — this bright young man — and he did not spot him!'. Or I could have been clever, anticipated all these, and told Lee Kuan Yew that I had approached Hsien Loong and he said his family situation was such and he was not interested. I could have left it as such. Then I delay it by four or five years, you see. And I could play the game and not bring him in in 1984, but wait till he was more ready in 1988 or even later. Then my position as successor would be stronger. But I was in politics for the country and not for myself.

Q: *Lee Kuan Yew said much later that Lee Hsien Loong could not succeed him directly and he used the analogy of the gears. He said the two gears would not engage properly. So, you are like the...*
A: Seat warmer.

Q: *He did not say seat warmer.*
A: Of course, he would not say so. It was the public who put it that way.

Q: He meant that he and his son could not engage correctly, they would clash.

A: He was correct. I think that is a nice way of putting it because Hsien Loong does have very strong views on certain things and the father also had certain views of certain things. And on some of these views — they clashed. I had seen in Cabinet, Lee Hsien Loong putting up a different view from the father. The father wanted one way and Hsien Loong said, no, and they would clash. Hsien Loong is not a yes-man on things he believed in. So, what would I be in the analogy — a lubricant? (laughs).

Q: So given all the rumours and allegations of a dynasty, why did you think it was still worth it to bring Lee Hsien Loong into politics?

A: The cost may be the rumours, but we do not worry about these things too much. We would go for the essentials. What is the interest and the truth? I can say all these quite sincerely and honestly because we know what happened in the selection process. What thoughts Lee Kuan Yew had — I did not know. But I know for a fact that he never told me that there was a bright young man in the armed forces; why don't you ask him? I got him in. Lee Kuan Yew also never asked what about Hsien Yang. No.[27] But one day, later on, he suggested his daughter. He said Wei Ling would make a very good MP.[28]

---

[27] Lee Hsien Yang is the younger son of Lee Kuan Yew. He was a brigadier-general in the Singapore Armed Forces before taking charge of Singtel, the state-linked telco firm.

[28] Lee Wei Ling, a medical doctor, is the only daughter of Lee Kuan Yew. She was the director of the National Neuroscience Institute.

Q: He did not suggest Lee Hsien Loong and yet he suggested Lee Wei Ling?

A: Wei Ling as an MP. MP is okay. And it was because of her social conscience, which was very strong. At that time, we did not have so many women candidates. We were looking for women candidates and it was difficult to find them. So, he was helping me. It was not because he wanted her, but he was helping me to look for candidates. It was in that context — here was a good candidate.

Q: When was this?

A: I cannot remember now, but probably when I was still DPM. I was looking for candidates. The reason LKY suggested her was that Wei Ling had very strong compassion for the down and out. She had a very strong sense of justice. Anything which did not seem just to her — she would push. So, he suggested. What did I do? Quietly, I sounded out George Yeo. He was chairman of Young PAP and he was politically significant. He said no. Then I sounded out Hsien Loong. Hsien Loong also said no. And that was enough. Then I kept quiet after that.

Q: So what did you say to Lee Kuan Yew?

A: I never replied to him. I just went mmm, mmm. Seriously. I had checked with George Yeo and Hsien Loong — both said no. Then I kept quiet, and Lee Kuan Yew also kept quiet. He had given me his daughter's name and if I did not want to pursue, why should he pursue? That was how we behaved. Had he pursued again, I was ready to tell him I had discussed with two politically significant persons and both were against the idea, and therefore, I was not pursuing. I had done my checks. It was not that I shunted her out, but I had checked with two people. So, again, I respected Lee Kuan Yew — he never came back on Wei Ling.

Q: But with Lee Hsien Yang — it never came up?

A: He never mentioned Hsien Yang. I thought of Hsien Yang, but I did not recommend him because I think he would be outshone by his brother. Having two brothers in Parliament was okay — Bernard Chen and Kenneth Chen, at one time.[29] But in Cabinet, how could I succeed as a PM if the father was there, the elder son and the second son too? Nobody would believe I am my own man, isn't it? With three — what chance would you have? I mean, that was how people would think, not knowing we are different individuals.

Hsien Yang, had he come in, he would be different from the brother. These are not yes-men. You see the situation now, he is fighting the brother.[30] He would be a different individual with different qualities. His value would be — had I been interested,

---

[29] Bernard Chen was one of the original Magnificent Seven and he served as an MP from 1977 to 2001. His brother Kenneth Chen served from 1991 to 2001.

[30] This interview was conducted in November 2017, four months after the first public airing of the dispute between Lee Hsien Loong and his siblings on the future of the family home in Oxley Road.

and that was later on — experience in the private sector. Hsien Loong did not have it.

So, it came back to the basics, because Lee Kuan Yew was a very honourable person. You think he would cause us to do things, but no. He would treat you as an equal and then respect your opinion and so on. It was not that he said, you do this, you do that. If that was the case, he would not have gotten Tony Tan, myself and Dhanabalan to work for him.

Q: Why do you think it is difficult for a lot of Singaporeans, as well as a lot of people around the world, to accept that you chose Lee Hsien Loong and the father did not?

A: Given Lee Kuan Yew's dominant personality, people would find it hard to believe. But he was an honourable man. That was why we were all prepared to work for him. He had his views and he would try to influence you. But on certain things and certain principles, he respected our decisions.

Let me give you an example which has stuck in my mind all these years. Soon after he stepped down as PM, I got a note from the secretary to the Prime Minister's Office. Mrs Lee had reported that their tailor had given them 10 of Mr Lee's favourite jackets — five for the father, five for the son. And they refused to accept it for free. The tailor said that for what he had done for the country, that was a small thing and he made the jackets just for them. He refused to accept any payment. Mrs Lee then declared the gift to the secretary and asked how much to pay.

Of course, the secretary reported to me and I asked if they had been doing this for a long time. Had they been paying the tailor in the past? The answer was yes.

So, I said okay, I approve. There was no need to ask for payment. Treat it as a gift from a friend. But the key is that Mrs Lee reported in the first place. She could have kept quiet, isn't it? This is what I know of Lee Kuan Yew and Mrs Lee — in my dealings with them, they were very correct.

When he suggested Lee Wei Ling, it was not because he wanted to push the daughter in. It was because we were looking for women candidates. He was trying to be helpful. And Hsien Loong could have said that it was a good idea as he would now have another Lee in Parliament. But he just said no. He did not think she was suitable and he was absolutely right. I was not in favour but I never said anything. I just checked quietly first.

Q: Speaking of women candidates and the Lee family, did you speak to Ho Ching at any point about joining politics?[31]

A: I knew you would ask! I did approach Ho Ching and ask her if she would be interested in politics. It was quite early on. She was about 28, 29 or 30, before she married Hsien Loong. I spotted her in Mindef and thought that she had the intellect and attributes we were looking for. I knew she was a President's

---

[31] Ho Ching is the wife of Prime Minister Lee Hsien Loong and was in the Defence Science Organisation in the early part of her career. She is the chief executive officer of Temasek Holdings, a Singapore investment firm.

Scholar, but I didn't know her well — only superficially because she was in the science part of Mindef. Through briefings and so on, I could see that she had a lot of substance. She would have made a good minister, a different kind of minister.

She did not say no. She said not at this stage. She was still young. After that, I was overtaken by events! She and Hsien Loong got married. As she was part of the Lee family, I never approached her again. I would not have asked her to be a politician. Hsien Loong would be against it. She would be against it. And Singapore would be against it.

Goh outlined on December 31, 1984, two main aims of the New Guard Cabinet: first, to understand why the PAP performed so poorly in the election; second, to realise the vision of the younger leaders for a more developed, higher income Singapore with a better quality of life. *The Straits Times* called it the "My two goals — by the striker." When he and the new Cabinet were sworn in two days later, PM Lee Kuan Yew, a leader well known for his lukewarm enthusiasm for sports, wrapped up his speech by using football language.

He categorised his political career into three stages of football positions. From 1959 to 1980, he was the striker. From 1981 to 1984, he fell back to midfield, he said, allowing the younger leaders to be tested out as potential strikers. From 1984, "I shall now play goalkeeper," he said in the Istana. The new striker already had ideas of how he wanted to score his two goals. In just two weeks after he was sworn in as First Deputy Prime Minister, moving at a speed which surprised even his closest confidants, Goh would begin to implement a vision of a more inclusive democracy. As he said on December 31, 1984: "Personally, I would like to encourage greater participation of Singaporeans in shaping the destiny of Singapore."

Chapter 8

From Nanny to Buddy

"Goh Chok Tong was not seen to be this hardline person.
He came across as somebody who listened."

Academic-turned-diplomat Chan Heng Chee, in an interview for this book.

A month after Goh Chok Tong became First Deputy Prime Minister of Singapore in January 1985, he had lunch with Prime Minister Lee Kuan Yew at the Istana on February 16. The new striker told the goalkeeper that he had a goal in mind: to create a body which would try to find out what Singaporeans were thinking, their concerns in life and reactions to government policies. Even before the PAP produced its post-mortem report of the 1984 general election, Goh instinctively knew what were the causes behind the party's poor performance. "At that time, the government was seen as not listening enough, shoving things down people's throats — it was quite a common perception," he said. The raw form of his idea was the old Public Complaints Bureau, which was disbanded in 1979 because of dipping popularity. Lee gave his blessings and Goh took off with lightning speed.

Within days, he was sounding out Cabinet colleagues, with Community Development Minister S. Dhanabalan quickly drafting a proposal to flesh out the idea. When the discussion reached the Cabinet, one of the issues discussed was what to call the new body. Goh recalled: "Senior Minister S. Rajaratnam asked us what we intended the unit to be. I said to gather feedback. So, he suggested, why not call it Feedback Unit? I said it was a good idea."[32]

On April 15, 1985, the Feedback Unit was launched, with vocal backbencher Tan Cheng Bock as its chairman.[33] The country's first institutional state feedback mechanism took only two months from genesis to birth, an efficiency which was unheard of even in the famously fast-moving city. Goh was in a hurry not only to make his mark, but also to reorientate the ethos of the government. Asked why the Feedback Unit was created at such a breathtaking pace, his reply reflected the urgency he felt at that moment: "It had to be done." Clearly, he knew the ground had shifted and the government needed to move accordingly and seen to be such. By forming the Feedback Unit, he was signaling to the people that he was ready to move from a top-down "nanny state" approach to a more "bottom up" style. The nanny would morph into a buddy.

There wasn't a grand theory underpinning Goh's thinking. He said quite plainly he was "not a great reader" of philosophical works. He was not an ideological leader. In fact, it was quite the opposite. His thinking was based on a straightforward diagnosis of the ailments and its most direct, simple and effective cure. Call it Goh-style pragmatism.

---

[32] I am grateful to Dr Shashi Jayakumar for allowing me to read the section of his forthcoming book on the history of the PAP that sheds light on the formation of the Feedback Unit.

[33] The unit was renamed REACH — Reaching Everyone for Active Citizenry @ Home — in 2006.

The era of top-down governance was over, he reckoned, and the time had arrived for a sustainable and genuine bottom-up drive. "The government must make the decision and initiate, but you must have a bottom-up flow to have a participatory democracy," he said. In such a new eco-system, there would be more than one point of reference, as power became decentralised. It would be messier, but to Goh, it was necessary.

He was prepared for this even in the realm of the military, where he introduced the concept of Total Defence as Defence Minister in 1984. It sought to involve every Singaporean in protecting the country. "A united community that feels and throbs as one, has no cracks for others to exploit," he said in a speech in 1984. "You therefore have a role to play — you, your wife or husband, and your children. Any potential aggressor must not just fight against our bullets, but also our whole people. Our defence must be total."

The motivation for such a change in his style of governance came from four sources. First, his assessment of the ground that Singaporeans wanted a greater say. Second, the vision he wanted to realise in the country, tapping on an emerging zeitgeist. "It was not an inspiration," he said. "It was a sense that this was the way society was moving and you liked the way it was moving and you encouraged it." Third, his own experience in business and politics, where he saw the merits of an extensive consultation process such as the MediSave and the efficiency of decentralisation during his days in the private sector. Last, it was more in sync with his personal leadership style, one characterised by openness and accessibility, said Lee Hsien Loong. "He listens. He takes advice and he is able to get good people to work for him," he said. "And he sees the point clearly. So, when you persuade him, he understands and he embraces your point of view."

Lee Kuan Yew was not fond of some of these makeover moves, admitted Goh. "He might not agree with many of the things I did, such as a consultative government," he said. "He said before 'Why consult? I just decide'. To Lee Kuan Yew, if you consult, it takes too long." But Lee lived up to his word to take a backseat, even though he was still the Prime Minister. He respected the new man in *de facto* charge, said Goh, and the pair enjoyed a chemistry in the early adjustment of their master-disciple relationship. "He recognised that I was in charge and that was the wisdom of the man," he said. "He would not be in charge forever. If he wanted things to be the way he wanted until his dying days, then what would happen after that? When the leader departs or passes away, then it would all be reversed. Just look at Donald Trump. Whatever Barack Obama had done, Trump is trying to reverse it. So, Lee Kuan Yew was a wise man — change gears and let the new person and new generation move forward the way they want to. Whether he thought it was fast enough or bold enough, he would just give his views but he would not interfere. He did not always agree, but he never stopped us."

And off Goh went. After the Feedback Unit, he introduced a spate of major policies in the late 1980s, giving a sneak preview of the participatory democracy which his premiership would later be known for. In particular, three new ideas would overcome initial controversies and resistance to become entrenched as accepted norms in Singapore's political system. The first is the town councils. For some years, Goh had felt that having the HDB as both the developer and estate manager of all public flats was an unsustainable arrangement. As the number of Singaporeans in HDB flats grew to above 2 million by the 1980s, there was too much for HDB to handle. Centralised control was slowing initiatives on the ground. "On the ground, as an MP, when I wanted something done, HDB would say it is a good idea," he looked back. "But if you change this year, it must be applied to all the HDB flats in Singapore. Therefore, please wait until we are ready."

The snail's pace frustrated him. "While the HDB has discharged its responsibilities admirably, it has done this at a price. This price is uniformity and a rather inflexible set of rules," he said in Parliament in 1988. "A central agency must be strict and must be uniform in its decisions. It cannot exercise flexibility nor make quick decisions at the constituency level. If it is generous to one constituency, other constituencies will immediately demand equal treatment."

He wanted to replicate what he did in health with housing. Just as he decentralised public hospitals to improve efficiency and service standards, he had a similar plan with public housing. Instead of HDB running estates, it would be devolved to each town to manage its own homes day-to-day. In this way, he hoped that people would be less dependent on the government. In 1988, he said: "The more HDB decides for the people, the less the people know how to do things for themselves. This is not conducive to developing self-reliant communities and community leaders. It certainly does not foster the development of a vibrant and creative people."

The idea evolved gradually, from a concept paper in 1984 to a pilot in central Ang Mo Kio town two years later. By 1988, it was implemented nationwide, with each town council having three MPs, one of them acting as the chairman. Goh did not shy away from saying the policy had a strong dose of politics in it. After the 1984 election, he was keen to put in what he called "stabilisers" in Singapore politics. It was to address a peculiar electoral behaviour which was emerging in the country then. While the voters wanted the PAP as the government, they also wanted to vote in some opposition to check the ruling party. Such a scenario might lead to a freak election when the PAP was voted out when in fact few intended for it to happen.

The town council was one such stabiliser. By giving more power to MPs, Goh hoped that voters would be less cavalier with their ballot slips. But he insisted that the policy was never meant to disadvantage the opposition. He said in 1988: "Town councils will make it harder for weaker candidates to win, whichever political party they come from. It will not prevent the stronger ones from winning. They will, in fact, help opposition parties if they are able to assemble strong candidates." He likened it to flying a plane. "If (a new party in Singapore) finds itself unexpectedly in government, it would be like an aspiring pilot taking over the controls of an SIA jumbo in mid-air, before he has flown solo in a Cessna," he said. "This cannot be in the interest of passengers in the jumbo. If any party aspires to displace the PAP government, its first step must be to try and acquire some experience in a town council. Town councils are the Cessnas of our political system. In the interest of Singapore, any party which wants to form the government should prove it can run town councils first."

Looking back, with the benefit of 30 years of hindsight, Goh believed his argument still stands. "Does it favour the PAP or the opposition? My thinking then was that it was neutral," he said. "It was probably in favour of the PAP at that time, on the basis that we could do a better job than them... But once they won over Potong Pasir and Hougang, and showed they could run it, then it becomes double-edged." Time has proven him right. The Singapore Democratic Party built on its management of Potong Pasir to win two more seats in the 1991 general election. Similarly, the Workers' Party used its sound work at the Hougang town council to land a breakthrough win at neighbouring Aljunied GRC in 2011.[34] "They said, 'Look, I can run a town council very well. Next election, let me have another one'. So, it is not static. The balance is dynamic. In the first part, we had the advantage. But over time, the advantage is lost and they can build on their track record."

Goh was intent on the devolution of powers and the decentralisation of authority. In the second of his signature policies in the 1980s, he would introduce the Government Parliamentary Committees, or GPC, to enhance the powers of the backbench. MPs would be grouped into policy domains which largely mirror the ministries. Their jobs were to scrutinise the policies in their committees and question the frontbench. To help them, they would get regular briefings from civil servants. The

---

[34] Opposition politician Chiam See Tong won the Potong Pasir ward, in south-eastern Singapore, in 1984 and held it until 2011. The former chief of the Singapore Democratic Party and current Singapore People's Party secretary-general was the longest serving opposition politician in Singapore until he was overtaken by Low Thia Khiang of Workers' Party. Low won the Hougang seat in north-eastern Singapore in 1991 and took the Aljunied GRC in the same region in 2011. He is still in Parliament.

GPCs also have resource panels, made up of experts who advise the MPs voluntarily. Goh's aim was to give MPs in the PAP more teeth in parliamentary debates.

For decades since the PAP came to power, Singapore's political culture had been shaded by an ultra-dominant government and an especially powerful Cabinet. "Is this the best formula for the future?" he asked in 1987 when speaking on the thinking behind the GPC. He did not want to diminish the Cabinet's power. But he saw no contradiction in increasing the effectiveness of the MPs, offering them more say in the making of policies. "I believe in a strong government and a decisive Cabinet," he said. "The government must remain politically dominant but I believe we can work our system better by giving MPs a more effective role."

The GPC would also give parliamentary debates a more even spread. "Before the GPC, I noticed that the MPs would speak on their favourite topics and those topics would be confined to the usual social services, economic development and so on," he said in an interview for this book. "And there was a lot of overlap and repetition. There were other areas where you should discuss but they would not discuss because they were not, shall we say, interesting enough for the MPs. So, to ensure that all subjects were discussed and all ministries were being examined by the MPs, you formed GPCs."

In the last 30 years, a new narrative has emerged on the creation of the GPC, arguing that it was set up by Goh to outflank the opposition. Former GPC chairman Aline Wong, for instance, told *The Straits Times* in a report in 2017: "Because of the lack of opposition in Parliament, and the population's desire to see some, Mr Goh came up with the idea that we should become some kind of internal opposition or proxy opposition." But Goh said that was not his intention. "GPC is not meant to be an opposition," he said. "It is to get PAP MPs to be more insightful in their criticism. It was not just to say, 'go and act as the opposition'. You want to have more considered, in-depth criticism, and not just your own ideas but the resource panel to help you. We allow them to have briefings by ministries… then they can make considered speeches."

The desire to raise the quality of Parliament and allow the people a greater role in the decision-making process of the legislature led him to his third, and possibly most controversial, policy as First Deputy Prime Minister. In 1989, he suggested having non-elected MPs, a scheme which would come to be known as Nominated MPs, or NMP. Lee first raised the issue in 1972, lamenting the failure of the opposition parties to have men of calibre, but nothing came of it. In 1989, Goh was determined to go one better than his mentor. His reasoning for NMP was succinct and crisp: "I felt the quality of people who might come in, at that point of time, in the opposition, was not the kind of people I wanted to do the check and balance. They were just chaps who could throw stones, who were good politicians who could argue, but who would not offer you possible solutions to a problem. So, NMPs are meant to be functional. People who are experts in the particular areas and they come in. They do not make flowery speeches, but they can offer ideas and they can criticise."

The proposal drew brickbats from both within the PAP and external voices. They slammed it as an attempt by the ruling party to ensure a "friendly opposition" in Parliament. An unnamed mid-level civil servant told *The Straits Times*: "The idea is corny. An elected government is trying to seek legitimacy for itself by inviting people to come in and criticise its policies. If you want to be in Parliament, go and earn your mandate from the people." The counter suggestions thrown up were for these experts to give their views outside the Parliament, including to the Feedback Unit set up by Goh. One of the loudest voices against the scheme was his old friend Tan Cheng Bock. "He was a bit upset with me," said Tan, with a laugh. "But he didn't boycott me or show his anger. He's too nice a guy!"

It was a mark of Goh's style that he also chose not to block his friend from speaking up against his policy in public. Goh explained: "I told him he could object. He was very, very agonised. He told me that he could not support this, but I told him not to worry — he just needed to speak his mind. He was not attacking me but attacking the concept. But he said it was my idea. I said, yes, it was my idea, but it was a concept and we have a debate. So, I asked him to speak freely and he did." While Tan was against it on ideological grounds, Goh did not share his thinking. "Cheng Bock and others were against it on certain basic principles. They said that all MPs must be elected — that is all. I said, who said so? Senators in Malaysia are not elected. The lords in the UK are not elected," he said, referring to the House of Lords in the United Kingdom whose members were all appointed.

The Goh-style pragmatism came forth strongly again. If the objective was to include more good people in politics, and improve Singapore as a result, he would not be stymied by dogma. He found a strong supporter in S. Rajaratnam, who had retired from politics by then. The Old Guard said: "I would be dismayed to hear someone say that I don't want a bright chap in Parliament who is not elected by me, but I'd rather have a crook elected by me."

Goh had another reason for NMP which was less well known. He saw it as an avenue for the government to plug key appointments in the Cabinet if the preferred candidates had lost in an election. Specifically, he was concerned with finding the right men to be Finance Minister and Law Minister. "I was very worried about those two positions," he said. Given the domain knowledge and expertise needed to fill the two jobs, he wanted a back-up plan in case the PAP ministers with these qualifications were not elected. The NMP scheme would give him a chance to appoint a suitable person from outside the PAP for the job and ensure the government could continue to function well. "But after one term, they must contest the election because you should not have an unelected minister for more than one term," he explained. "It is not right in principle. They have to face the electorate on the basis of their performance."

Such a scenario did not come to pass, with the PAP able to have two men holding on to the portfolios for long periods, and still winning their electoral fights. S. Jayakumar stayed as Law Minister for 20 years from 1988 to 2008, while Richard Hu was the Finance Minister for 16 years from 1985 to 2001.

Q: *These changes which you introduced in the 1980s had your imprint of a participative democracy. But some have argued that they were also meant to disadvantage the opposition, who would not have been as well-equipped to run a town council and who would not have the expertise of NMPs. Was that your intention?*

A: Town council was probably in favour of the PAP at the start, on the basis that we could do a better job. Of course, during the elections, we asked if the electorate wanted garbage to pile up — this is election hyperbole. So, that was to our advantage. When the opposition won Potong Pasir and Hougang, their management of the estates was worse than ours in terms of cleanliness, arrears and sinking funds — objectively speaking. But their S&CC rates were lower.[35] And we discovered that Singaporeans were prepared to live with a little messiness outside, provided that their S&CC charges were low. So, we had a disadvantage there. More recently, Hougang and Aljunied GRC had governance issues and that helped us. But then we forced them to put things right, and if they do, it would not help us anymore.

On NMPs, has it checked the opposition? When we started the scheme, there was only one elected opposition in Parliament. Now, there are six. They have not stopped the growth of the opposition. Even if the opposition rises to take up 20 per cent of the seats, I still think NMPs should be there. They contribute to Parliament. Look at their speeches. Do they contribute? The

---

[35] S&CC refers to Service and Conservancy Charges.

answer is yes. Do they restrain the growth of opposition? No. So, they are not related. I do not think Singaporeans look at NMPs as opposition. Singaporeans still want what they call genuine opposition. In fact, the problem is that the Workers' Party now is seen to be too gentle on the PAP. A significant group of people want somebody who, metaphorically, can throw stones, somebody like Chee Soon Juan.[36] Then as spectators, they watch. What we want is sharper questioning by opposition MPs. Some of them do question you very sharply, they do their homework, they are very well prepared. That is the kind of troublesome opposition that you want. They are troublesome but that is correct — they ask sharp questions.

It's the same for the GPC. When I introduced it, I wanted it to be only for the PAP. There was only one opposition MP in the Parliament then, so there was no point in involving him. But at the back of my mind, one day we may drop the G. One day, when Parliament changes, it becomes more 60-40 type, then you drop the G. Then both sides can be on the committees.

Q: Do you think the time is now?
A: No. I hope not (laughs).

---

[36] Chee Soon Juan is the leader of the Singapore Democratic Party.

Q: There are nine Workers' Party MPs, including Non-Constituency MPs, in Parliament now.[37]

A: Perhaps it is not a bad idea for me to suggest that they join — then they would be seen as part of the government. They would lose clout with their supporters. In the end, they ask the same questions as we do because when you know the background, then how can you ask different questions? They would not join.

Q: What vision of Singapore were you trying to build with these major institutional changes?

A: I asked myself what kind of a system we want to be sure that our politics would be stable in Singapore. Being stable does not necessarily mean it has to be the PAP all the time. If your thinking is that you must have only PAP, then you will get into trouble somewhere down the road. I was thinking about a stable and good government, with good people in charge. That was my starting point. After being in politics for some time, I asked myself why I was in politics. Why was I taking this job of being a PM for which I was not very trained in the aspect of language and other abilities? What was I in it for? And why was I picked? So, I come back to what I have said quite often: Keep Singapore going.

Keep Singapore Going — I kept it simple on purpose. I did not want to raise expectation nor be weighed down by the enormity of the task. So, no highfalutin or pretentious slogan.

---

[37] Non-Constituency MPs are legislators from opposition parties who were the best-performing losers in a general election.

At the back of my mind, I was deeply concerned that Singapore must survive, grow, prosper after Lee Kuan Yew had left the scene, and that the responsibility has fallen on me and my colleagues. I have seen many new countries disintegrate after the first-generation leaders passed away. I did not want that fate to befall Singapore.

That is my responsibility. And once I accepted the job, it was to keep Singapore going. Then these other things followed. How do I do it? The obvious things would be to grow the economy. But the politics was very important too. You had to get the politics right. Of course, I wanted to win elections. But I wanted to win in a fair way. I was prepared to win some and lose some. But ultimately, even if I lose completely, if the politics is right, Singapore is kept going.

I did not assume the PAP was the only one who could keep Singapore going forever. If we can have good people in Parliament, regardless of party, then you do not have to worry who runs the government. Then whether A or B is in charge, you worry less. And we have toyed with the idea of that model. When the PAP had 100 per cent of the Parliament, Lee Kuan Yew and the younger leaders talked about whether we should split the party into two. Then there are all good men and women to well, then, satisfy the people. We would have real debate — not *wayang* — but real debate between two groups.[38] But both

---

[38] *Wayang* means "shadow" in Javanese. In Singapore's context, it is often used colloquially to mean "acting" or "pretence."

groups are the PAP people. So, when they changed government, it is PAP 1 or PAP 2.

Q: Why didn't you go ahead?

A: The resources were so limited. So if you divide the PAP team into two, you would weaken the government right away. You can get MPs, but the government — to get, say, 15 or 20 people — you do not divide your first team into two. You just cannot. So, we used to joke about this. Supposing I am PM on one side and Tony on the other side. Then I pick Ong Teng Cheong and he would pick Yeo Ning Hong. Then I pick Wong Kan Seng, he picks Jayakumar. See, that is how you would pick your football team in school right? But would this be better for Singapore? I said no. We must have our strongest team available to play against another school, the rest of the world.

Q: So, you had seriously discussed it?

A: Yes. We discussed it, albeit not that seriously as to proceed with it. We discussed many times.

Q: Wouldn't that suggest that you believe a two-party, one-man-one-vote system is a more stable one?

A: We had a deep suspicion of one man, one vote. Democracy favours the man with the most persuasive tongue, with the most populist policies, and he will win. But you have no other way and you must get a mandate from the people. So we worked out a system where you put in stabilisers into your democratic system. Then the good people would be in charge. So, it is geared towards getting good people into Parliament.

Without the Elected Presidency, anyone can make all sorts of promises during elections, promising free healthcare and free this and that. But with the Elected Presidency, you don't hear as much of such promises from the opposition. So, by their not doing so, we have actually taken out populist politics in terms of giveaways. There are other kinds of populism, but populist politics in terms of giving away things — they cannot do that now. You must know that the PAP is a fluke. Because Mr Lee was so strong and he instituted the system and we are now trying to replicate it. And most Singaporeans accept it. But it does not mean it will last forever. That's why we need to have stabilisers in our political system.

Q: *Since the goal is to get good people in, it should please you that the Workers' Party is increasingly attracting candidates whom people say are like the PAP's?*

A: When they get good people, it is a challenge to us. But it is better that you are challenged by good people and you may lose to them than to be challenged by people who are shady characters but very able politicians. Able politicians, but who are crooks, or if not crooks but have short-term, populist thinking — they will bring us down the wrong route and go into spending and spending, just to win the elections — it would be troublesome. Good people in opposition is a challenge to us, but it is better for us because if you lose, the next morning, when you get up, the country will go on. Of course, we hope we would not lose.

Q: *So, you do like the opposition being able to attract better candidates?*

A: Yes. That is good for them and for us. That they can attract better people with slightly different or sometimes fundamentally different points of view. That is okay — we can debate it out. But are they honest? Are they committed? Are they doing this for Singapore? That is what you want to know. I am not passing any judgment. But if you get good, honest people on the other side, that is all right. Then you have a real debate and the quality of Parliament is different. Your quality of government would be very different. So, whether you lose or win, it then does not become a disaster for Singapore. Other than for those people in charge, you do not lose sleep over it. Then Mr Lee would not turn in his grave and I would not turn in my grave.

Q: *That is very enlightened. Would future PMs hold the same view?*

A: Don't get me wrong. You must fight to win because you are the better team. You must believe that, isn't it? But I am saying if they are a better team, and when you lose, you are not going to see riots in the streets tomorrow. You are not going to be charged by the other party. First of all, you do not worry because you did not commit a crime. You did not take money and put them under the pillow or somewhere. But the big worry would be whether the other chap is trying to undo everything.

But look, you think the opposition will not face the same problems as us if they become the government? They are heroes now in their position. But once they are in government and the MRT breaks down, they get the same blame. That is the nature of the system, isn't it? If Low Thia Khiang is in charge and a few things break down, things are not well maintained, people will blame his government. And we will blame the government. That is the nature of politics. The moment they have a chance to be government, the fight will start in the party — who would be the finance minister, who would be the foreign minister? I do not believe that when they are in charge, they will not have any problems. That's the way it goes in politics. But nevertheless, if you have honest people in charge, they can do all this and the country will not go too far wrong.

It comes back in the end to an intelligent electorate, which I think we have. Generally speaking, the results turned out all right and the people would know how to signal the government where they are unhappy. What we want is a vigilant electorate. They say, this chap — Chee Soon Juan — I do not trust him and the electorate does not trust him. He may be intelligent, but a bit slippery — better don't trust him. Sylvia Lim — she is not as good as Shanmugam, but okay, she is an honest woman, so yeah, okay, we need her.[39]

The fourth PM would be challenged more severely than me and Hsien Loong electorally. Would I be worried that he would be challenged by a very able person? The answer would be no. Would I be worried if he was challenged by a very slippery kind of a politician? The answer is yes. If that person can knock out our team, then that is worse for us.

Q: When you introduced these changes like the Feedback Unit and town councils to give the people a greater say in governance, did you expect it to translate into a higher vote share?

A: These things are meant for the longer term. It is the way you want to govern and involve the people. You do not expect these things to help immediately or that people on the ground would vote very differently. They vote differently not only on the basis of your Feedback Unit and so on. I would tell you how they vote, from just one example. A resident whom I have known for many years said to me after the 2011 election that she voted against the PAP. I said, why? I said I knew her and she knew me, so why did she vote against me? Then she was a bit sheepish and she said she wanted to plant something in the community garden and they would not allow her. So, because the community garden and the RC did not allow her to plant something of her choice, she just voted against the PAP. So, of course, I said, she

---

[39] Sylvia Lim is the chairman of the Workers' Party and K. Shanmugam is the Law and Home Affairs Minister.

should have told me about the plants earlier. She walked away very quickly.

And from the Meet-the-People sessions, I could tell right there and then if there was someone whom we were not going to get his vote. Usually, it is because they cannot get what they want. Singaporeans who have, say, married Vietnamese wives, who want to get a permanent residency (PR) for the wife. You explain why you cannot, but after he had come to see you three times, do you think he will support you? He is a Singaporean, he married a Vietnamese wife, he wants to give her PR — which is fair — you do not give it to them. They would be very polite because they still need you to try and appeal. I am very polite because I need their support. But do you think they will vote for you? My guess is two out of three would not vote for you. Maybe one would say yes, it is not your fault, it is the policy. But I am prepared to bet that two out of three would not vote for you. Votes are generally decided by very personal interests.

But overall, if you create an environment where people feel that they have a say in their country, whether they are down at the bottom or higher at the top, yes, over time, they will say yes, you are putting into action what you believe in and that this system is a model they can support.

Q: *During this period after 1984, you were in charge but yet Lee Kuan Yew was still the PM. How did you strike a balance between making decisions and yet knowing not to overstep your boundaries?*

A: The analogy would be that he was the chairman and I was the CEO. You cannot have it all your own way because the chairman has the final say. Supposing I began to swagger around, then I walked in front of him. Of course, he would say this chap, even before he became PM, he was already displacing me. That is overstepping the boundary. But in terms of work, I had a free hand. If I wanted to change the constitution to do certain things, I had the free hand. But this was provided my team supports it. But then why are you changing the constitution? To entrench whose power? Lee Kuan Yew would check me if he found out that I was trying to create some institution to perpetuate my power. That would be overstepping. I'm sure he would have stepped in and said 'No, this chap is dangerous. Power has gone to his head'.

Q: *So, you knew how to behave in the right way?*

A: No no, you were not conscious about these things. You were DPM, self-renewal was taking place, you were going to be in charge, and this was the period when he wanted you to learn, he wanted to test you, he wanted you to do things, so you just did it. And you did not worry about being under test and hence you did everything cautiously. Then he would say this chap was too careful and he didn't dare to take risks.

Q: *This is where the public perception was different. The public believed that he was always there, active chairman and you were...*

A: I was just his puppet?

Q: *Executor.*

A: You couldn't go 'PM, what is it you want me to do? Should I create the GPC?' No. You did what you thought should be done and you were conscious of the fact that he was still the PM. So what you wanted to do must in the end be cleared in Cabinet. In there, he was the PM. So, you must do things where you believed the PM would support. Where he did not support, you must be able to persuade him. But first, you have to persuade your own cohort.

Between me and Lee Kuan Yew, it came quite naturally, in the sense that having worked with him, there was the comfort level. We had regular one-to-one lunches. I knew his purpose. I knew my purpose, the role I was in. His purpose was to have a smooth transition with the whole team with me in charge. And he had already removed many of his own Old Guard, very painfully. People did not know till much later that the removals hurt him a lot. It was very painful for him to have to do so. People thought he had no heart — how could he remove all these people who worked for him for years? And it was not just the Old Guard ministers, but Old Guard MPs too. The reason was so that we the second generation could move in. That was the big purpose. It was not that he was trying to bring in his friends and cronies to be in charge, to look after him later on, like Mugabe would do with his wife, and look after his wealth and so on. It was not him. He did not do that.

So, it was the larger purpose — you move in, you knew this was your job, you did your job. You did not think: Was I overstepping my limit? You just got things done and persuaded your colleagues to go along. And colleagues were looking at you: Did he have ideas? If I were just in charge and had no ideas, just went through Cabinet papers put up by the ministers, my colleagues would wonder what kind of PM I would be. They wanted to know if I had ideas, if I was a risk taker, or if I was reckless. So, these were being assessed by your colleagues and also by the PM.

Q: *This balancing act being the CEO when there was a very strong chairman around couldn't have been simple.*

A: It was not difficult to do because Mr Lee had picked a team of people who knew what the team was for and they knew the mission. So, in terms of character, competence and commitment, we were more similar and therefore, it was easier to do. I am not trying to make it seem simple, but I have not seen the complexity. But had there been different types and they were not gathered by Mr Lee, then it would not be so easy. This would be because each of us might have a different mission. Not just to be the PM but a different mission of what Singapore should do.

But all of us knew that we were here to keep Singapore going. In other words, all of us have gone into the same boat, we have to row the boat or sail the boat or whatever it was to a destination we knew we should be heading, with the people behind us, carrying them. Who can captain the ship better — that was the test. It sounded easy because the team was a good team, picked by Lee Kuan Yew.

While Goh and his second-generation team were eager to inject new participative features into the Singapore political system, they had not swung to the extreme of populist policy making. As Dhanabalan said when announcing the Feedback Unit's formation in 1985, the outfit would enhance communication. But it did not mean that the government would govern by conducting referenda or opinion polls for every issue. "We cannot become populist in policy making," he stressed. The PAP said as much in its post-mortem report of the 1984 general election. "Despite the population's reluctance to accept tough measures, the substance of the PAP government's policies cannot change. Policies must remain firmly based on logic, not emotions, however uncomfortable the logic may be," it said.

Singaporeans and the rest of the world would soon realise that while the Old Guard was tough and hardheaded, the New Guard was not a bunch of softies. They might not have entered politics as a result of a world war, colonialism and fought with communists for survival, but they had a bite and were not afraid to leave a rough mark if they had to. Goh, in particular, would prove more than capable in making tough and unpopular calls in economics, diplomacy and internal security.

Chapter 9

Mr Porcupine

"He doesn't look it, but he makes tough decisions."

Lee Kuan Yew on Goh Chok Tong, in 1988.

Singaporean Maznan A. had been making regular trips to Skudai, a small town in Johor, Malaysia's southern-most state, for special training with a group known as Budi Suci Sejati (BSS). They practised a spiritual form of *silat*, a traditional Malay martial arts, and the training involved ritual baths and the recitation of Quranic verses. Midway through the sessions in early 1987, Maznan was told to spread the word that racial clashes were going to happen in Singapore and to build up a BSS unit back home which could help foment a riot. The former police officer was ordered to gather a team of 10 and send them to Skudai for training. He was promised reinforcements from BSS cells in Kuala Lumpur and Johor once fighting breaks out in Singapore.

The 30-year-old worked fast. Within days, he managed to put together a team of four, including himself, a police constable, a driver and a student. The word they put out in April 1987 was that racial violence would take place around May 13, the anniversary of the 1969 riots in Malaysia which had spread to Singapore, killing four in the republic. Meanwhile, they stepped up their training in *silat* in anticipation of the strife and began sharpening and "charming" *parangs*, or long knives. Red sashes were also prepared and distributed, because the bands were supposed to render the wearers "invulnerable" during fights.

Unbeknownst to the group, Singapore's Internal Security Department (ISD), the country's domestic intelligence and security agency, had caught wind of the chatter. They briefed Goh Chok Tong, the First Deputy Prime Minister, to obtain permission to arrest the quartet. "They were quite firm about the rumours," said Goh. "Then I asked if they had physical evidence of weapons which were being collected for use in the racial riots. They said, no, they did not have physical evidence. But they were quite sure that there would be a cache of weapons." Despite the incomplete clues, Goh had to decide if he should give the green light.

And he knew the timing could not have been worse. The Ramadan fasting month was round the corner. The Malay community was also "quite restive," he remembered, because of the Herzog incident. In November 1986, just six months earlier, Israeli President Chaim Herzog had visited Singapore, the first by an Israeli head of state. The trip did not go down well with Singapore's neighbours, who were, and still are, largely Muslim. Malaysia, Indonesia and Brunei expressed displeasure and urged Singapore to be sensitive to the feelings of the Muslims, who are sympathetic towards the Palestinian struggle against the Israeli state. Such sentiments were true among the Malay-Muslims in Singapore too, and the Herzog visit led to a more serious controversy over the issue of Malay loyalty to Singapore and Malays in Singapore's military. "The Malay ground was not entirely with us," said Goh. "There were groups of Malays challenging the Malay leadership. The ground was not so calm. So, if I agreed to the arrests and if there was no cache of weapons, it would be seen that the government was against the Malays and just detained people without good reason."

Despite these concerns, Goh trusted the intelligence and gave approval for an immediate arrest of the *silat* group. "That was a risk I had to take," he said. "There was no consultation. I was alone. I didn't tell ISD to 'Let me check with Mr Lee Kuan Yew, the PM, let me speak to everybody'. They came to me with their judgment and I was in charge. I said go ahead." On April 24, 1987, ISD detained the quartet, who admitted their culpability and directed the investigators to their stash of weapons. Five *parangs*, two *keris* (short daggers with wavy blades) and a sword were found in one of the arrestees' flat.

The incident is illustrative of a man who was known to speak softly but rarely seen to wield a big stick. Yet, during a period when he was given *de facto* run of the government, he showed he was not afraid to bare his teeth on more than one occasion, in areas as wide ranging as economics, politics, diplomacy and, as the *silat* case has shown, even the highly sensitive field of domestic security. While he was keen to bring government closer to the people, he did not shy away from making difficult and even unpopular decisions. Lee Kuan Yew summed it up when he described Goh in 1988: "He doesn't look it, but he makes tough decisions."

A fitting metaphor would be a porcupine. In the latter half of the 1980s when Goh was also Defence Minister, he used the analogy of a "porcupine" to describe Singapore's military doctrine of deterrence. It would have been just as appropriate to describe the genial man himself. When necessary, he had spikes which could prick and draw blood. By 1987, he and his team had shown enough courage to reverse major policies, some of which bore the very personal imprint of Lee, who was still the Prime Minister. In May 1985, the highly controversial Graduate Mothers Scheme was reversed. The next year, the CPF withdrawal issue from the Howe Yoon Chong Report was resolved.[40] In March 1987, Goh personally announced the reversal of the Stop at Two family planning programme in light of declining fertility rate among Singaporeans. His new slogan? Have Three or More if You Can Afford it.

When Singapore was hit by a major recession in 1985, its first since independence, he would demonstrate his strength in economics by leading and steering the country out of trouble. Two decisions in particular played a critical role. First, despite the majority of his colleagues pushing to devalue the Singapore dollar, he was not in favour. He argued that it would raise the cost of living, hurting the poor more than the rich. He managed to convince them. Lee praised him three years later: "From a minority position he argued his way into a majority position. But that required a tougher decision."

---

[40] In 1984, the Government issued a report by a high-level committee formed to looked into Singapore's greying population. The committee was headed by then Health Minister Howe Yoon Chong and the report became widely known by his name. Its most controversial suggestion was to increase the withdrawal age of CPF from 55 to 60 so as to allow more funds for the elderly in retirement. The public uproar against the recommendation led to the idea being shelved.

It led to the second critical call Goh made. In order to help business stay afloat, the alternative to currency devaluation would be for salaries to come down. The Cabinet approved a 10 per cent cut on employers' contribution of CPF to the workers every month, even though some members, including Goh, believed a 15 per cent slash was more effective. Goh knew it would be hard to convince workers to take such a sharp cut. When he met union leaders, he saw an opening to sell 15 per cent. "I saw fear in their eyes — fear of recession and loss of jobs," he said. "I did not use any of those multimedia tools in my talk to them. I just used a simple chart and drew a few lines. At a 10 per cent wage cut, this was what would happen. The share of the profit of multinationals would increase by so much. If you do 15 per cent cut, we get a bigger margin for the multinationals and the investors. So, I say, if you ask me, let's do a 15 per cent cut. And I used very simple logic. 10 per cent's impact was neither here nor there. The investors would say you lacked courage. You do 15 per cent — it would be painful for you, but investors would say Singapore was a good place to do business in. The workers could take pain. They agreed. I said, okay, let's do 15 per cent cut. On the spot, I decided on it." It worked, and by the second quarter of 1986, Singapore rebounded from the recession quicker than expected. In 1988, Lee lauded it a "major triumph, not attempted anywhere else in the world." "You wouldn't even dream of doing it. Your unions will immediately go on strike," he said.

But more explosive crises were in store, requiring Goh to make tough and unpopular decisions in some of the most dramatic political incidents in the history of Singapore. The first came almost immediately after the *silat* arrests. The ISD was involved again. The agency, together with the Minister for Home Affairs, revealed to Lee in his office that there was a Marxist plot to subvert Singapore, said Goh, who was present. Unlike the earlier incident, when Goh took the briefing and the subsequent decision, this incident was of a larger national significance and Lee was in the picture right from the start.

The intelligence was that there was a group of ex-student activists, some with connections to Malayan Communist Party (MCP) elements, who were looking to use legal organisations, including the Catholic groups as a "cover" for subversive activities. They comprised Catholic lay workers, social workers, theatre practitioners and professionals. Intelligence pointed to Tan Wah Piow, a former student leader in self-exile in Britain since 1976, as the mastermind. Through his contacts in Singapore, including Catholic Church worker Vincent Cheng, Tan wanted the activists to infiltrate groups like student and religious organisations, and the Workers' Party so as to put pressure on the government, leading to eventual open confrontation. ISD revealed to Lee and Goh that several Malaysian and Singaporean activists from the former University of Singapore had joined the MCP in the early 1980s, and believed that the party was trying to make inroads into English-educated groups. These developments were of concern, as MCP had issued a directive in 1979 calling for the penetration and subversion of open and legal organisations.

For these reasons, ISD recommended the arrests of the activists, said Goh. But "the decision was not taken immediately," he recalled. "Mr Lee asked a lot of questions and, of course, we (the younger ministers) also raised many questions, essentially to be sure that the conspiratorial activities reported by ISD were indeed prejudicial to Singapore's security." Besides the MCP, the intelligence also pointed to how some of the activists were influenced by the liberation theology — popular in South America in the 1970s, seeking to help the poor and oppressed through the Catholic Church getting involved in politics. According to ISD, Cheng, for instance, had visited the Philippines where he learnt about liberation theology and the church's involvement in the political struggle there. Lee and the younger ministers were satisfied with the intelligence of an MCP hand behind the group, said Goh. When Lee asked Goh: "Should we do this?" Goh replied: "Yes." Lee approved the arrests.

On May 21, 1987, ISD arrested 16 people in a pre-dawn raid named Operation Spectrum. Six more were detained the next month, while four of the original 16 nabbed were released. By December, all were released except Cheng, as ISD assessed that they were no longer a serious threat to security. But that was not the end. In April 1988, nine of the detainees released a joint statement recanting their confessions, claiming they were made under duress and torture by the ISD. The move presented an immediate dilemma to Goh. Lee was in Italy at that time and as Acting Prime Minister, Goh had to make a decision in his absence. Lee called him from overseas, asking him what he had decided to do.

But Goh hadn't decided yet. "I was pondering what to do. I called a meeting of the younger ministers in my house," he said. "So, what were we to do? We had some discussion and, at the end of it, we said we have to re-detain them. They were denying the basis of their arrests and detention, saying it was unjustified. So we had to re-detain them to confirm that the earlier decision to detain them on security grounds was the correct thing to do. In other words, they had not repented. They did not recognise that they were wrong; there was therefore every likelihood that they would resume their former activities. They were instead saying that we were wrong and they were tortured into confession. So, we had to re-detain them — that is it."

A day later, eight of the nine detainees were arrested again.[41] The 24-hour delay did not please Lee. He said in a talk at the National University of Singapore (NUS) in 1988: "If it were me, the moment that statement was issued, there would have been a response immediately. Because that's the way I act." He expressed his unhappiness with Goh at a Cabinet meeting. Then Environment Minister Ahmad Mattar revealed that Lee had tried to reach Goh at home during the incident but he could not get through because Goh's phone was engaged for a long time. It was found out later that Goh's son was using the phone.

Upon returning to Singapore, Lee chaired a Cabinet meeting and revealed his frustrations and anger in trying to get hold of Goh on the phone. "He then turned to Goh Chok Tong, who was seated opposite him, and in front of everybody in Cabinet, angrily remarked 'If Loong is not my son, I would have asked him to take over from you now'," said Ahmad. "I didn't know how Chok Tong felt at that time. But I certainly felt embarrassed and infuriated by it," he added.

---

[41] One of the nine detainees who issued the joint statement was away in Britain and has remained overseas till today.

Ten days after the second arrest, the eight detainees retracted their joint statement and said their original confessions were true. The government released further information showing connections between the MCP, which was still fighting an armed conflict in Malaysia at that time, and Tan Wah Piow.[42]

While more than 30 years have lapsed, the controversy surrounding the Marxist Conspiracy has refused to end. In 2017, its 30th anniversary, activists protested on a subway train in Singapore, urging justice to the ex-detainees of Operation Spectrum. The incident had also divided the establishment somewhat. Goh first revealed in *Men in White* that former Cabinet minister S. Dhanabalan left the Cabinet in 1992 because he did not fully agree with the arrests.

When interviewed for this book, Dhanabalan elaborated on his decision, saying he was "not convinced at all" about the conspiracy. "I certainly asked for the individual reports to go through because I was not prepared to just accept the conclusion," he said. "I felt that maybe two or three — I cannot remember the names now — were up to no good, but the rest were being manipulated and that they were do-gooders who felt that certain sections of society would be ignored or left behind, therefore they had to fight for the interests of those groups."

Deputy Prime Minister Tharman Shanmugaratnam, who was a personal friend to some of the accused and questioned by ISD for a week, expressed doubts during his induction into politics in 2001.

---

[42] Tan Wah Piow's connections with the MCP were detailed in government press statements in May 1987 and again in April 1988. Separately, the Malaysian Special Branch had also uncovered links between Tan and the MCP, made public by Kuala Lumpur in March 1988.

"Although I had no access to state intelligence, from what I knew of them, most were social activists but were not out to subvert the system," he said. He was part of a study group led by Tan Wah Piow in London. Similarly, Mary Turnbull, a noted historian on Singapore, went as far as to call the alleged conspiracy a myth.

Dhanabalan said Goh shared Lee's views about the activists. "I remember Chok Tong being very persuaded that this group posed a danger," he said. "He himself was very clear and he saw these people as dangerous people. He had a deep conviction that these people were up to no good." Goh agreed, citing two factors behind his assessment, in his first extensive comments on the incident. First, since he and the second-generation leaders took charge in 1985, they had had regular briefings from ISD. "We got to know how ISD worked. More importantly, the purpose was to know the people working the system — how they collected intelligence, how they analysed it, how they came to certain judgment," he said. "We got to know them and the kind of people in charge. It was not just the head of ISD, but also the people working because if you do not know them and you do not trust them, and they are in charge of intelligence, they could be manipulating the leadership with the intelligence. So, we knew the people behind the arrests."

Second, the *silat* arrests. "Because of that incident, my faith in the ISD increased. In other words, the Marxist Conspiracy was not the first time they gave me intelligence," he said. "It was never 100 per cent certain because it was intelligence. If it was 100 per cent certain, you would have arrested and charged them in court and so on. In ISA arrests, intelligence could lead to more... and you suspect that this will lead to something very troublesome for security. Based on that, you arrest and you obtain intelligence from them."

Looking back, Goh pointed out that subsequent information confirmed the government's judgment and actions. He revealed that in 2004, two months after he stepped down as Prime Minister, he met former MCP leader Chin Peng in the Istana, Singapore. Chin acknowledged that the MCP had elements in Singapore. He had earlier stated in his memoirs first published in 2003 that the MCP had "successfully recruited a number of university students in the mid-1970s from universities in Singapore and Malaysia" for their radio station in Hunan, China, called Voice of Malayan Revolution. The station was aimed at subverting Malaysia and Singapore and was closed down in 1981 after Lee Kuan Yew's historic meeting with Chinese leader Deng Xiaoping in 1978. Goh was present at this meeting. Several of these students were close associates of Tan Wah Piow and one of them, Juliet Chin, joined the MCP. Chin Peng told Goh that he had met Juliet Chin and Irene Koh but for Tan Wah Piow, "not recently."

Goh said that making a decision based on intelligence was always a difficult judgment call, whether it was the Marxist group or the *silat* group. But it had to be made. "Mr Lee, my colleagues and I took the right decision. You will never know the full facts until later. They might be just do-gooders, but when you suspect them of engaging in questionable activities and being manipulated, you do not know where it would lead to," he said. "So, if you do not stop such activities and the problem worsens, it becomes too late. And the point we are making is that whatever mission you have, if it is above board, there is no problem. Take us on openly — that is not an issue. Your mission to help the foreign maids, to help the dispossessed — that was entirely right. But do not do it in such a secretive, subversive way. The right thing to do was what Teo Soh Lung did years later — she stood for election in 2011."[43]

The issue is not likely to disappear any time soon, said Goh, and he was prepared to live with it. "It would not go away, just like many of those who were detained by Lee Kuan Yew. They said they were heroes: 'We played a part in Singapore's history'. Yes, they played a part. They can claim to be heroes. But if they were in charge, where would we be? As Mr Lee said, my fingernails would be pulled out. When we are in charge, they just get locked up and get fed by the state. We released them, so the ex-detainees must defend what they did."

The Marxist Conspiracy segued into a diplomatic crisis. In April and May 1988, two high-profile lawyers who represented the detainees, Francis Seow and Patrick Seong, were also arrested. Seow, in particular, was well known in Singapore as a former Solicitor-General and Law Society president. He was found to have been cultivated by an American diplomat based in Singapore, E. Mason "Hank" Hendrickson, to stand for elections and take on the PAP. Even though it was during the Cold War and Singapore was a staunch ally of the United States, Goh said the decision was taken quickly to expel Hendrickson. "Whether it was a US diplomat or not, as far as we were concerned, it was immaterial. You cannot interfere in domestic politics," he said. "He was telling

---

[43] Teo Soh Lung is one of the detainees. In 2011, she contested the general election as a candidate of the Singapore Democratic Party. She obtained 33.14 per cent of the vote and lost to PAP's Grace Fu.

Francis Seow to stand for election against the government. That was interfering. That was the US supporting an opposition figure. And, later on, they could be supporting, if we were not careful, an opposition party to stand against us. We cannot allow that. It is for Singaporeans to decide how Singapore should be governed."

Seow released a sworn affidavit admitting that he had visited Washington D.C. to meet Hendrickson's superior in the US State Department. Seow was assured of refuge if he had to leave Singapore — an offer which he eventually took up, for life. The US Embassy in Singapore said that Hendrickson did not act improperly but it acceded to the government's request to withdraw him. In a tit-for-tat response, the US also expelled a Singaporean diplomat, Robert Chua Hian Kong, in Washington. Once Seow was released from detention, he stood in the 1988 general election as a Workers' Party candidate and came close to winning. His three-man team banked 49.11 per cent of valid votes in Eunos GRC, losing to the PAP. He was accused of tax evasion after the polls and fled Singapore for the US, where he died in 2016.

Washington was keen on getting Seow into politics because of the PAP's dominance, said Goh. "We did not distrust the US. At that time, we still believed the US was a benign force," he said. "They did not like the fact that the PAP was totally dominant. It was not democratic by their definition. Democracy means there must be another party, there must be a change in government every four, eight or 12 years. That is their belief." But while the Americans had a long track record of regime change overseas, both through overt and covert means, Goh did not believe the Hendrickson Affair — as it has come to be known — was an attempt by Washington to get rid of the PAP. "We came to the conclusion that these chaps were trying to encourage opposition to stand against us and have more of them in Parliament. It was not trying to overthrow the government," he said.

The series of action taken by the New Guard earned them praise from Lee. In a forum with NUS students in 1990, he said: "The team has shown guts in tackling tough, sensitive and potentially vote-losing issues. We tackled them because the problems were critical for our survival." Goh regarded it as a compliment from Lee, although that was never the objective of him and his team. "We never set out to show guts. We did what we thought was correct," he said. "I was not trying to show that I was a tough guy. It was not important. In the *silat* case, the ISD said this is our intelligence, they are spreading rumours, this is what they want to do, we recommend you arrest them — would you agree? I did not say, I am a tough guy, I agree. There is no such thing. You have to be very responsible, ask questions and in the end, you trust the judgment of ISD. It is a very serious matter."

Q: *What is your view on the Internal Security Act (ISA) today?*

A: We told the people in the late 1980s that it was their right to campaign for the abolition of the ISA. If they win, they do away with ISA. But if I am in charge, the ISA is very important. Supposing we abolish it, you think the JI will not be creating problems for us?[44] The government has arrested self-radicalised Muslims. They surf radical websites, they read, they get very angry, and they want to go to Syria to fight for ISIS. Are there security grounds for detaining them? You are going to have more and more radicalised Muslims, whether self-radicalised or otherwise. By the time they have 100, 1,000 such radicalised Muslims who believe in violence to attain their ends, the security problem will be too big to handle. Bring them in, question them, detain them, rehabilitate them.

Somebody said they were just looking at the websites, self-radicalised, they were not doing any harm. All they say is that they want to go to Syria. You have Malay women here who said they wanted to be a bride of a fighter in Syria. Don't detain; this is her wish — she has every right to go to Syria and marry a fighter.[45] Okay, but if you look around and there is not just one case, but many such cases, then it is a thinking that is going to cause the larger Muslim community to be distrusted in multi-

---

[44] JI refers to Jemaah Islamiyah, a terrorist group in Southeast Asia which wanted to establish an Islamic state in the region. Its plot for a bomb attack in Singapore was foiled in 2001 and 2002 when about 40 members were detained under the ISA.

[45] In June 2017, Singapore detained its first female citizen for radicalism. The 22-year-old infant care assistant wanted to make her way to Syria and marry an ISIS (Islamic State of Iraq and Syria) fighter.

racial Singapore. Then you better bring them in. At the end, you must win the support of the Malay-Muslim community and the leaders. Which was what we did — we said we are helping the community. We are not against Islam.

What is the danger of self-radicalisation? Self-radicalised individuals may resort to violence and launch terrorist attacks, as shown in the numerous incidents around the world. Indeed, the self-radicalised individuals who were detained under ISA had made plans to undertake violence either here or overseas, or engage in activities that pose a serious threat to security.

So, abolish ISA? *The Straits Times* can put up articles against ISA. The opposition can campaign, which is fair because if you are in charge of the government and you say you do not believe in ISA — that is fair. But around the world, more people have introduced preventive detention than the other way around.

Q: But I think the fear has always been abuses of ISA.

A: That is correct. But, do you allow the fear to therefore do away with the ISA and have more fear after that? That you do not even know what happened, subversively — which is a greater fear? I know we have honest people in charge. Lee Kuan Yew, myself, Lee Hsien Loong. How did the arrests in 1987 advance our political purposes? We lost ground in the 1988 general election because people who were unhappy thought we were wrong, that we were overreacting in hauling in some 'innocent people', 'do-gooders'. But if we had abused the act, we would have been out.

Let me give you a personal example. After the Marxist arrests, I found out that one of the girls detained was a sister of my classmate, who was, and remains, a very close friend of mine. My classmate and his brother came to see me to appeal. They said their sister was not doing anything wrong. I said this might be so, but this was what the evidence was. What I could do was arrange for them to see ISD, then ISD could explain to them the part the sister played. ISD told them the basis on which they decided to detain their sister… she was part of a group, without knowing she was being manipulated. My friend and I still see each other today and he is in my circle of close friends. In other words, he trusted me, that I didn't abuse my position. He might not have agreed fully with me. Whether he accepted ISD's explanation of his sister's role, I do not know. But my point is, we are still friends today.

Q: Francis Seow was connected to the Marxist Conspiracy. You mentioned earlier of undesirable characters who should not be in Parliament. Would he be one of them?

A: Francis Seow was detained in connection with the Hendrickson Affair. No, I would not use the word undesirable against him. I knew him very superficially. As a civil servant, I was working in Finance Ministry and he was working in the Attorney-General's Chambers. So, very often, we would cross one another on the way to lunch and we would nod and so on. Of course, there was tremendous respect for him at that time. I was a very young civil servant. He was Solicitor-General and he certainly was a very polished man. So, I would not put him in the category of undesirable or troublemaker.

Q: *In other words, if he had won in 1988, you believe he might actually bring something to Parliament?*

A: He could debate, but he was known to be not very hardworking. If he came into Parliament, he would not have taken on the responsibility seriously. He would not be like a Jeyaretnam or Low Thia Khiang. But on certain matters which he knew well, on the legal side, you could expect a debate with him. But he was not seriously interested in politics.

Q: *You said earlier that you had no problems talking to Jeyaretnam when you saw him. Would it be the same for Francis Seow?*

A: When I went to Williams College for my honorary doctorate, Francis Seow turned up. And we said hello. He turned up and sat in the front row. He was quite gentlemanly. He went there and he listened. I made a short speech and was part of a panel discussion. He sat through. So, when the thing was over, I came down, I spoke to him, he spoke to me, we had a chat. He was not out to create trouble. With me, he was okay.

Q: *What about someone like Tang Liang Hong? Would you talk to him if you bump into him?*[46]

A: Again, after all that had happened, when I was in Australia as PM giving a talk, he turned up! My security officer was starting to get worried. Tang Liang Hong said 'Hi, Mr Goh'. I said 'Hi, Liang Hong, how are you? Are you doing all right?' He said he was doing all right in Australia. So, it is nothing personal. As a person, he was all right. But politically, he was using Chinese language and Chinese culture to win votes. That is not right because if you allowed him to use that, then the Malays would say that we are killing the Malay language and would ask to be voted in to defend the Malay language. So, you got to say that you cannot do that in Singapore.

Q: *Do you think Lee Kuan Yew would say hi to Tang Liang Hong?*

A: I knew Tang before he entered politics and we knew that he was very active in promoting Chinese culture. Whereas Lee Kuan Yew would not know him personally. It was wrong of Tang to campaign on that, but we had won and he had lost the battle. He was not coming back to fight us. He was destroyed personally. For Lee Kuan Yew, never leave a wounded tiger — he would fight to the death. On language, racial and religious

---

[46] Tang Liang Hong is a lawyer and former Workers' Party candidate who contested and lost in the 1997 general election in Singapore. During the campaign, the PAP accused Tang of being an anti-Christian Chinese chauvinist. After the election, he was sued by PAP leaders, including Goh, for defamation. He also faced charges for tax evasion. Tang left Singapore and eventually settled in Australia in self-imposed exile. He has not returned to Singapore.

issues, Lee would not tolerate any divisive views and activities.

Some years later, during a visit to Australia, John Howard intimated to me that Tang had asked for residency in Australia. It was not as a refugee, but he just applied for residency in Australia. Howard said they were going to give it to him. He was not asking for permission but just telling me. I said, that is good. Okay, that was the end of the conversation on the subject. At least Tang would have a place to go. If they did not give it to him, he must come back. If not, where was he going to stay? China? Had he come back, he owed a lot of money, his house was sold and he would be in trouble. So, I said that is good.[47]

Q: *Would you be friendly with long-time opposition MPs like Chiam See Tong and Low Thia Khiang too?*

A: I regard Chiam as a friend.

Q: *As a friend?*

A: As a friend, yes. I have seen him at dinners outside. He would come to me and I would go and talk to his wife and so on. If I see the wife, I would ask her how Chiam is. He was a gentleman politician. He had his own purpose in politics, which is to create a two-party Parliament. There is nothing wrong with that. We did not like it, but we said you try, so he tried.

---

[47] John Howard was Australia's Prime Minister from 1996 to 2007. He is the country's second longest serving Prime Minister.

Q: *Would that be the same towards Low?*

A: It is the same with Low. In fact, with most of the people, it is the same thing. We always watch. What is the purpose, their aspirations, their goals and would they bring Singapore down? Or would they be just difficult opponents for us? Then we got to be better than them. So, if they are honest and honourable and want to do good for Singapore even though it is in a different way, well, we can have a debate on that. But if your views are totally wrong in our view, like promising a welfare state and using the reserves, then we would fight you. We would fight you tooth and nail on your wrong-headed and populist approach.

Q: *So who would be someone whom you would not speak to?*

A: Chee Soon Juan.

Q: *Is it because he was your toughest opposition opponent?*

A: No. His character is so flawed, he cannot be a tough opponent. To put it in a general way, the toughest opponent is actually PAP's success. And the wish of the people to have alternative voices in Parliament. That is the toughest opponent because we have succeeded and won so many seats and the people, not just opposition, say, no, they want to hear alternative voices. We could encourage, as we did, PAP MPs to be critical, to be honest in their criticism, to speak out. But the people say — all of you are of the same mould; they want somebody different. That is the toughest opponent. In other words, it is a situation of success and total dominance.

So, if you ask which individuals would pose problems? They are not troublesome, but they are tough in a sense that they would fit the mood of the people. So, Chiam would be tough to get out of Potong Pasir because he fitted the thinking of the people and is decent, a middle-of-the-road kind of an MP. If you want to campaign against him, it would be very difficult to get him out. So, it was tough in that sense. Low would also fit that mould. Once he had won, it would be difficult to get him out. Politically, he is sharper, compared with Chiam. If you want to debate against him to get him out, it would be difficult. He is shrewd.

Chee is flawed. He tried so many times but people have sized him up. They would not want him. Chee flew all the way to Williams College to slam Singapore during my conferment. On another occasion in the States, he went without an invitation to a by-invitation event where I was speaking. He entered the room midway through the forum and asked a question on Malays, how we treated the Malays. That is a troublemaker. Francis Seow and Tang Liang Hong suffered more politically than Chee, but they were respectful and friendly. Chee Soon Juan, wherever he was, was my opponent.[48]

---

[48] Chee Soon Juan is the leader of the Singapore Democratic Party. He has contested and lost in five elections in Singapore since entering politics in 1992. When Goh was conferred an honorary doctorate by his alma mater Williams College in 1995, Chee went to Williamstown to join a protest against the award. During the 2001 general election, Chee heckled Goh in public.

Q: *Is there a second person whom you would not acknowledge?*
A: No.

Q: *Only one?*
A: Yes. One is bad enough, you know.

Q: *Let's go back to the difficult decisions you had to make in the late 1980s. Amid all the ISD-related incidents, there was also the introduction of the Group Representation Constituency (GRC). You were the face of the scheme, explaining it to the public. What was the toughest part of the job?*
A: It started with Lee Kuan Yew's idea of twinning, pairing a Chinese with a minority to stand for election: a two-member constituency. We were against that one. The Malay leaders, in particular — Ahmad Mattar — were dead against it because it was obvious to everybody that the Malay candidate was to be carried by the Chinese. So the younger leaders came up with a suggestion that it would be better to have a three- or four-member constituency where the Malays were not seen to be carried. In some instances, the Malays could carry the Chinese in a Malay-dominant or high percentage constituency. It is a tripod. In a tripod, who carries who is more difficult to say. If it is just two legs, it is easier — the left leg is stronger or the right leg is stronger.

So that was one example where we took LKY's idea and we changed it. He said okay and he accepted it. Then he said why not go up to six? That was the way he worked, to think ahead. But during that time, it was not going to be popular to have six-member GRC. So we had the provision to have six members in a GRC but in 1988, we kept it to three. We convinced Singaporeans that the idea was meant to introduce multiracial representation in the Parliament.

Q: But minority candidates have beaten Chinese candidates in single seats both before and after the introduction of the GRC. So how true is it that minorities needed the GRC to guarantee representation?

A: Yes, there are exceptions. People do not want to say so, but the biggest concern for us is whether the Malays, who are in the minority in all constituencies, can win on their own merit in sufficient numbers. Our concern was that they would be under-represented in Parliament. Like it or not, race still plays a part in elections. Go and ask yourself that. Be honest with yourself. What is your answer?

Q: But as the GRCs expanded, it diluted the argument that it was meant for minority representation.

A: There is another explanation for that. Why have six? We can then introduce new candidates. And Lee Kuan Yew justified that when Teo Chee Hean came in, in the 1992 by-election. He liked to say that without the GRC, Teo Chee Hean on his own, standing in a single ward, might not win against somebody like Chee Soon

Juan. Teo was a young, fresh person from SAF. But after one term, he was on his own. Look at him now. So, that is the merit of the GRC.[49]

Q: Why do you need something like this when earlier politicians like yourself, also without political experience, were able to stand on your own?

A: The ground has changed. Earlier on, the PAP brand name was very strong. Many candidates could come in. But later on, as we became dominant in Parliament, with more or less 100 per cent of the seats for two or three elections, the electoral mood changed. People thought this was not quite good for the country; you must have an opposition voice. Then for us, it was a question of bringing in good people to stand for election and to take the country into the future. Political succession was our motivation and we bring in good people through this. Of course, the press and the opposition put it in colourful language — under the armpits and so on.

Q: Coattails.

A: Coattails. Not armpits. That is a nicer way of putting it.

---

[49] Teo Chee Hean is the Deputy Prime Minister of Singapore. He was a former Chief of Navy in the Singapore Armed Forces, before joining politics in 1992 in a by-election in Marine Parade GRC. Among the opponents during the by-election was the team from the Singapore Democratic Party, which included its star recruit Chee Soon Juan. In the 1997 general election, Teo moved to Pasir Ris GRC to head the PAP team there. He has remained there since.

Q: *But if you look at the development of the GRC system, it became a little perverted, with ministers who did not contest at all for several elections and never really had the chance to face the voters.*

A: No, that is not the result of the GRC. That was because of the poor quality of opposition candidates and the interest of, shall we say, able people who wanted to go into opposition politics. So, they could not produce the candidates. We went on principles. The GRC did give the incumbent an advantage. It must be so. You have a minister there, a new candidate, in a team of three or four. Or even twinning. It would give the incumbent an advantage. That is a fact. And there is nothing wrong with that. Everybody has his advantage in incumbency. The public says, no, you must not have the advantage. But that is not life. Every incumbent, everywhere, if he has done a good job, has an advantage. Where the incumbent has not done a good job, incumbency can become a disadvantage.

We are prepared to say that the GRC has sort of served us, but it is a level playing field. The only advantage is the incumbency. So, perversely, we saw a silver lining in our loss of Aljunied GRC. 'See, I have told you that it is even. If you have good candidates, even if you are up against ministers, you can win.' So, six, seven or eight-member GRC — there is no problem. It is the mood, the campaign and how you exploit the situation. So, in retrospect, were we right or wrong? We were right! Incumbency gave us an advantage but there was no guarantee.

In Aljunied, we had three high-level, powerful and hard-working ministers — George Yeo, Zainul Abidin Rasheed and Lim Hwee Hua. What more do you want — there was a Chinese, a Malay, and a woman? And still we lost.[50]

Q: What would you consider to be the optimal size of a GRC today?

A: It should be a mix. I do not know what PM's thinking is. I find that four would be quite good because having four people is easier to run a GRC. Three may be a little too small. It is either single, four and maybe some fives and very few sixes. Maybe you can argue that sixes would be the constituencies of your strongmen — the PM and maybe Deputy PM. Then the reason is you bring in five other MPs, you are stronger in Parliament. But one day, when the PM is unpopular, you see what happens. You may lose six seats. It does not mean that the PM will always win. John Howard lost his seat.[51]

---

[50] The PAP lost a GRC for the first time when its team in Aljunied GRC was defeated by the Workers' Party in the 2011 general election. The PAP team included then Foreign Affairs Minister George Yeo, Minister in Prime Minister's Office Lim Hwee Hua and Senior Minister of State Zainul Abidin Rasheed.

[51] In Australia's 2007 federal election, Prime Minister John Howard lost his own seat of Bennelong in the Sydney area, to Labor candidate Maxine McKew. Howard was the second sitting Australian PM to lose his seat since Stanley Bruce in 1929.

By 1988, Goh and his team had been in charge for four years and proved that while they had their own style, they could still deliver the twin goods of a strong economy buttressed by a stable political system. When necessary, the tall man with the gentle smile was more than capable of wielding a big stick. He was ready for the big job. Yet just when all seemed to have gone according to plan, a major curveball was thrown in his way — by none other than Lee Kuan Yew himself.

Towards the
Istana

"

Part 4

By 1990, I was ready.
In my heart, I was ready.

"

Chapter 10

This is Me

"The good thing about Goh Chok Tong was that he did not try to be another Lee Kuan Yew. He was himself and that appealed to people. And people were ready to have a leader who was not Lee Kuan Yew."

S. Dhanabalan, in an interview for this book.

G oh Chok Tong settled into an upholstered red chair in the front row of the Kallang Theatre, a seat which he had become accustomed to for some years. As the heir apparent to Singapore's Prime Minister Lee Kuan Yew, he had been taking prime spot among the 1,800 in the audience for the annual National Day Rally speech. The event, unique to Singapore in its style and length, had become a national tradition, a platform where Lee addressed the country on major challenges and policies. After more than a decade in the crowd, Goh had also picked up some useful habits before the annual proceedings. For one thing, he made sure he visited the toilet before he entered the auditorium, knowing full well that few bladders could withstand the oratory tour de force of Lee, an uninterrupted lecture in three languages which could last up to four hours.

It was no different this year, in August 1988. Sandwiched between Lee's wife and fellow Cabinet minister Tony Tan, Goh was comfortably dressed in a light blue short-sleeved shirt and dark pants. He knew what Lee was going to speak on. As First Deputy Prime Minister, he had a sneak preview of the speech when Lee asked for views and corrections, if any. But Lee was known to ad-lib liberally and Goh knew those were usually the most colourful, at times humorous, bits of the speech. He did not bargain for what was to come.

After touching on corruption, birth rates, Westernisation and a host of other issues, Lee reached the end of his speech. He cautioned that his concluding note was "a sober one." "Yes, we have done well. Yes, there's a team in place to provide continuity," he said. "But I want to add a caveat. I don't want to be blamed if anything goes wrong. I have done my best and I think this is the best in the circumstances." He then gave, for the first time in public, his appraisal of Goh and his batch of so-called "second-generation leaders," shocking Singaporeans when he said that Goh was not his first choice. "I put Tony Tan No. 1 because, although Goh Chok Tong has got a faster mind — and he has, he has a fast, quick brain — there's a decisive quality about him (Tan)," said Lee. "He listens, takes all points of views and decides. After listening, you can't keep on listening. After listening, you sit down and you listen to your conscience, your judgment, and you say, 'Right, we will do this. And if it's wrong, I will take the responsibility.' I told Goh Chok Tong, 'Look you are trying to please too many people.' Even the pressmen, they badger him. He keeps on obliging with answers. I said, 'Just cut them off'."

The crowd laughed, and Goh, who was ranked second by Lee, smiled awkwardly. But in his first extensive comments on the incident in 30 years, he revealed he was shocked by Lee's bombshell. "I was perplexed, stunned and dumbfounded by his revelation. You have to live with the awkwardness of facing the big crowd after the rally. You had to be very wooden when you came out," he said, making light of an infamous jibe which Lee made a week later. "What else could you do? People looked at you and just shook your hand and said, hello. What was there to talk about?" The front bench was confounded. Tan told Goh: "A very curious speech, a very curious speech." S. Jayakumar was reported by *The Straits Times* to be "puzzled." Lee Hsien Loong said he could not recall how he felt, but added with a broad smile: "I imagine I would be feeling squeamish on behalf of the people who were being talked about."

Goh told his old friend Ahmad Mattar that he would "walk out" if Lee did it again the next year and Ahmad replied: "I'll walk out with you." Ahmad shared his feelings 30 years on, in a rare interview post retirement, that he had felt "very embarrassed" for Goh. "It means he wasn't the chosen one, the one preferred by the incumbent Prime Minister," he said. "But we had agreed among ourselves that he should lead and Lee Kuan Yew had accepted our choice. Why must he make it known to the people, to the population, to the world that his successor is not the man he would like to be?"

It was the question on Goh's mind too. "I was bewildered and trying to figure out why he was doing that for," he said. He arrived at two conclusions behind Lee's intent. First, it was the caveat which Lee had lodged at the rally — he did not want to be blamed if Goh failed. Unlike most strongmen in Asia, Lee bucked the trend by intentionally not choosing his successor. "So, he was saying that he was getting a successor who, in his view, could fail and would not be the best man," said Goh. "So, he was not going to get the blame." Second, Lee wanted to remove Goh as his heir apparent. "This is a possibility which had crossed my mind many times," said Goh, revealing his uncertainty of his own status at that point. "That he was trying to manipulate or manoeuvre for the team to reconsider and put Tony Tan as No. 1. Maybe, he was just sort of opening the possibility for — not for himself — but for others to change."

The rally speech, which was incidentally among Lee's most memorable, stunned Singaporeans who had assumed the leadership succession was long a done deal. In fact, Goh had told visiting Indonesian journalists just a month earlier, in July 1988, that he was confident of becoming the next Prime Minister. "Two months ago, we met again and I asked them (the younger ministers) who they wanted to lead them and all of them, including BG Lee, renewed this confidence in me," said Goh in *The Jakarta Post*, referring to Lee Hsien Loong. "So I have no choice." But the news report said Goh "hastily added that politics usually is full of uncertainties." It was strangely prescient. While Lee Kuan Yew did not explicitly restart the race, his hard truths at the rally suggested that he was not completely satisfied with Goh as the next Prime Minister. As Goh approached the last mile on the winding road to the top, he would hit the most severe of road bumps in the shape of his mentor, the indomitable Lee Kuan Yew.

The background to the 1988 speech is useful here. While Lee had never made known when he would retire, he had said on occasions that he had admired the model of American corporations, where chief executives retire at 65. "Several years before a CEO's retirement, he had to put before the board one or more candidates for them to choose one as his successor," he wrote in *From Third World to First*. "I resolved that I must not be found wanting in this respect, and that I must place Singapore in competent hands before I retired." In 1988, Lee turned 65. In other words, he was expected to hand over to Goh that year.

But the rally speech gave a strong hint that he was not ready to completely relinquish power yet. Besides criticising Goh, Lee also left the door open for himself to take on the new job of the Elected Presidency, a rumour which was rampant at that time. Lee did not quash it. "It is a possibility, which I will consider, when the time comes," he said. But he added that he did not need to be the president to retain control. "Given me and my links with so many people, all I've got to do is to stay secretary-general of the PAP," he said. "I don't have to be president. I stay secretary-general of the PAP and I can decide, I will have a very strong last word on policy. I don't have to be president and I am not looking for a job. Please believe me."

And if anyone had still not gotten the message, he would deliver one of his most famous quotes: "I belong to that exclusive club of founder members of new countries — first prime ministers or presidents of a new independent country. And even from my sick bed, even if you are going to lower me into the grave, and I feel that something is going wrong, I'll get up. Those who believe that when I have left the government as prime minister, that I've gone into permanent retirement, really should have their heads examined."

To Goh, on hindsight, it was clear the speech was carefully planned to signal to Singaporeans that Lee was not about to retire. "When he made the speech, he must have already decided that he would not hand over just yet. So, maybe, he was also preparing the ground because people might quote him and say that he had said he would retire at 65," he said. "So why was he not retiring? He had to square with me. He had raised the expectation that I would take over in 1988, so he had to square with me publicly, with the whole team, that I was not quite ready yet. So, this could be the reason why he did all this."

If Lee's intent was to get the younger ministers to choose a new leader, it failed miserably. Within a week, the two candidates most likely to replace Goh — Tony Tan and Lee Hsien Loong — both separately renewed their public support of Goh. "I see no reason at all why that decision should be changed," said Tan, referring to their original unanimous choice in 1984. For Lee Hsien Loong, he said in an interview for this book it "was not on the cards" for him to succeed his father. "None of the ministers or MPs would have believed that," he said. "Mr Lee had the prerogative of saying these things. We had discussed it among ourselves and we had settled on Mr Goh, and we were not intending to change our minds. We did not think it would be helpful to change our minds. We were happy with it, we were making it work. There were some adjustments along the way, but we did not see any reason to change." That was why he quickly made public his continued support of Goh. "In that situation, if you do not state a clear view, there would be even greater speculation and excitement going around," he said. The backing "pleasantly surprised" Goh, who shared that he had never asked the pair why they felt compelled to do so.

But Lee Kuan Yew was not done yet. A week later, during a forum with students at the National University of Singapore (NUS), he brought up the topic of leadership succession. In particular, he explained and elaborated on his criticisms of Goh. "If I am just one paean of praise, it's like selling detergent, it's a waste of time," he said. Lee complimented Goh effusively, praising his integrity for being incorrupt in NOL, turning the shipping line around, and being unafraid of competition. Of the 61 new candidates fielded by the PAP in the 1980, 1984 and 1988 elections, 30 of them were talent-spotted by Goh. "He's not afraid of able men," said Lee.

However, he also brought up Goh's weaknesses again. "He is unable to convey publicly through television and through mass meetings what he can convey in individual, face-to-face or small group discussions," said Lee. "I don't know why. I have suggested to him, perhaps, a bit of psychological adjustment, maybe a psychiatrist, something holds him back. He is, before a mass audience, he gets wooden — which he is not. When you speak to him one-to-one, he has got strong feelings. Get him on television, it's difficult. He has improved, I will say about 20 per cent. He needs to improve by more than 100 per cent."

As is usually the case, and as predicted by Lee, his praises of Goh at NUS were quickly forgotten. Instead, it was the brickbats, especially the "wooden" comment, which went viral at an age when the word "viral" was usually associated with the spread of viruses. It might as well have been, such was the infectious impact of the "wooden" label. In fact, it would not be an exaggeration to say that the word, for better or worse, has remained closely associated with Goh since. Even Goh himself admitted his memory of the event has been reduced to that one comment. "All I remember was 'wooden.' The rest I cannot remember," he said candidly.

But he refused to let it break him. "Just take it one more time. I did not fall the first time. What is one more time?" he said. "It was not the 'wooden' part that disturbed me because I knew my own communicative abilities — that was not a problem. The part that upset me was to see a psychiatrist because that could be thoroughly misunderstood by people. So, what else could you do? Had I gone out to explain why I would not see a psychiatrist, then of course, I had to see one. People would laugh at you. So, I just shrugged it off." It upset others in the Cabinet too, such as Ahmad. "I was infuriated and upset when I heard the advice he had given to Goh Chok Tong. Psychiatrist? See a psychiatrist to loosen up?" he said, his voice raised. "To me, a psychiatrist is a medical practitioner specialising in the diagnosis and treatment of mental illnesses. Is nervousness when facing a crowd a mental illness?"

For Goh, a deep trust in Lee helped him cope during that dark month of August 1988. "He did not do this to destroy me — I was not his political opponent. If I were his political opponent and he wanted to destroy me and put somebody of his choice up, like his son, then that would be different," he said. "It was not behind the back sort of stabbing. It was very open, so you did not get angry with that."

Instead, the "humiliation" — Goh's word — acted ironically as a release valve of sorts in the unnatural politician. Having been slammed so openly by his leader and mentor, it was as if he had hit rock bottom in his political career and could go no lower. Goh turned the personal crisis into a turning point to embrace himself for who he was, and urged Singaporeans to do the same. After the NUS forum, he said in public: "Do not be too upset or confused by PM's remarks about me. Take me for what I am. There is not going to be any change in leadership after the Prime Minister has eventually relinquished his position. The second-generation leaders had decided and that's that!"

He redoubled his efforts to improve communication, stepping up his training with voice and speech coach Sue Greenwood. "She was my 'psychiatrist'," he joked. The British trainer, who also worked with other Cabinet ministers, taught him breathing technique whilst he lay on the floor (to develop his capacity to project his voice); to speak while walking and kicking a pillow at the end of each sentence (to force him to expel all his breath at the end of each thought, replicating punctuation); and even to interpret various passages from literature (to improve his connection with what he was saying). Gradually, it worked, and he began to feel the difference. "He said to me one day, 'In the past, I was just saying words. Now I know I have to put my feelings into them. My ear is better. I know how to listen with discrimination'," Greenwood recalled.

Goh's self-belief shot up, and now that Lee's criticisms were out in the open, he embraced it with good humour — one of his key strengths. He said in 1988: "Better for the public to know me for what I am than to expect great oratory out of me! I am not President Reagan. I am not good at one-liners. Neither am I Prime Minister Lee. I am not good at making three-hour-long speeches." By September 1988, even Lee liked the new and more relaxed Goh. He said during an election rally: "I said: 'Speak up! Be yourself if you are angry, say so!' The result? He's no longer inhibited. He can talk about his inability to react naturally with crowds and in the process, has come through."

Lee urged Singaporeans to support Goh: "I think I have helped and you should help. Laugh with him, laugh against him, but cheer him on." They did, said S. Puhaindran. "What the old man said got Goh a lot of sympathy from the people. They wanted him to succeed and prove Lee wrong." By April 1989, observers had discerned a slightly different man. "Today, he enjoys a vastly different image," wrote *Asia Magazine*. "He is the regular Mr Nice Guy, the common man who mingles with the masses, stops to kiss babies, plays billiards with the lads. He smiles an affable smile and has a warming home-spun style of speaking. The wooden face, the inarticulate, stiff style are yesterday's man."

Looking back, Goh said that episode freed him from the demands and desire, both from within and without, to be like Lee. After it, "there was a certain confidence that I would do things my own way," he said. "Before, there was some pressure that to be a leader, you must be like Lee Kuan Yew. So, by 1990, I said no, I would do things my own way. I would communicate in my own ways." It worked, said Chan Heng Chee. "Goh Chok Tong spoke the Singapore English and he was not a slick speaker," she said. "But in a sense, it became a bit endearing to the population. He is like us — 'Hey, I talk like that too'."

Goh's confidence continued unabated even after the rally, when Lee confirmed Goh's suspicions that he was not ready to step down. "After the rally, one day when we had lunch, he told me he did not think I was ready to take over yet and asked if it would be all right if he carried on for two more years," said Goh, revealing for the first time that it was Lee who wanted to stay on. "And I said, of course, you carry on. So, he carried on for two more years."

Q: As you approached 1990, what were your thoughts on what kind of leader you would like to be?

A: The first thing you would ask yourself and your colleagues would ask you is whether you stood for change or continuity. That was also the question Lee Kuan Yew asked me. And he asked me because I was thinking of, at that time, to move into the Istana Villa and making it my office.[52] It was very clear in my mind that I was not going to move Lee Kuan Yew out of his room.

---

[52] The Istana Villa is a small standalone structure, separate from main building in the Istana compound where the Prime Minister and the President work. The Villa is closer to the Orchard Road entrance of the Istana.

Q: Why?

A: Because too much of him was in there. I did not want to take over the room. I mean, it is not a joke, but to me, the room would smell of Lee Kuan Yew. Everything there would have his spirit. You could not operate. Also, out of respect for him, he should stay there; it had been so many years. But it is the thought that you were stepping into something which was his — it was like going into his home to run the family of Singapore — it was very difficult. So, I was thinking of moving the Prime Minister's office out. I was thinking that I could go to the Villa. I quite liked the idea of a small Prime Minister's office (PMO) in a villa instead of at the Istana main building.

During Lee Kuan Yew's time, the staff strength was very small; and my time, it was very small. There was just myself, a PPS, a Press Secretary who was based in MCI, and two secretaries.[53] That was all my staff. That was also the staff for Lee Kuan Yew. That was Singapore's 'White House'. The Cabinet secretaries are not part of your inner staff. They handle Cabinet papers and they are more administrators. The Singapore system is that the PM would deal directly with the ministers and ministries. So, if I had to do something on economy, I would go through the minister and the minister has the whole ministry. So, it is a very lean PMO. Of course, CPIB and a few other places come under

---

[53] PPS refers to Principal Private Secretary, the key aide to the Prime Minister. MCI refers to the Ministry of Communications and Information.

PMO — that is different.[54] Election's Office — that is different. But the Istana staff was very small. So, this was all I had and I was thinking it would be very nice to go to the Istana Villa. It would be a very cosy kind of a PM's office.

So, I gave LKY my view and I told him continuity in policies. He advised that if I was for continuity, then do not move out. If I moved out to a new place, I was signalling change. And I would be distancing myself from the old regime. He said he wanted me to take over his room, it is the PM's room. I said no, I did not want to take over.

Q: *If you had taken over his office, where would he have gone?*

A: In other countries, that was their problem, not the PM's problem. You are out, you are out in the streets. John Major and Tony Blair — they are out, going all over the place.[55] That is the system. Ours works out differently and very well now; there is a certain system in looking after the former PM. At that point, there was no experience. So, I said, stay where you are. Seeing that I would not change my mind, Lee Kuan Yew told me that there was a place available above his office. It was his dining room. The whole floor was empty and only a little corner was marked out to be his dining room. The place was quite big and I could use it. I asked him where he would then have his lunch. He said that there was no problem — he created a small room on a different

---

[54] CPIB refers to the Corrupt Practices Investigation Bureau.
[55] John Major and Tony Blair are former prime ministers of the United Kingdom.

level from his office to be his lunch room. We are all very practical; we are not looking for grand things. So, the third floor was renovated to be my office. I decided on the carpet and picked the furniture.

Q: And you were comfortable with this arrangement to be literally above him?

A: Yes, I was above him. No, that is a joke. Let me share another story with you. I had to decide on the furnishings. I was wondering if I should have a soft sofa or a hard one? His was hard. He prided himself — wooden frame, very thin cushions. So, I had to decide. Do I show frugality by following his example or do I upgrade? I went for a soft sofa. I chose that because I thought it was 1990, and if I was receiving visitors, I did not have to impress them like Lee Kuan Yew about how frugal we were.

He came to have a look at my place and he said it was very good. Then, somebody told him he had better upgrade his room. So, he asked my permission to use my room while his was being refurbished. My room was ready a few months before I became PM. So, I said yes, carry on. So, he was the first PM to use this room, not me! He was the first to occupy it and I succeeded him in my new office. It turned out to be very comical. Later, I went into his room after it was renovated. And no more wooden sofa with thin cushions. He had also changed to a soft sofa!

Q: *How were you able to have such a relationship with him, especially after how he criticised you publicly?*

A: We were quite frank with each other. I trusted him. I never doubted his honesty, motive and integrity. I never doubted that he wanted me to succeed. If anything, he was exasperated with my lack of public communicative skills. And if he wanted Lee Hsien Loong to be in charge, he would have told me. That was why I could work with him. I came to the conclusion early that he did not want the son to take over from him, and he was looking for somebody other than Loong. That was quite clear. The public conclusion was that he wanted me as a seat warmer. But I knew him and I went in knowing I was not to be a seat warmer and I was to be in charge for as long as I could. In other words, he was looking for a real successor outside his family.

Q: *How did you know that you were not a seat warmer?*

A: It was interaction and confidence in him. If I suspected that he was just putting me to be a seat warmer for his son, and just for two, three years, what is the point? Then I would have said 'Let us find a way for Lee Hsien Loong to take over from you.' There was no need to have me. There was no point. But I never worried about the seat warmer joke. In my heart, I knew that Lee Kuan Yew never meant for me to be a seat warmer. Politicians must have some thick skin and be able to laugh it off because in my view, that is not what Lee Kuan Yew regarded me as. You must have self-respect. If Lee Kuan Yew used me for his own purpose, then what is the point for me? History would laugh at you, isn't it? I had the self-confidence. I was prepared to do the job and I knew he was honest with me, with my strengths and weaknesses.

Q: But did it cross your mind that after you become the PM, he could remove you any time?

A: In the first year.

Q: Why only in the first year?

A: It was because he was still the secretary-general of the PAP.[56] He told me that normally it is the secretary-general who becomes the Prime Minister. I am handing over to you, but would it be all right if he stayed on as secretary-general? So, what does that tell you? He was not sure if I might change or could succeed. Many people change after becoming Prime Minister — you remove all the old guards and have your own team. Power could cause a person to change. So, he asked me if it was all right if he carried on as secretary-general. So, you know my style, and I said yes. In other words, he had the right, as secretary-general of PAP, to remove me. It was understood. He could decide to kick me out of the party. Once I am out of the party, I would lose my seat. That was how I would be removed.

But I wasn't insecure about him staying on as secretary-general. I had self-confidence. I mean, in the end, he would step

---

[56] Lee Kuan Yew handed over the premiership to Goh Chok Tong in November 1990. But he remained as the secretary-general of the PAP until 1992.

down. If I said no to him and he went out of the party, he might be a Mahathir or do a Mahathir.[57] Look at what Mahathir has managed to do, even at 92! LKY would be the same if he felt that something was wrong with the country. So, if he remained in the party, we could discuss, we trusted one another and we sorted out any doubts. The biggest compliment was in 2004 when I told him I wanted to step down and he asked why, there was no hurry. So, I explained to him that I was not old but my deputy, Hsien Loong, was getting old. Then he understood.

Anyway, from his point of view, it was not my character which he was concerned about. I think he was not sure if I could do the job. In other words, the doubt over my ability to win elections. It is not governing. The key is, always, can you win elections? That is the same question I asked of the fourth-generation leaders now. They can govern, but can they win elections? That is the question. Can you mobilise and will people follow you?

Q: *And even when he said some very nasty things, you put it all aside because you absolutely believed in his larger purpose?*

A: That is correct. It was not personal. He was not out to humiliate me for personal reasons, even though I felt humiliated.

---

[57] Mahathir Mohamad is the fourth and seventh Prime Minister of Malaysia who became a vocal critic of his former party, United Malays National Organisation (UMNO), after retirement. In 2018, he led an opposition coalition to unseat UMNO.

Q: *Some people may not agree with your analysis and still believe that he may have some other purpose. But for you, you believed it and therefore you behaved in a certain way and it worked?*

A: That is correct. So, I may have been naïve. People think I have been naïve and used by him; that I was his stooge and I did not even know I was his stooge. People would come to that conclusion that I was stupid. I was indeed flexible, but I was not a stooge. Ours was a close interaction, the regular lunches, and he spoke frankly. In a sense, he moulded me and because I knew him and his purpose, I trusted him, and he learnt not to force me to be someone I'm not.

My team worked very well and the main thing was that the three of us — Lee Kuan Yew, myself and Lee Hsien Loong — we worked very well. We never doubted each other's intentions. Hsien Loong, I never doubted. He was never impatient. If he was impatient in taking over, my attitude would have been very different: 'You are ambitious and you want the job and you are impatient.' In his case, he wanted the job but he was not impatient. He was prepared to support me all the way. And the father, towards the end, was very happy that the arrangement was working and I was doing well.

Q: I am sure you have heard of the saying: Father, Son and the Holy Goh. What do you think of it?

A: I am not a Christian, so I have only a rough idea of what it means. To me, the three work as one — Father, Son and Holy Goh — and the three work together positively.

Q: But the more serious question is, with father and son in your Cabinet, did you think about how it would be?

A: No. Once you are in the Cabinet, there is no father-and-son thing because Hsien Loong would also have to convince the other Cabinet ministers that he was his own man. And that is very important. At times, he disagreed with the father. And most of the time, he would be on my side because we would discuss issues at our pre-Cabinet and various meetings, so he would know my thinking. And then, the father would raise something and Hsien Loong would state his view or, sometimes, he would state our views. So, each of us was our own man.

Q: Speaking of Cabinet, when you became PM, you chose Ong Teng Cheong and Lee Hsien Loong as your Deputy Prime Ministers. Why did you select them?

A: I did think of Tony Tan. But I wanted to have a complement and that complement was Teng Cheong — he was Chinese-educated. He was able, reliable and trustworthy. And on the Chinese part, he could help me to rally the ground. Tony Tan was more like myself. Initially, I decided on only one DPM — Teng Cheong. Lee Kuan Yew wanted to know my choice.

Q: *What was Lee Kuan Yew's reaction?*

A: His reaction was not very good. He asked why Ong Teng Cheong. He did not say, why not Lee Hsien Loong. But from the way he asked, I could sense it, that he was thinking of the future and the future lay with Lee Hsien Loong, not with Ong Teng Cheong. Lee Kuan Yew was worried about the future. His thinking was that Hsien Loong had the potential to be the Prime Minister. If something happened to me and Teng Cheong would take over, future political succession would be disrupted.

I am not saying he wanted to put Hsien Loong there because Hsien Loong was his son, but he wanted to put Hsien Loong there because he thought this was a better man. So, he asked why Teng Cheong and I gave the reasons. Later, I came to the conclusion that, for myself, I should have two DPMs. I wanted and needed Teng Cheong more than Hsien Loong to engage the Chinese ground. But why not have Hsien Loong as DPM as well? This was for the future and you signalled that Hsien Loong had the potential to take over.

Q: *When you say signal, it was to Lee Kuan Yew?*

A: No. It was to the public. It was in my interest and the country's interest. In my interest, I wanted Ong Teng Cheong. In the country's interest, I put Hsien Loong. But of course, I spoke to

Teng Cheong that for the future, Hsien Loong is the one in my team who had the potential to take over. So, if I were to go on leave, I would appoint Lee Hsien Loong as the acting PM.

Q: But Lee Kuan Yew did not mention Lee Hsien Loong? So, he said enough for you to know what he was thinking?

A: He did. But I never came to the conclusion that he wanted to place the son there because Hsien Loong was his son. If that was the conclusion, I would not have gone ahead. I am against dynastic politics. But if Hsien Loong was the best man for the future, we should not cut him off just because he was the son of Lee Kuan Yew.

Q: How did Lee Kuan Yew tell you that he was ready to hand over to you?

A: I was quite happy he was doing the job of PM. He was still young and I was in no hurry. But in early 1990, over lunch, he told me that I should take over now. I was to pick a date and take over. So, the man was true to his words that he would hand over. He could not do so at 65 as he felt I was not ready. In 1990, he just said I was to take over. So, I said yes. That was all. That was how transition took place in Singapore. Elsewhere, they fought and so on.

He added that he thought he should stay on in Cabinet. Was it because he wanted to play a role or was he not fully confident in me? I think he was not fully confident. Indeed, he would not be immediately confident in anyone taking over from him. He wanted to guide and help; not to direct or control.

Q: *When he said he should stay on in Cabinet, did that come as a surprise to you?*

A: Not really. I was quite happy. It was better to have Lee Kuan Yew inside than outside! Remember his remark about rising from the grave if things went wrong? If things went wrong, would he have kept quiet? Would he have said that this is a new PM, he would watch and he would not interfere right away? In 1988, I was very relieved he was going to carry on for two more years. By 1990, I was ready. In my heart, I was ready.

On October 16, 1990, at a press conference at the Singapore airport before leaving for Hong Kong, Goh announced he would take over from Lee on November 28. "I did not consult any astrologer," he quipped. In typical pragmatic fashion, he explained that he chose the date because it was a Wednesday and he wanted a mid-week swearing in so that the new Cabinet could put in some work that week. It was independent Singapore's first leadership transition, and yet, it was almost just another day in the life of Goh and Singaporeans in general. "It was a non-event because Lee Kuan Yew had always wanted elections to be a non-event," he said. "People expected PAP to win and we win. The next day, we just work. So, to me, the changeover should be a non-event. I had been prepared for quite many years; he would be around in Cabinet and he was not kicked out by me and there was no revolution. What was there to celebrate?"

But, he acknowledged, Singapore "had to mark the occasion." Since he wanted to emphasise continuity over change, Lee suggested to Goh to hold the event at City Hall, where Lee was sworn in as Prime Minister in 1959. "I went to have a look at the place. It was nice and I said, yes, this place could be the venue. So, we settled for City Hall," said Goh. "That was the comfort between us. He was guiding me because I never had a handover before in my life."

On November 27, 1990, Goh was formally appointed Prime Minister by then President Wee Kim Wee at the Istana. In a folder which Goh submitted to Wee, he listed the details of the first Goh Cabinet. Lee

Kuan Yew would be Senior Minister, while two Deputy Prime Ministers were appointed — Ong Teng Cheong and Lee Hsien Loong. The only new member of the Cabinet was George Yeo, who would helm a new Ministry of Information and the Arts.

A day later, Goh was sworn in at City Hall, televised live. He had neither a new suit tailored, nor wore a new shirt. The crowd included politicians, civil servants, grassroots leaders, unionists and diplomats from mainly ASEAN countries. "It was a smallish event," said Goh. A crowd gathered outside City Hall, mostly made up of his supporters from Marine Parade. When he learnt that they were there, he walked out of the building and waved to a cheering crowd. Lee Kuan Yew followed behind, along with the rest of Goh's new Cabinet. And in an iconic photograph snapped of the historic moment, Lee was shown in the background for the first time in decades, as Goh strode to the fore. The symbolism was not lost on Goh. "I've got the photograph at home," he shared.

And that was it. Goh, ever the unromantic when it comes to politics, went home right after the event. There was no party, no celebration, no champagne. "It was a formal event. We did not do things for the TV," he said. "As I have said, I was not wanting this job and looking for the day I would be Prime Minister. It is just another milestone, part of a continuum of taking over from Lee Kuan Yew. And he was still very vigorous, at 67. The most powerful man had decided to plan for this succession and this was our duty, my duty and my group's duty, to take over and make sure that Singapore continues. There was the sense of responsibility. This was our succession. That was all."

The change held a significance far beyond its ceremonial simplicity. To Lee Hsien Loong, it signalled the country's sustainability. "It means that you are going to make a system that should work beyond the career and lifetime of one man," he said. "And you must have this ethos that it is your responsibility to look after the place and to look after it so as to be able to hand on to somebody else in good time to take over from you and carry the job beyond your working life. And it is possible for this to work."

The people were prepared for a leader after Lee, said both the second-generation leaders and observers. "People were ready to have a leader who was not Lee Kuan Yew," said Dhanabalan. "Chok Tong tapped that desire among the electorate and he was very successful in winning over support." Political commentator Cherian George, writing in *Singapore: The Air-Conditioned Nation*, believed that "Goh was the ideal PAP leader for the times." He said: "People sensed that when he said he wanted to make Singapore a more forgiving, second-chance society, he meant it, for surely he knew how it felt to be held up to impossibly high perfectionist standards."

On the eve of taking over, it was a sense of the ground which Goh shared too. "People wanted a change," he said. "Lee Kuan Yew was there for a long time and people wanted a change. And people knew that I was not Lee Kuan Yew and they accepted me. In fact, they wanted a more ordinary kind of prime minister. A more human one." He may not have wanted this job in the first place. He may not have been Lee's chosen one. Politics may not have been his choice. But Singapore was about to enter a new, and golden, age with him in charge. The tall man had pulled off the tall order.

> I did not choose politics,
> but I chose to serve my country.

Afterword by
Goh Chok Tong

L ooking back on seven decades of my life is not as easy as looking into a telescope. I cannot see the entire picture clearly. Peh Shing Huei did the research and used his telescope to focus on what he thinks will interest the readers. The book is not to benefit me. I have no need for it. It is about Singapore's transition from Lee Kuan Yew to the next generation, with me as the protagonist.

I answered Peh's questions directly and as clearly as I could recall. What I could recount best were not the details but the emotions and thinking behind certain decisions.

Singapore is an improbable country. Lee Kuan Yew and his generation fought for its independence. It was a gripping tale of struggle, sacrifice and survival.

Mine was an unlikely and unexpected political journey. My generation had to keep Singapore going. This seemingly mundane mission did not fire the imagination. Few appreciated the need for succession planning and the enormity of the task.

But some of us did, after we were helicoptered into politics. We understood the need to discharge our responsibility to future generations. Being improbable politicians, we "struggled, sacrificed and survived" when thrown into the political pit. We built on the foundation laid by the first generation.

Singapore is now a successful, rich little country. Five decades of steady growth, interspersed only with a few quickly solved crises, had lulled Singaporeans into believing that growth, prosperity, stability, social harmony, peace and security are par for the course. If we are not careful, we can become victims of our own success. As the Chinese saying warns, "Wealth does not last beyond three generations" (富不过三代).

The world is changing quickly and becoming more divisive and complex. So is Singapore.

I hope my story will inspire more Singaporeans to come forward to serve the country.

Chapter 1, The Coup

My great-grandmother, grandfather and father died within a few years of each other. I can remember the crying and wailing, especially that of my grandmother. But I cannot picture my great-grandmother and grandfather. I also cannot recount the time spent with my father, save for a trip with him to visit his friend in Chinatown.

My mother was close to her mother and siblings. She visited them during the school holidays in Kluang and Batu Pahat, and later in Singapore. I went along. I got to know my maternal uncles and aunts, and cousins around my age.

I appreciate the extended family ties. As the eldest of my generation, I host an annual Chinese New Year gathering to exchange greetings and encourage the younger generation to continue with these family ties. But it is not easy. The Goh and Quah extended families now number more than 100 on each side. The younger generation of Gohs and Quahs do not know each other well.

When I visited my ancestral village in Yongchun after stepping down as Prime Minister, I could feel the ancestral tug at my emotion. I can trace my family roots back 17 generations. They produced a few scholars, government officials and generals. It was a farming community, growing mandarin oranges. Yongchun oranges are now imported into Singapore.

I was interested in where my ancestors came from, partly because of the stories my grandmother told me. Shu Er, eight years older than me, shed additional light on my roots and childhood in her interview for this book. She was a good student but could not proceed to secondary school because her family could not afford it.

My interest also came from growing up with traditional religions, practising ancestral worship. I visited my elders' graves during *Qingming*[58] for tomb-sweeping. You remember where you came from when you worship them.

---

[58] *Qingming* is a Chinese festival, during which Chinese families visit their ancestors' tombs to clean the gravesites, pray, and make ritual offerings.

My children and grandchildren are different. They worship God. I hope this chapter will arouse their interest to learn about their ancestors.

Chapter 2, The Corporate Bureaucrat

My formative years in the civil service shaped my values and attitudes.

I had the good fortune to work under two of the best minds in government: Dr Goh Keng Swee and J. Y. M. Pillay.

Goh Keng Swee, Minister for Finance, was as frugal with government expenses as he was with his own. I gathered statistics for his Budget speeches. He told me with a wry smile that whenever a minister stepped into his room, he would say "no," even before the minister spoke. He knew the purpose. When the minister asked for an increase in his ministry's budget, Goh Keng Swee would still say "no." Only when the minister persisted would he then listen.

Today, there is constant pressure to spend more, and even to dip into our reserves. The public appetite for spending is insatiable. Like Goh Keng Swee, our Finance Ministers must be disciplined and say "no" unless a strong case is built. We should take a long view in our budgeting.

Unfortunately, I had on one occasion disappointed Goh Keng Swee. Up to today, I feel bad about it. He had arranged for me to work in the World Bank for three years soon after my return from Williams College. He wanted me to gain experience and build contacts so that Singapore could borrow money from the Bank!

I had to turn it down because my wife had just delivered a pair of twins. It was financially and logistically impossible for us to cope in Washington. Goh Keng Swee was quietly furious.

But he did not write me off. Soon, I headed a team of young officers in the Economics Division. Years later, when I became the Minister for Defence, he gave me a crash course on what I had to learn and do.

J. Y. M. Pillay, who was my superior in the Economic Planning Unit (EPU), set the course for my future. He got me to Williams College to study Development Economics. Upon my return, Lee Kuan Yew wanted me to be his Principal Private Secretary. Pillay muttered to me, "I did not send you to Williams to be PPS of PM." I stayed back in the EPU.

Later, at my request, he seconded me to NOL. The company was losing money. As the Permanent Secretary in charge, he joined the board to put things right. After the Pakistani Managing Director resigned, the board appointed me and the Executive Director as Joint Managing Directors. Though two heads are usually better than one, this joint arrangement did not work out. I became the sole Managing Director.

Goh Keng Swee and Joe Pillay personified the values, ethos and innovativeness of our pioneer generation of ministers and civil servants. They created value out of almost nothing — SAF, Jurong industrial estate, Bird Park, SIA, DBS and NOL are just a few examples.

They took an interest in their staff and went out of their way to develop them.

Chapter 3, "Marine Palade"

Looking back, it seemed easy for an ex-civil servant with some experience in the business world to work the ground as a Member of Parliament (MP). The PAP brand equity was strong. Lives of all Singaporeans were getting better as strong economic growth lifted all boats. The people were welcoming.

Marine Parade was a new constituency. It had no party branch or grassroots network. My Elections Agent was NOL's administration manager.

I drew on my experience in NOL to organise the branch and community network. Very quickly, many residents, market stallholders and supporters stepped forward to help.

I had to assess people I had not met before. I appointed Tan Kin Lian and S. Puhaindran to key positions. Both were effective organisers. Kin Lian later upgraded to a private home outside Marine Parade, and left the party branch. Puhaindran remains in Marine Parade, and still helps out.

Former civil servants have an advantage in politics. They know how government works, its philosophy and values. They know some ministers and many former colleagues. Values-wise, they are generally not chasing fortunes.

They make good office holders. Yet, too much of a good thing is bad. If good, able people from the corporate world avoid being "enlisted" into politics, Cabinet will increasingly lack diverse talents and thinking.

Why do high-flyers in the private sector shun politics? Changes in lifestyle, loss of privacy, lack of personal freedom, family considerations and the heavy responsibility of a Minister are the main factors. The sizeable loss in income is also a factor. We are also victims of our own success. When the country is doing well, successful Singaporeans would rather pursue personal aspirations and ideals than be scrutinised, and even vilified, in politics. Social media and fake news only make things worse.

I hope highly able Singaporeans would not wait till the aircraft engine is sputtering before deciding to come on board to fix it.

If the country fails to assemble the best team to serve, Singapore will slide into mediocrity. Getting the best to serve Singapore goes beyond the interest of the People's Action Party. It is our common interest. It is our responsibility.

Chapter 4, The Magnificent Seven

The methodical process of political succession is unique to Singapore.

Technocrats like Ong Teng Cheong, S. Dhanabalan, Lim Chee Onn, Tony Tan and myself, were not natural politicians. Unprepared but not reluctant. No initial fire in the bellies but the ember grew over time. We were no less passionate in playing our part in Singapore's transition to a new phase.

National and global circumstances have changed dramatically. A different batch of leaders more attuned to the young and the new domestic and world order is needed to take Singapore forward.

Lee Kuan Yew stepped down as Prime Minister at 67. I retired at 63. Prime Minister Lee Hsien Loong said that he would like the 4G team to take over before he crosses 70.

The careful and systematic preparation of the 4G team and its predecessors reflects how challenging it is to ensure a smooth handover. Factionalism, vested interests, strife, dysfunction and discontinuity are more often the reality in political succession.

We must avoid a situation where a former Prime Minister has to come back and save his country at the age of 92!

Chapter 5, Anson

The unexpected loss of Anson broke PAP's aura of invincibility. It brought home the reality of electoral politics. No matter how well we had governed, current livelihood issues on the ground will determine the local results.

It was instructive to watch how Lee Kuan Yew responded to the loss. He summoned the MPs, analysed the reasons for the loss, discussed and decided on the next steps to avoid future losses. He shored up confidence among his troops, not chopped heads. Fortunately. It would have been my head!

The knee-jerk reaction to the loss of a seat is to "punish" the opposition ward so that other wards would not follow suit. Slaughter the rooster to scare the monkey (杀鸡吓猴). But the reality is that Singapore is edging towards a vested-interest, liberal democracy. The electorate wants fair play and contestability on the ground.

Will the Singapore model of stable democracy and planned political succession endure? Will the current situation of a dominant party and a significant opposition voice in Parliament be the way forward? Or will Singapore experiment with a musical chair government?

Politics everywhere has become more transactional. It seems to be "ask not what you can do for your country, ask what your country can do for you," turning President Kennedy's famous quote on its head.

Democracy is faltering in many countries. How will ours continue to work?

Chapter 6, Reformer of Health

I did not set out to be a Reformer of Health as Chapter 6 might suggest. I had no ideological mission to shift healthcare from a subsidised socialist model to a market-based system. I only brought with me my economic training, corporate diagnostic experience, and plain common sense.

I found out there was a "them and us" attitude. The doctors in the private sector were not regarded as part of the national health system and those who had left the public sector hospitals were treated at an arm's length. I set out to put that right. I held several meetings involving both public and private healthcare practitioners to build up understanding, trust and share the common responsibility of looking after the health of Singaporeans.

Healthcare is a barometer of a country's governance and its well-being. Our infant mortality rate is amongst the lowest in the world. Our people live longer than most. The current emphasis on preventive healthcare is surely meant to make us live even longer and healthier.

But fast forward, the national expenditure on healthcare will balloon. If each person lives longer by just three years, collectively, there will be more than 10 million man-years to care for!

Will Singaporeans be of healthy mind and body throughout their lives? Or will we limp along the way, handicapped by debilitating illnesses and weighed down by medical bills?

The government has introduced universal health insurance and long-term care insurance in MediShield Life and CareShield Life. It is right to provide this safety net but we need to beware the buffet syndrome, both from medical providers and patients.

Watch the Health Ministry's budget like you should your waistline.

Chapter 7, Striker Takes Charge

Leadership succession in Singapore is not dynastic. It is not a dog-fight. It is not a jerky changing of the gears. It is based on identifying

Singaporeans who have the potential and to lead and to serve their fellow Singaporeans.

A leader must have the ability of getting his Ministers and MPs to work together. He is more than just an efficient manager or Party Whip. He has to deal with a strong and competent Cabinet and independent-minded MPs. And he has to unite the people with their diverse views. A shared mission is absolutely necessary. So is trust.

When I became Prime Minister, I mulled over who I should appoint as my deputy.

I decided to appoint Loong as 1DPM and Teng Cheong as 2DPM. Teng Cheong was five years my senior. Loong, being 11 years younger, would be more in touch with the younger generation.

Teng Cheong selflessly endorsed my decision. He, too, looked towards the future.

Loong gave me his full support. He was not impatient to become PM. He must be the longest PM-in-waiting. No British or Australian DPM would wait 14 years!

How did I succeed as a "Goh-between"? It was because father and son did not "sandwich" me.

Fourteen years later, I surprised Lee Kuan Yew when I intimated that it was time for me to hand over the position to Loong. I was at my political peak. He said that I was doing well and should carry on. That was a pat on the back.

I am happy I could choose my time to step down and hand over Singapore in good working order.

Chapter 8, From Nanny to Buddy

Lee Kuan Yew wanted me to govern Singapore with a strong, firm hand, instilling fear into opponents, dissidents and troublemakers.

By 1990, Singaporeans had been more exposed to the concept of democracy as practised in the West. More were English-educated. More had gone to polytechnics or universities. We were Asians but increasingly westernised. The Confucian tradition in which children were not allowed to talk back to their father has weakened.

I wanted a kinder and gentler society. I believed that a consultative, participative democracy would release the energy to drive Singapore to its next phase. I wanted all Singaporeans to play a part. I wanted them to be stakeholders in shaping Singapore's future with the government.

Lee Kuan Yew was initially disdainful of my consultative style. He thought it wasted time. But it worked for me, and Singapore. I stayed true to my pledge that I would walk in my own pair of shoes, not his.

"Kinder and gentler" also led to the tilt towards a more liberal film censorship rating system. However, while the younger, English-educated Singaporeans supported this tilt, the conservative segments, particularly the non-English educated, were uncomfortable.

As an aside, Lee Kuan Yew was more liberal than we think. Or more practical. When the tourism sector was down, he floated the idea of allowing a nudist colony in Sentosa or an offshore island to bring them in! The younger Ministers vetoed him.

Society is not frozen in time. Each successive generation of leaders must express their own and Singaporeans' ideals for Singapore.

Find your own style of government and ways to gain the people's trust.

Chapter 9, Mr Porcupine

I am not a prickly person. But Chapter 9 characterises me as a porcupine. I suppose Peh has to write to catch eyeballs.

He sees me through his journalistic lenses and relies on confidential materials provided by me and publicly-available resources. For this chapter, I had to refresh my memory in order to provide the background and context to the security risks posed by the Marxist group through its link with the Malayan Communist Party.

I am aware that some people were not fully convinced of a conspiracy to subvert Singapore. They believed many of the people arrested were "do-gooders." Dhanabalan was one of them.

Dhanabalan was in fact the first minister to comment on the arrests of the Marxist group when he spoke to the Foreign Correspondents Association in June 1987. Whatever his reservations, the Cabinet had decided and he was bound by collective responsibility.

Nevertheless, I knew the burden he carried. He decided to leave my Cabinet. Lee Kuan Yew was angry that he should abandon me, having chosen me to be Prime Minister. I let Dhana go because I knew that he could not live easily with his conscience.

Dhana did not rock the boat. He never publicly expressed his reservation on the Marxist arrests. To ease the burden which he quietly bore, I decided to reveal his disquiet over the Marxist arrests in *Men In White*. I also asked Peh to record his position in this book. Dhana played a big part in my Cabinet. He was a strong, supportive 2G member. I should free him of the burden of collective responsibility in the Marxist arrests.

This Marxist event brings me back to my innocent brush with the Special Branch — ISD's predecessor — in my Cambridge 'O' Level year in Pasir Panjang. In the dead of night, I was awakened by the incessant barking of dogs and heavy footsteps outside the house. Then a loud knock on my door. I opened it and saw many men outside. They were from the dreaded Special Branch. They asked for my Identity Card, took a look and returned it. I was not the one they were looking for.

A few months later, a few Special Branch men returned, this time in broad daylight. They searched my study table, and took away a few Chinese books which belonged to my left-leaning uncle, Kah Peck. I feared for him.

I learnt later from the newspaper that they had found their man. He was a Malayan relative of the Lim family, co-tenant of the house. He had visited the Lims a couple of times. After his release a few years later, I met him when he came to the house. He was an earnest, friendly young man.

Communism had posed a serious threat to Malaya and Singapore since 1948. Though only 14, I followed with deep interest *The Straits Times* reports on the Baling Talks in 1955 between Chin Peng, the MCP leader, Tunku Abdul Rahman, Chief Minister of Malaya and David

Marshall, Chief Minister of Singapore. There was great excitement when Chin Peng emerged from the jungle.

The then Singapore Government saw communism as a serious threat to the security of the country. It made hundreds of arrests. In October 1956 alone, over 200 people were arrested in connection with mass rioting instigated by MCP-penetrated organisations. Further arrests were made in 1958. You can say that I had been sensitised early to the potential security threat posed by MCP.

The internal security risks to Singapore now do not come from the communists but radicalised Islamic extremists who are prepared to kill and use violent means to attain their goals. While the new threat is clear, identifying the extremists requires good detective work.

Our security agencies do not sleep, so that we can. Thank goodness for their vigilance.

Chapter 10, This is Me

It feels strange to read your own biography. A person has three selves: who he thinks he is; how others see him; and who he really is. I have not faked good in the interviews with Peh. He has researched the literature on me. He has interviewed my childhood friends, colleagues and comrades. What he has written seems to be who I am.

The book should capture my unexpected journey to become Singapore's second Prime Minister, and my trials and missteps along the way. I soldiered on, even in the midst of criticism, because I could not afford to fail. It was not the humiliation of personal failure which I feared but the failure of planned political succession and its consequences on Singapore.

So really, this story is about Singapore's transition from the Lee Kuan Yew era. I was merely the chief protagonist.

The book has made the governing of Singapore appear simple, mainly because I am looking back with satisfaction, and not regret.

I did not choose politics, but I chose to serve my country.

Acknowledgements

Writing a biography of a Prime Minister should be daunting, stressful and challenging. Or so I was told. In truth, it was fun, enjoyable and I lost count of the number of times I laughed out loud in the Istana. I'm most thankful to Emeritus Senior Minister Goh Chok Tong for his patience and willingness to share, even when asked to recall events from decades back. He was not irritated with the hard, and at times intentionally pointed, questions. Instead, he chose to respond with charm and a self-deprecating humour which I discovered only when I began on this process as his biographer. I can't wait to start on Volume 2.

It is usually lonely when writing, but I never felt alone in the production of this book. Marine Parade grassroots leaders Ng Hock Lye, Patrick Ng, Chua Ee Chek, Kok Pak Chow, and Tan Jack Thian offered generous advice. Pak Chow in particular was consistently forthright with his feedback, and I am appreciative of his honesty and dedication. ESM Goh's aides, press secretary Heng Aik Yeow and special assistant Bernard Toh, connected me to the many whom we interviewed, dug out almost archaic information and were indefatigable in their support. I'm also grateful to Chan Heng Chee, Tan Yong Soon, Tan Tee How and Shashi Jayakumar for reviewing an early draft; their comments led to a stronger final product.

During our search for old photos, it was particularly tricky to locate those from the NOL days. Without the National Library Board's Sabitri Devi, Lee Mei Chen and Timothy Pwee, we would not have made a breakthrough. Thank you to shipping line APL for granting us permission to use those photos. I would like to also thank Vanessa Too from the Ministry of Communications and Information for her help in sourcing for photos.

I had the good fortune of working with my former boss Han Fook Kwang from *The Straits Times* again, allowing me and my team to benefit immensely from his institutional knowledge of Singapore politics, history and government. His critique of my drafts was what I have come to expect of him: sharp but always kind and gentle.

My publisher World Scientific was unstinting in their backing and passion for this project. I do not recall an instance when they said no to my requests and suggestions. Such ease in the working relationship between a writer and his publisher is a privilege. Many thanks to Max Phua, Chua Hong Koon, Khoo Yee Hong, Jimmy Low, Daniele Lee and Jiang Yulin. Editor Triena Ong gave my copy a shine which I'm most appreciative of.

I have been seduced by the work of designer Truong Quoc Huy for some time, swooning every weekend at the beautiful covers he drew for *This Week in Asia*, a publication of the *South China Morning Post*. So it was a little personal coup for me when he agreed to design this book's cover. I'm thrilled to see the classy work he has done, giving my words a stylish home.

This book would not have been possible without my team at The Nutgraf. In particular Sue-Ann Chia, Aaron Low and Pearl Lee joined me at the interviews in the Istana and conducted several on their own of other newsmakers to bolster my efforts. Their insights, observations and camaraderie helped sharpen the drafts and I'm heavily indebted to them for their honest feedback. They helped me shoulder my other work responsibilities so that I could focus on this book. Pearl was relentless in the tedious work to find, curate and caption the photographs, even during the final trimester of her first pregnancy. It was a team effort to produce this book and I'm glad I'm surrounded by some of the best in the game.

Finally, I am most thankful to my family for their love and belief. My parents, my sisters, my in-laws and my partner in work and life, Sue-Ann, are all quiet fans of my writing, giving me the strength to pursue a life adventure carved out of words. My father, in particular, was a fantastic sounding board on this project given his intimate experience with politics. I couldn't have asked for a better *pro bono* adviser.

Peh Shing Huei

Photo Credits

The publisher acknowledges the following for their kind permission to reproduce photos in this book:

- Goh Chok Tong Collection
  p. xiv (first 2 photos)
  p. xv (first photo)
  pp. xxxii–1

- Ministry of Information and the Arts Collection,
  courtesy of the National Archives of Singapore
  p. viii
  p. xii
  p. xiv (middle photo)
  p. xviii
  pp. 50–51
  pp. 120–121
  pp. 226–227
  pp. 254–255

- National Archives of Singapore
  p. xiv (bottom photo)
  p. xv (bottom 2 photos)

Index

Published by

World Scientific Publishing Co. Pte. Ltd.

5 Toh Tuck Link, Singapore 596224

USA office: 27 Warren Street, Suite 401-402, Hackensack, NJ 07601

UK office: 57 Shelton Street, Covent Garden, London WC2H 9HE

National Library Board, Singapore Cataloguing in Publication Data
Name(s): Peh, Shing Huei, 1975– .
Title: Tall order : the Goh Chok Tong story, Volume 1 / Peh Shing Huei.
Description: First edition. | Singapore : World Scientific Publishing Co. Pte. Ltd., [2018]
Identifier(s): OCN 1052763550 | ISBN 978-981-32-7613-0 (paperback) |
    ISBN 978-981-32-7604-8 (hardcover)
Subject(s): LCSH: Goh, Chok Tong, 1941– . | Prime ministers—Singapore--Biography. |
    Politicians—Singapore--Biography.
Classification: DDC 959.57052092--dc23

British Library Cataloguing-in-Publication Data
A catalogue record for this book is available from the British Library.

For any available supplementary material, please visit
https://www.worldscientific.com/worldscibooks/10.1142/11149#t=suppl

Editorial Adviser: Han Fook Kwang
Editor: Triena Ong
Desk Editors: Daniele Lee, Jiang Yulin
Cover Designer: Truong Quoc Huy
Designer: Jimmy Low
Research and Interviews: Sue-Ann Chia, Aaron Low, Pearl Lee

Printed in Singapore